# PARADIGMS
# OF
# PUBLIC ADMINISTRATION
# AND CIVIL SERVICES

# PARADIGMS OF PUBLIC ADMINISTRATION AND CIVIL SERVICES

*Edited By*

R.K. Pruthi

DISCOVERY PUBLISHING HOUSE
NEW DELHI-110002

First Published-2005

ISBN 81-7141-981-X



*Published by*

**DISCOVERY PUBLISHING HOUSE**
4831/24, Ansari Road, Prahlad Street,
Darya Ganj, New Delhi-110002 (India)
Phone: 23279245 • Fax: 91-11-23253475
E-mail:dphtemp@indiatimes.com

**Printed at**
**Arora Offset Press**
**Laxmi Nagar, Delhi–92**

# Preface

Systematic study of approaches to public administration and bureaucracy can be traced to 19th and early 20th century. During the period classical, human relations, behavioural, social psychological and ecological paradigms were discussed. Particular set of belief and shared values were examined to raise the level of organisational efficiency of public administration.

This book aims at providing to our readers interesting and important material on the organisational approaches and the civil service. Every possible care has been taken to select useful essays for students and teachers.

While preparing this work we have incurred indebtedness and gratitude of authorities on the subject. We record our respectful acknowledgements.

Librarians and their staff members have been kind and co-operative. We thank them all.

I have always received every help and a real hard work of my publisher and his staff members. They deserve my readers love and patronage.

**R.K. Pruthi**

# Contents

# Introduction

The importance of Public Administration as a specialised subject of study was well brought out by Woodrow Wilson, the founder of the discipline. In his celebrated essay on 'The Study of Administration' published in 1887, he characterised government administration as the practical or business end of government that could be separated from the rough and tumble of politics'. Urging for the establishment of an autonomous field of academic inquiry. Wilson observed:

"There should be a science of administration which shall seek to straighten the paths of government, to make its business less unbusiness like, to strengthen and purify its ogranisation, and to crown its duties with dutifulness."

## I

Since government has to respond to diverse public needs, Public Administration's first and foremost objective should be to efficiently discharge the public's business. The Wilsonian definition of the subject as an efficiency-promoting, pragmatic field was first explicitly articulated statement on the importance of a separate discipline of Public Administration. This view of the discipline emerged at a time when there had been a felt need for increased social productivity and for a positivistic role of the government as the chief regulator of the social order and a facilitator of socio-economic development.

Classical administrative theory reigned uninterrupted for about three decades since the beginning of the present century. It laid special emphasis on improvement in the machinery of government. As the tasks of modern administration increased enormously, it was just proper to look into the causes of administrative incompetence.

The Haldane Committee Report (1919) in Britain and the President's Committee on Administrative Management (1937) in the United States are examples of official efforts to streamline Public Administration to make it a fit agency of social development.

In India, also several committees had been set up during the British period as well as after independence. One of such major effort was undertaken by the Administrative Reforms Commission (1966) which was set up with the identical purpose of making Public Administration a suitable agency for effective and efficient socio-economic development.

The overdependence of administration on "Politics" was criticised by the reformers of Public Administration. On the basis of studies made by the practising administrators and academicians, a new faith was born in the form of a 'science' of administration that would have great applied value in scientific restructuring of Public Administration.

The classical 'principles' of administration have severely been criticised. Despite criticisms they have never been totally discarded. These were the precursors of later day sophisticated methods of techniques of administrative improvement such as cost-benefit analysis, operations research, etc.

- With increasing social complexity and international tensions, governments everywhere had gradually come to assume more and more interventions postures. Trade, Commerce and Industry expanded and new kinds of productive enterprise sprang up. There were increasing social demands for State intervention in industrial regulations. Poverty, malnutrition, illiteracy and other social evils had become central concerns of public policy. The era of the laissez-faire state had thus come to an end. Instead, a positivist-interventionist welfare state has emerged steadily.

- The State's increasing concern for social regulation and general social welfare meant a quantum leap in governmental activities. The academic interest in the study of government and administration accompanied this historical expansion in state activities.

As Leonard White has put it:

"In their broader context, the ends of administration are the ultimate object of the state itself—the maintenance of peace and order, the progressive achievement of justice, the instruction of the young, protection against disease and insecurity, the adjustment and compromise of conflicting groups and interests—in short, the attainment of the good life".

- Rising popular demands and expectations from government coincided with a liverly interest in 'efficiency' in Public Administration. How can governmental activities be made more cost-effective? How can the budgetary practices in government be streamlined and made more and more management-oriented? Are there better ways of organising the administrative machinery? What could be done to ensure a steady and timely flow of skilled and motivated personnel within the governmental machinery? After all, it is popular satisfaction and fulfilment of popular demands that provides the rationale for Public Administration, what methods could be invented to monitor popular reactions to administrative action? How can people's satisfaction be measured? Apart from these, larger issues of public policy formulation, policy execution and monitoring and evaluation of policy outcome had come to assume crucial significance in governmental operations. After the seminal contribution of Herbert Simon to decision-theory, Public Administration has received policy science orientation. This has greatly enhanced the utility of the discipline for practical policy analysis and policy improvement in the government. Writers like

**Dror and Die have greatly enriched policy analysis as a major area of Public Administration.**

- **These objectives and practical requirements of government gave a fillip to the academic development of the new discipline of Public Administration. The importance of the new discipline came to be recognised, as sustained academic inquiry and interest started producing new techniques and methods of improving governmental performance.**

Public Administration's increasing practical concern for public problem-solving has steadily legitimised its place in the larger family of Social Sciences.

Complexity and larger scale of governmental operations have prompted innovations in organisational designs. In order to meet the needs of rapidly changing social situations, governments have been groping for new organisational formats that would match the specific situational needs. Organisation theory has, in recent years, assumed the character of a well-developed discipline. The theories of organisation have been co-opted by Public Administration and there is widespread application now of organisation theories to administrative design problems. The organisation theory perspective is now an integral part of Public Administration discipline.

This has made the discipline much more useful then ever before for organisational development and structural experimentations in government. Thus in recent years the discipline has acquired considerable strength. It is in a position to suggest alternative ways of organising government activities to optimise the results.

Application of behavioural science knowledge has also facilitated more sophisticated analysis of public personnel systems. Research as on motivation and morale, group and intergroup behaviour, and interpersonal relationship have produced rich conceptual and theoretical toolkits that are currently being used by Public Administration analysts. The crucial importance of the human element in administration, which was largely ignored in the classical model, is currently being emphasised. As an applied science. Public Administration has thus been of direct use in public personnel management.

## II

Since government touches on almost all aspects of life in the contemporary world, how the government is organised and how it operates in practice should naturally attract our attention.

The importance of Public Administration as social science lies in its methodical study of government and in attempts to organise knowledge about governmental structure and operations. In this role. Public Administration as a discipline is more interested in providing scientific explanations rather than merely solving public problems.

Administration is looked at, in this perspective, as a social activity. Hence the concern of academic inquiry would be to understand the impact of government policies and operations on the society.

What kind of society do the policies envisage? To what extent administrative action is class oriented? In other words, how is Public. Administration and what are the immediate and long term effects of government action on the social structure, the economy and polity.

From this social science perspective. Public Administration, as a discipline, has to draw on a variety of sister disciplines such as History, Sociology, Economics, etc. the objective being to "explain" and not just to "prescribe".

## III

Public Administration's special status in the "developing countries" has been widely acknowledged. The post-colonial, "third world" countries have everywhere embarked upon speedy socio-economic development. These countries have naturally to rely on the government to push through speedy 'development'.

This means Public Administration, has to be organised and operated to increase productivity quickly. Similarly social welfare activities have to be efficiently and effectively executed.

The government sponsored planned development activities have necessitated the birth of new sub-discipline of "Development Administration".

Based on a series of country studies, Development Administration has emerged as an extremely useful field that has great practical utility in the special circumstances of the developing countries.

The emergence of 'Development Administration' is indicative of a felt need for a body of knowledge about how to study the third world administration and at the same time to bring about speedy socio-economic development with government intervention.

All the developing countries in the third world depend on the government's aggressive role in nation-building and socio-economic reconstruction. Development Administration, therefore has emerged as a special sub-discipline to serve the cause of development. This is a distinct branch of the discipline, serving a distinct cause, viz. development.

## IV

Another general utility of Public Administration as a discipline lies in its contribution to creative citizenship. In a democracy, the citizen must be well-informed about what the government does or does not do. Governmental literacy is a sine-qua-non of good citizenship. People must get to know about the organisation of government, the activities it undertakes and the manner in which these are actually performed. As a discipline, Public Administration has ample scope to educate the lay citizens about the machinery and procedure of work in the government.

## V

The expanding role of government in every country, especially in the developing nations, has encouraged many-sided inquiries into governmental operations. Since government touches on almost every conceivable aspect of life in a democratic society, the citizens must have access to information about government and about how it is actually organised and preserved into social regulation and citizens' welfare. Public Administration as an intellectual discipline has, therefore, been gaining an importance with the increasing interventionist role of government in social life.

The importance of a well-developed discipline of Public Administration lies in its five kinds of major contributions to organised social life.

- epistemological
- technical
- ombudsmanic
- liberal-educational, and
- professional

**Epistemological**

The first type of contribution arises out of the discipline's capacity to build up a rigorous, systematic and scientific body of knowledge about governmental structure and operations. Public Administration alone has the exclusive responsibility to study the government in action in all is aspects. In discharging this responsibility, it has been striving to collect reliable information and data, analyse administrative structures and operations, and build explanatory theories for enhancing knowledge about administrative practices.

**Technical**

The second type of technical contribution of the discipline flows from its first major role as stated above. Since the days of the pioneers like Woodrow Wilson, it has been the endeavour of Public Administration specialists to apply knowledge to actual public problem solving. With reliable theoretical equipment and on the basis of "clinical" studies of administration situation, the technical consulting capacity of the experts in the discipline has increased considerably. Advising government and solving practical problems in administration are legitimate expectations from Public Administration analysis.

**Ombudsmanic**

The third type of contribution of the discipline can come out of investigative studies of critical sectors of Administration. Case studies on citizens grievances, administrative red tape, corruption, etc. may be widely circulated to familiarise the general public, the press and the legislature about the actual going-on inside the bureaucracy. By disseminating knowledge and information, the experts in Public Administration can play a socially useful role akin to the ombudsmanic institution as established in many countries.

**Liberal Education**

Public Administration as a discipline has the fourth important responsibility to create enlightened citizenship. In a democracy, knowledge of how the government and the administration functions must be universally disseminated. This is what can be called governmental-administrative literacy. Public Administration is the only social science discipline that can perform this role of a universal educator of "government and administration" for all the citizens.

**Professional**

Public Administration has also served the cause of vocationalism. The discipline has been greatly useful in training civil servants and equipping students to join the professional stream of practising administrators. Institutes and school of Public Administration, Public Affairs and Public Policy Analysis are engaged in the organisation of professional courses.

The importance of Public Administration as a discipline has been highlighted. Subsequent developments in the discipline in response to both practical problems and academic questions have further enhanced its importance as an autonomous field. In the contemporary world, the burden of public duties on government has been steadily increasing. To expect that the days of laissez-faire would return again is mere day-dreaming. The positivistic-interventionist role of government would automatically find reactions in academic inquiry. The importance of Public Administration as a discipline has been closely associated with the increasingly activist role of government everywhere.

In the 'developing' or 'third world' countries, 'Development Administration' as a sub-discipline has a special role to play to systematise knowledge about 'development' as well as to facilitate successful and effective governmental intervention in radical socio-economic reconstruction.

From the time of Plato and Aristotle of ancient Greece to the 18th Century. Social Sciences have been regarded as a single subject of study. With analysis of different aspects of it, it has split into different disciplines. Their development was hastened by the Industrial Revolution which gave rise to issues requiring investigation by specialists. The broad division of Social Science into Economics, History, Political Science, Public Administration, Sociology, etc. has proved inadequate to the understanding or the solving of several problems posed by social phenomena.

This has led to specialisation in different areas of a subject (e.g. Economics into Applied Economics, Econometrics etc. Politica' Science into Political Sociology, Political Anthropology, etc.). As a result it has become increasingly difficult to realise an integrated perspective of social events. Indeed, the writings in Social Sciences in the 20th century testify to the phenomenal expansion of specialisation.

However, too much specialisation may lead to unrealistic results ignoring social phenomenon in its totality. It is like missing the wood for the trees. This is so, because, no social events is *unidimensional* nor does it occur in isolation. It is linked with, economic, political, administrative and social systems of a country.

In order to understand the role of administrative system of Public Administration in a social setting, it is necessary to know the relationship between Public Administration and other Social Science not only to understand the nature of social phenomena but also to know whether Social Sciences can be regarded as Sciences;

what features Public Administration has, as a Social Science and how it is related to other Social Sciences.

## Social Phenomena: Their Integrated Nature

No social event can be studied in isolation without reference to other events. Consider for instance, the policy on Reservation. A good section of people are supporting it and an equal number are opposing it. If it is viewed only as a policy for raising or reducing the percentage of reservations we would be facing difficulties. We have to take into consideration its root cause which is the outcome of the historical development of the Indian society.

This means that we have to analyse the social, economic, political and cultural aspects of reservation policy in order to be able to formulate it in such a way as to meet the ends of social justice and ensure national progress.

Likewise, with regard to the problem of growing inefficiency in public offices you have to take into account a whole spectrum of policies ranging from the recruitment policy through educational policies to the absence of 'achievement' motivation. Then only you will know what has caused it. If you view inefficiency only as a matter of discipline in the offices you may not be able to solve the problem of inefficiency.

## Public Administration as a Social Science

One of the problems faced by almost all Social Sciences is the absence of some important feature of a Science. The main features of a Science are (a) exactness, (b) validity and (c) predictability.

Sciences have laws which are verifiable. Sciences follow a systematic procedure of observation, investigation, experimentation, the building of a hypothesis, verification of the hypothesis by facts, tabulation, classification and correlation of facts, etc. in order to arrive at conclusions that can be put forward as generalisations. Thus exactness, universal validity and predictability are ensured.

As observed by Aristotle, Art is to do and Science is to know. If Science is called a systematic body of knowledge, it can be acquired only through the application of the scientific method.

At first, knowledge was viewed as a single entity in which various subjects of study could be regarded as different dimensions of it. Later, we find subjects divided into sciences such as Physical Sciences, Life Sciences and Social Sciences. But just as the way we call Physical Sciences which deal with physical phenomena as exact Science or Sciences, we cannot call Social Sciences which deal with human beings as Sciences.

The reason is that, the social phenomena in which human beings play a major role cannot be studied in as rigorous a way as the physical phenomena can be. Moreover, no Social Science can claim such exactness as to be able to make predictions.

This, however, does not mean that it is impossible to evolve valid laws about human behaviour. The contribution of Sigmond Freud to Psychology cannot be ignored. The point is that the level of exactness which is attainable in Physical Sciences is not possible in Social Sciences. 'Facts' in Physical Sciences, unlike those in Social Sciences, need not be related to any prescribed setting or context.

To be regarded as Science, Social Sciences have to have principles which are of universal applicability and validity. While some subjects in Social Sciences can claim to have developed such principles, the others can prove no such claim. The reason is that human behaviour is so complex that it is difficult to account for it, using the same principles in every context. For example, no political scientist can trace certain political developments to any one cause. However, you should not assume that there are no principles in any discipline of Social Sciences. Not all Social Sciences have such principles to which the criteria of exactness, universal validity and predictability can be strictly applied. The scientific methods which are used for arriving at accurate results, are now being borrowed by Social Sciences. The behavioural movement which has called for extensive use of empirical techniques for the scientific study of human behaviour, has made inter-disciplinary approach possible. It is against this background that we shall consider Public Administration as a Social Science.

Public Administration deals with certain aspects of human society. Various public organisations are supposed to serve the public in different ways. To the extent to which the administration deals with the public. Public Administration can be called a Social Science. Public Administration is a Social Science having techniques and abstractions of its own concerning the concepts of action and its own problems of theory. It is vially concerned with the integration of knowledge in other Sciences, physical, biological, and psychological. Further, Public Administration relies on the method of observation rather than on that of experimentation. Although experimentation in a laboratory is not possible in he case of Public Administration, the advent of behaviouralism has made it possible.

Public Administration appears to be both positive and normative. Questions of 'What is' and 'What ought to be' are as much relevant to Public Administration as they are to Political Theory. Public Administration has been passing through various stages of theory building. In other words, it is a discipline in the making.

# 2

# Theories of Organisation

It is no exaggeration to say that we are living in the age of the Organisation Man, a man who accepts the organisation goals as the value premises of his decisions. "About the first thing we do to identify people today is to find out the principal organisation of which they are members." Organisations are important because a large number of people (particularly in highly industrialised countries) spend a big chunk of their time in them. Moreover, for many persons organisations represent a major part of their environment, tending to make their behaviour 'organisational'. Little wonder, then, if a lot of thought has been devoted in recent years to a discussion of the meaning, nature and scope of organisations, and to a study of the behaviour and attitudes of persons working in them. With the growth of organisations, which has been further complicated by the impact of science and technology, problems of organisation have attained a bewildering complexity.

Ever since the Hawthorne experiments of the late 'twenties and early 'thirties of this century shattered the implicit faith in the physiological or structural theory of organisation, a whole group of conceptual developments bearing on the problem of organisation have come to forefront. Thus, the current literature on organisation includes theories like behivioural theory, game theory, decision theory, informal theory, communication theory, group theory, concept of informal organisation, motivational approach, quasi-mathematical approach, human relations approach, and the like. Attempts have been made to explain organisaticnal behaviour in terms of political science, economics, sociology, psychology, anthropology, history, mathematics and biology. The problem of organisation has, thus, become the focus of several disciplines.

**Meaning**

It would be pertinent here to explain the meaning of the term "Organisation". The Concise Oxford Dictionary defines the word ''to organize" as ''to frame and put into working order". The term ''Organisation" lends itself to three different meanings: the act of designing the administrative structure, both designing and building the structure; and the structure itself. Evidently, the idea of human relationship has not been conveyed in any of these meanings. Organisation is the method of dividing up work. Implicit in the term are two basic conditions; namely, firsts, a job is to be done; and second, division of work becomes essential if a group of persons is engaged in accomplishing the job. It is true that organisation would be informal even implicit in simpler situations. But, as the job gets larger, involving an increase in the number of people employed, it has to be more clearly defined. Organisation refers to a plan of action to ensure fulfilment of purpose or purpose which a group of individuals has set for realisation, and towards the attainment of which they are collectively bending their energies. In the words of Gaus, ''Organisation is the relation of efforts and capacities of individuals and groups engaged upon a common task in such a way as to secure the desired objective with the least friction and the most satisfaction for whom the task is done and those engaged in the enterprise." Gaus highlights the importance of the human element in an organisation. Gladden defines it as ''the pattern of relationships between persons in an enterprise, so contrived as to fulfil the enterpriser's functions."

It would be of utmost significance to stress that Organisation is not merely a structure; in fact, it embraces structure as well as the human beings who run it in order to realize the preconceived objective. This is clearly borne out in the following observation—''Organisation is the systematic bringing together of interdependent parts to form a unified whole through which authority, co-ordination and control may be exercised to achieve a given purpose. Because the interdependent parts are made up also of people who must be directed and motivated, and whose work must be co-ordinated in order to achieve the objectives of the enterprise, organisation is both structure and human beings.... To try to deal with organisation merely as framework and without considering the people who make it up and those for whom its services are intended would be wholly unrealistic." We sum up by stating that organisational theory must also be basically human.

**Functions**

The function of organisation is to enlarge the resources and opportunities of those for whom it has been established. In it is implicit the idea of change. "An organisation that ceased to change is moribund." As Simon has stated, it influences the members by:

*(i)* dividing work among them;

*(ii)* formulating standard practices;

*(iii)* transmitting decisions downward, upward and crossways;

*(iv)* providing a communication system, thereby making known all sorts of information; and

*(v)* training them.

**Factors in Planning an Organisation**

What factors do the public administrators take into account while planning an organisation? The objectives of a governmental enterprise are laid down by the political policy-maker. After the objective has been laid down the public administrator sets out to plan the necessary organisation. The type of organisation will be conditioned by the type of the service that is, expected to be produced or supplied. The contemplated administrative activity may be collection of taxes, provision of services, or regulation of some activity. In each case, a different organisational pattern would emerge. Secondly, the availability of human resources also influences the type of organisation. When a new organisation is being created, the available human resources will determine its form, but afterwards the organisation itself starts influencing the employees. Thirdly, the availability of material resources, too, is an important factor. In activities like provision of postal facilities, for instance, the material resources play more important part in determining the type of organisation. Lastly, the geographical factor is also taken into account. A nationwide service requires a complex organisation, while a simple one will meet the needs in a local government enterprise. Thus, while planning an organisation the administrator has to weigh these various factors.

## Theories of Organisation

There are several theories of organisation, although, strictly speaking, the word 'theory' may not be very correct to use at the present stage of development of Public Administration. Yet we are employing this term because it has become a popular one. It is proposed to discuss four of them here: (i) Scientific Management, (ii) The Bureaucratic Theory, (iii) The Classical Theory, and (iv) The Human Relations Theory. The last one is of recent origin, the chief value of which lies in toning down the rigidities of the classical theory, and in this sense it really supplements it.

## Scientific Management

The first coherent theory of organisation is referred to as 'Scientific Management', which came to be formulated in the beginning of the twentieth century. At that time, the conditions in the factories were rather unplanned. There was nearly complete absence of standardisation of methods of work. The workers were left entirely to themselves in the matter of choosing the methods to be employed for doing the work. Not only this, they even used to bring their own tools for doing the work. Whether these methods were the efficient ones, and whether the tools were of the right kinds, were none of the responsibilities of management. It was against such a general background of managerial unconcern for methods and tools of work that Scientific Management emerged as a new philosophy of management. Frederick Winslow Taylor (1856-1915), an engineer by training, is regarded as the father of Scientific Management, for it was he who first advocated the systematic adoption of the methods of science to problems of management in the interest of higher industrial efficiency; Taylor himself did not employ 'Scientific Management' to refer to his thoughts. This concept was first used by Louis Brandies in 1910. From that time onwards Taylor also began using this term. He pointed out: "Management is a true science, resting upon clearly fixed laws, rules and principles, as a foundation." He argued that management comprised a number of principles which commanded applicability in all types of organisations, "the same principles can be applied with equal force to all social activities: to the management of our homes; the management of our farms; the management of the business of our tradesmen, large and small; of our churches, our philanthropic institutions, our universities and our governmental departments."

The overall goal of Scientific Management is higher industrial efficiency, but this is the goal of other theories also. What distinguishes Scientific Management from other approaches is its assumptions, specific objectives, and techniques. Taylor, whose thoughts go under the name of Scientific Management, made two assumptions, namely: (i) the application of the methods of science to organisational problems leads to higher industrial efficiency; observation, measurement and experimental comparison are these methods; and (ii) the incentive of high wages will promote the mutuality of interest between workers and managers which, in its turn, will lead to higher productivity.

Besides, several specific objectives are embodied in Scientific Management. It, for instance, seeks standardisation of working conditions—such as, the best temperature and humidity for achieving productivity. The second objective of Scientific Management is standardisation of work methods. What is the best procedure for doing a job is an example of standardisation of work methods. Taylor observed that the average weight of the coal scooped by a shovel ranged from 16 to 38 pounds. By standardisation of the implement, the production could be appreciably raised. He, for instance, developed a shovel holding 21-22 pounds, and by using it a worker could load twice as much coal in a shift. The third objective underlying scientific Management is the planning of large daily task, which too leads to industrial efficiency. Motion Study, which is the observation of all the motions that comprise a particular job and the determination of the best set of motions, is a technique of standardisation of work methods. Motion Study makes use of motion picture cameras. Time Study is the technique to be employed for the planning of a large daily task. This technique determines the time-content of a job; in other words, how much time does a job take to perform? A still another specific objective of Scientific Management is to encourage the 'high performer' to stay and the 'low performer' to leave. This is secured by what is called Taylor Differential Piecework Plan; under this Plan those who produce above standard receive higher wages than those producing below standard.

Scientific Management addressed itself to the problems of the 'shop floor'—that is, the bottom part of an organisation where the work performed is of a receptive and routine nature.

Taylor's Scientific Management was supremely concerned with organisational efficiency interpreted in only mechanistic terms. Scientific Management viewed man as but an adjunct of the machine; it, therefore, sought to make him *like* a machine, and as efficient as a machine itself. This is a rather degrading view, and unacceptable to a modern man. It must always be remembered that man is *not* a machine.

Secondly, Scientific Management over-simplified the worker motivation. To argue, as Taylorism did, that an employee is motivated by high wages is grossly to underestimate the meaning of human motivation'. Likewise, the assumption that an individual existed in isolation from his social environment is erroneous.

Scientific Management is also called the 'physiological organisation theory'. It is concerned with only that range of human behaviour which relates to production. Here, too, it emphasizes only a limited number of physiological variables; it completely neglects, for instance, the psychological aspects.

**The Bureaucratic Theory of Organisation**

The term 'Bureaucracy' lends itself to two usages; it refers to the task and procedures of administration, as well as is used as a collective word for a body of administrative officials. Frequently it also stands for inefficiency and an improper exercise of power on the part of officials, and thus has become a term of abuse.

The word 'Bureaucracy' was first coined by Vincent de Gournay (1712-1759), an economist of France. He had observed: "We have an illness in France which bids fair to play havoc with us; this illness is called bureaumania". The Dictionary of the French Academy accepted the word in its 1798 supplement and defined it as "Power, influence of the heads and staff of government bureaux."

But it was in the nineteenth century, under conditions of increasing state intervention, that the term came into regular use among European writers. In England, it became current in the 1830s during resistance to the centralisation of poor relief and public health measures. To Thomas Carlyle it was "the continental nuisance".

A sustained treatment of the concept came in 1895 in Gaetano Mosca's *Element di Scienza Politica,* translated in 1939 as *The Ruling Class,* where the author regarded bureaucracy as being so fundamental to the governing of great empires that all political systems could be classified as either feudal or bureaucratic.

It was, however, Max Weber (1864-1920) who founded the modern sociological study of bureaucracy, freed the term from pejorative connotations, and emphasised the indispensability of bureaucracy for the rational attainment of the goals of an organisation. Weber termed his formulation as "ideal type"; an ideal type is what an organisation (or, and other phenomenon) tries to be.

Following are the characteristics of bureaucracy, as enumerated by Max Weber:

1. The staff members are personally free, observing only the impersonal duties of their offices.

2. There is a clear hierarchy of offices.

3. The functions of the offices are clearly specified.

4. Officials are appointed on the basis of a contract.
5. They are selected on the basis of a professional qualification, ideally substantiated by a diploma gained through examination.
6. They have a money salary, and usually pension rights. The salary is graded according to position in the hierarchy. The official can always leave the post, and under certain circumstances it may also be terminated.
7. The official's post is his sole or major occupation.
8. There is a career structure and promotion is possible either by seniority or merit, and according to the judgement of superiors.
9. The official may appropriate neither the post nor the resources which go with it.
10. He is subject to a unified control and disciplinary system.

These ten features constituted Max Weber's ideal, pure or rational type of bureaucracy. The characteristics of bureaucracy were: precision, continuity, discipline, strictness, reliability. These characteristics made it technically the most satisfactory form of organisation. But bureaucracy has its dysfunctionalities also. R.K. Merton argues that demands on officials to conform to bureaucratic regulations lead to ritualism, defensiveness, rigidity, and difficulties in dealing with the public. This stream culminates in M. Crozier's *The Bureaucratic Phenomenon* (1964) in which the author uses bureaucracy to mean "an organisation that cannot correct its behaviour by learning from its errors."

The Bureaucratic Theory is characterised by rigidity, inflexibility, emphasis on means rather than ends and anti-humanist over-tones.

**The Classical Theory of Organisation**

The Classical Theory of Organisation, also known as the Mechanistic Theory or the Structural Theory, is the dominant one in the field (hence, called 'classical'), and has been enunciated most notably by Henri Fayol, Luthor Gulick, L.F. Urwick, J.D. Mooney, A.C. Reiley, Mary Parker Follett, R. Shelton, etc. These writers argue that administration is administration regardless of the kind of work being undertaken or the context within which it is performed. They then proceed to identify the important elements in the processes of administration as well as features common to all administrative structures. This exercise is preparatory to the development of a set of principles of organisation. Indeed, the single most distinguishing feature of the classical theory is its concern with the formulation of principles of organisation. The classical theorists addressed themselves to the task of discovering the true bases on which division of work in an organisation could be carried out, and devising effective methods of bringing about coordination in it. They, moreover, laid emphasis on precise definition of tasks and their inter-relationships, and advocated the use of authority and a system of checks to exercise control over personnel so that the organisational work gets done.

Let us begin with Henri Fayol (1841-1925). His *General and Industrial Administration* is a classic treatise and according to Urwick, this book "has probably had more influence on the ideas of business management in Europe, and especially in the Latin countries, than any other work." Fayol divided all activities in an organisation into the following six groups: technical, commercial, financial, security, accounting, and administrative. Administration, according to him, comprises the following five elements: forecasting and planning, organising, commanding, co-ordinating, and controlling. Henri Fayol propounded fourteen principles of organisation which may be enumerated below:

1. Division of work.
2. Authority.
3. Discipline.
4. Unity of Command.
5. Unity of Direction.

6. Subordination of individual interest to general interest.
7. Remuneration.
8. Centralisation or decentralisation.
9. Scalar Chain.
10. Order.
11. Equity.
12. Stability of Tenure.
13. Initiative.
14. *Esprit de corps.*

The most comprehensive enunciation of the classical theory is contained in *Papers on the Science of Administration* (1937), edited by Luther Gulick and L. Urwick. Luther Gulick summed up the principles of organisation in the word 'POSDCORB', each letter of which stands for a particular function. To quote Gulick, "Posdcorb is made up of initials and stands for the following activities:

Planning, that is working out in broad outline the things that need to be done and the methods for doing them to accomplish the purpose set for the enterprise.

Organising, that is the establishment of the formal structure of authority through which work-subdivisions are arranged, defined and co-ordinated for the defined objective.

Staffing, that is, the whole personnel function of bringing in and training the staff and maintaining favourable conditions of work.

Directing, that is, the continuous task of making decisions and embodying them in specific and general orders and instructions and serving as the leader of the enterprise.

Co-ordinating, that is the all-important duty of inter-relating the various parts of work.

Reporting, that is, keeping those, to whom the executive is responsible, informed as to what is going on, which thus includes keeping himself and his subordinates informed through records, research and inspection.

Budgeting, with all that goes with budgeting in the form of fiscal planning, accounting, and control.''

Mooney and Reiley enunciated the following four principles of organisation; the co-ordinative principle, the scalar (or, hierarchical) principle, the functional principle (or, division of labour), and the staff/line principle.

According to this theory organisation is a formal structure of plan, amenable to creation in accordance with clearly-understood principle, much like the plan of a building, prepared in advance by the architect according to some principles. This concept stems from two beliefs, namely—(i) there is a body of principles in accordance with which organisation plan can be spelled out to fit into the requirements of the chosen purpose or activity, and (ii) the requisite personnel must meet the requirements of this preconceived plan. It may, thus, be seen that this theory views organisation as a machine, considering the human beings who run it as mere cogs. In the words of L.D. White, "It is a formal declared pattern of relationships established in government by law and by top management. It is based on the nature and volume of work to be done and is dictated by the requirements of efficiency in the sense of securing the most effective use of men and materials and by the need for responsibility. The organisation is established and supported by authority and can be set out, although imperfectly, on a chart or diagram. It is normally the dominant set of work relationships." This approach "bears the stamp of the engineer seeking scientific precision, logical structure, and the one best way of performing each step, and of relating the parts to a unified whole." It is marked by an almost exclusive attention to the problems of the structure in the role's relations, i.e., activities and task laid down to ensure the most effective and efficient organisation. Focus is thrown, not on the human beings as such, but on the role as it (i.e., the role) relates to other roles in the context of the organisational objective. This theory manifests four features—impersonality. division of work, hierarchy, and efficiency. Further, it is marked by the following six philosophical characteristics:

1. It is atomistic in the sense that it sees the individuals in isolation from fellowmen.
2. It is mechanistic. It does not explain the dynamics of organisational behaviour.
3. It is static.
4. It is voluntaristic. It rests upon the naive belief that the individuals are immune from the control either by the groups or by social factors.
5. It is rationalistic. By rational behaviour is meant performance of task according to method determined by the principles of scientific work performance.
6. It does not take any note of non-economic incentives.

The classical theory of organisation is made explicit in organisation charts, rule books, manuals, rules of procedures, etc. It deals with what is called formal organisation—an organisation which is deliberately and rationally designed to fulfil the objectives of an organisation. The classical theory treats an organisation as a closed system, completely unconnected with, and uninfluenced, by its external environment. It is more concerned with what *ought to be,* and this kept it away from the study of actual behaviour in organisations. It under-estimated the human factor and oversimplified the human motivations. Besides, although this theory set out to develop principles of organisation, they were, according to critics, no better than mere 'proverbs', hardly providing any meaningful guidance to scholars and practitioners of the subject. Despite these limitations, the classical theory has made major contributions to administration which cannot be ignored. In the first place, this theory played a notable role in rationalising and even stimulating production. Secondly, it was this theory which first propounded the idea that administration itself was a separate activity, and was worthy of intellectual investigation. Thirdly, it formulated a set of concepts in administration and evolved a terminology which has provided a base for subsequent researches in this field. Finally, the limitations of this theory stimulated further researches in organisational behaviour, thus becoming an important milestone in the development of organisation theories.

## The Human Relations Theory of Organisation

The single greatest influence which made the classical or the mechanistic theory of organisation fall into disfavour, came from the Hawthorne Experiments which were carried out in the U.S.A., in the late 1920s and early 1930s. So 'unorthodox' were the findings from these studies that it seems necessary to describe these experiments.

The experiments were carried out at the Western Electric Company (owned by the Bell Telephone Company) at Hawthorne (near Chicago), under the leadership of Elton Mayo and his colleagues of the Harvard Business School. They are ably discussed in *Management and the Worker* (by F.J. Roethlisberger and William J. Dickson), published in 1939.

In one 'experiment', the activities of a group of workers engaged in making telephone switches were observed. These workers were operating under a piece-rate system, and the management believed that this would stimulate the workers to earn more. For, has not Taylor talked about the interests between workers and management promoted by the device of high wages? The workers, however, reacted quite differently. Contrary to management's expectations, they worked to a level which ensured them what they considered to be adequate earnings, and, thus, refused to work more to earn more. They feared that if they produced more, some of them may face retrenchment or even the wages may be reduced. It was discovered by the researchers that these workers constituted a small, well-knit social group which was governed by a code which effectively discouraged a 'rate-buster' (who does too much work), a 'chiseller' (who does too little), and a 'squealer' (who passes unfavourable information about his colleagues to his superior).

In another experiment some girls were separated from the rest and placed in a special test-room for observation. Physical conditions under which they worked, were changed frequently, but according to a plan, to evaluate their effect on production. Sometimes the lighting in the room was improved, sometimes made worse. Some rest-pauses were introduced sometimes; they were discontinued sometimes. But under all such changes the production of these girls was continually showing an upward trend. This proved that there was no positive correlation between the physical variables and production. Both the researchers and the management were puzzled by these findings. In the first experiment the workers' reaction to management's plan (i.e., piece-rate system) was negative; in the second one, it was positive. In the second experiment, the girls knew that they were separated from the rest and selected for an important experiment. They, thus, knew about their special position, and felt important. They, therefore, co-operated with the management and were giving their best.

The Hawthorne Experiments proved that men are not inert or isolated creatures; on the contrary, they react in their own way... responding, for example, to a motivational variable other than the lighting. These studies proved that an organisation was (also) a social system, a group of people behaving.

The Hawthorne Experiments contained many startling findings on employee attitudes to work and supervision, and disclosed the tendency on the part of employees to form small social groups with their own status system, behavioural patterns, beliefs and goals which may be different from... or even opposed to ... the stipulations and prescriptions of the formal organisation. So new, indeed, were these that they gave rise to a new theory of organisation, called the Human Relations Theory.

To contra-distinguish it from the formal organisation of the classical theorists, the human relations theory focuses on what is called informal organisation. In the words of Roethlisberger, "Too often we try to solve human problems with non-human tools and in terms of non-human data. It is my simple thesis that a human problem requires a human solution. First, we have to learn to recognize a human problem when we see one; and second, upon recognising it, we have to learn to deal with it as such and not as it were something else. A human problem to be brought to a human solution requires human data and human tools."

There essence of the human relations theory lies in its dominant emphasis on people, on human motivations and on informal group functioning—in contrast to the classical theorists' exclusive concern for principles. The human relations theory of organisation rejects formal institutionalisation: it considers the informal, day-to-day functioning of the structure more important and revealing than the charts, maps, etc. It assumes that organisational behaviour is quite complex, subject to a wide range of influences impinging on human beings from all directions. For analysis and solution of the organisational problems, therefore, it is of the utmost importance to comprehend the multi-dimensional nature of man. This theory has been termed human relations theory, socio-economic theory, or humanistic theory. It is, as White remarks, "the set of work relationships that grow out of the mutual interactions of persons working together over long period of time...The informal organisation is more subtle, reflecting such matter as social and economic status, race or language differences, educational levels, and personal likes and dislikes. It is customary, not enacted; it is not written and it is not subject to neat diagrams. The formal organisation tends to be relational and impersonal; the informal, emotional and personal. The two usually overlap, may nearly coincide, or may be far apart." By informal organisation. Simon means "interpersonal relations in the organisation that affect decisions within it, but either are omitted from the formal scheme or not consistent with that scheme." It is "the whole pattern of actual behaviours—the way the members of the organisation really do behave—in so far as these actual behaviours do not coincide with the formal plan."

The informal organisation is customary, not enacted. It is not written and manualised; it is not portrayed in organisational charts. An informal organisation is the set of work relationships that grow out of the mutual interactions of persons working together over a period of time. It reflects matters, such as, social and economic status, race or language differences, educational levels, personal likes and dislikes, etc.

There are always and everywhere departures from the official versions of an organisation. The 'informal overlays' portray the patterns of these informal deviations from manualised behaviour. There are many types of informal overlays which describe the relationships that are superimposed on the formal structure, but the principal ones are five:

1. *The socio-metric overlay* describes the pattern of relationships growing out of the feelings of social attraction or rejection that people have for each other.

2. *The functional overlay* refers to contacts, such as, those between the staff specialist and those in the organisation who directly seek his guidance or co-operation outside the formal channels.

3. *The decision overlay* describes the relationships based on going directly to the people who have the real influence in reaching a decision and by passing the formal lines.

4. *The power overlay* indicates the key-people who can accomplish something because they "know the ropes," they are in intimate touch with the formal decision-makers, or they are highly respected in spite of their relatively low position in the organisation.

5. *The communication overlay* reveals the actual pattern of pathways which information, such as, correspondence takes in moving through the organisation.

It must be noted that informal organisation is based on and could not exist without the formal structure as the point of departure. The informal organisation allows an organisation a measure of flexibility which is a functional necessity; but it must not be in total disregard of the formally structured organisational arrangements. Some features of informal organisation may, indeed, be co-opted in the formal organisation. The greatest weakness of the informal organisation, however, is its utter instability; it goes on changing, and its behaviour cannot be predicated. One should also add in the end that the informal organisations in the West tend to be more formalised than their counterparts in many developing countries like India. This is largely because the organisational thrust has been the heaviest in the West, and has only now begun to be experienced in a country like India. The tea-club, for instance, is used in the West for sorting out, among others, many organisational problems while it has hardly such functions in India.

**Relative Importance of these Theories**

A study of the behavioural pattern in an organisation may reveal a disparity between the formal organisation, visualised in charts, manuals and the like, and the informal one. The disparity appears inevitable, as no formal plan however skillfully drawn, can be deemed complete. Vacuum being abhorrent to nature, informal patterns soon fill up the deficiencies thereby making the plan workable. The disparity grows wider as the specifications of the charts are modified, diluted, even supplanted by such considerations as social and economic status, language differences, educational levels, caste considerations, regionalism, to name but a few.

The informal organisation is not necessarily an evil. In truth if it does not already exist, it will have to be created. It germinates administrative vitality and ensures access to group opinion by extending and broadening the avenues of institutional planning and thought. We sum up the discussion by making the following observations made by Pfiffner and Presthus.

1. The informal organisation may or may not be identical.
2. An informal organisation may or may not be subversive in the sense that it resists and seeks to thwart management objectives.
3. The informal aspects of organisation being inevitable, management should attempt to utilize them in accomplishing management objectives.

4. A management institution in which the main outlines of formal and informal organisation coincide is a healthy and happy one.

These two approaches are not mutually exclusive alternatives. They, in fact, deal with two different sets of functions in organisations—the 'binding between' and the 'binding in' functions. These two sets of functions—and the resulting two sets of problems—confront every organisation and, therefore, have to be dealt with, keeping in view their inherently mutual relationship. The formal organisation theory is "likely to be in accurate and incomplete," unless it is 'corrected' by what the informal organisation theory has to offer. But exclusive or even excessive emphasis upon the informal organisation is also not conducive to happier results. It runs the danger of becoming a disorganising force, if not judiciously controlled. It may mullify the advantages accruing from division of labour, and segregation of function; and undermine official responsibility. "The problem of the student of Organisation.... is to create a unity out of what would otherwise be a confusing duality. The obvious challenge to the present generation is to work out a single theory of organisation where heretofore there have been two."

# 3

# Principles of Organisation

A question is at times raised as to whether there are general principles of organisation. There are writers who dismiss these principles as just "myths" and "proverbs". According to Herbert Simon, "Most of the propositions that make up the body of administrative theory today share, unfortunately, this defect of proverbs. For almost every principle, one can find an equally plausible and acceptable contradictory principle. Although the two principles of the pair will lead to exactly opposite organisational recommendations, there is nothing in the theory to indicate which is the proper one to apply." It must be admitted that the principles of Public Administration are not axioms and laws of physical science which are true at all times and at all places. Nor are these principles conceived *a priori;* they are in the nature of inductive generalisations and are the consequence of keen, informed and continuous observation of administrative phenomena. These principles of organisation are neither rigid nor absolute. Flexibility and capability of adaptation to every need are in the essence of these principles. In the words of White they "suggest only working rules of conduct which wide experience seems to have validated." The responsible administrator must know the principles and apply them with judgement in terms of his immediate situation. Henri Fayol has defined these principles as "acknowledged truths regarded as proven on which to rely."

## Hierarchy

It is difficult to conceive of an organisation without some form of hierarchy. Organisation is essentially the division of functions among a given number of persons. The distribution of functions and responsibilities is both horizontal and vertical. An organisation structure grows both vertically and horizontally. When additional levels are added in an organisation structure, it is called vertical growth. But when more functions or more positions are added without increasing the number of levels it is called horizontal growth. Vertical distribution create levels like Top Management. Middle Management, Supervision and the level of specific performance. Strictly speaking, these levels connote no inherent superiority and inferiority. However, due to the difference in the nature of responsibility of various levels, the difference in the salary scales as between different levels and the difference in the qualifications and qualities of the personnel manning various levels, superior-subordinate relationship does emerge in the organisation. "Hierarchy consists in the universal application of the superior-subordinate relationships through a number of levels of responsibility reaction from the top to the bottom of structure." Mooney and Reiley call it the "scalar process".

All organisations are hierarchical, and there is no escape from it how hard one may try. A hierarchical organisation is like the following:

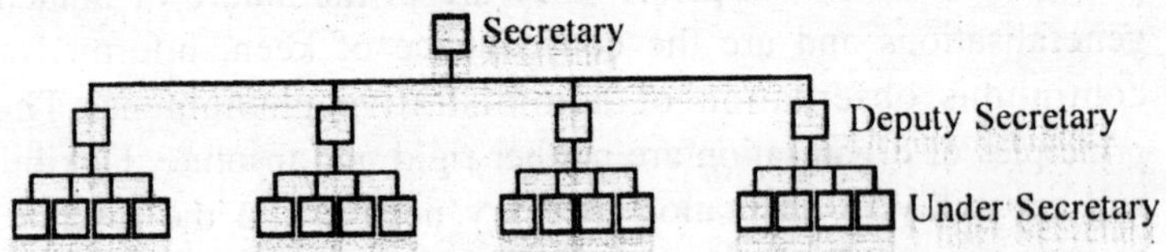


The above organisational chart is a very simplified one, but the point to be noted is that the functions of an organisation are divided both vertically and horizontally, and a pattern of relationship is established.

The principle of hierarchy has come in for a lot of criticism. It has been blamed for creating superior-subordinate relationship in the hierarchy. Procedure through proper channels, red-tapism and delay in disposal of cases are other criticisms levelled against it. However, hierarchy performs very useful purposes in an organisation. Hierarchy provide the much-needed channels of communication in the organisation from the top to the bottom and from the bottom to the top. It is also built-in device to achieve consensus in the organisation. It also facilitates delegation of authority. The many and varied functions of hierarchy have been graphically described by Appleby as, "Within the executive branch general functions of hierarchical structure include the following: fixing responsibility; providing leadership with areas of discretion at successive levels; providing means of exerting influence and exercising fellowship; making any particular organisation and the general executive government manageable; making it acceptable; determining levels at which decisions of various kinds may be made; providing for ready movement of decision making from one level to another under agitation; bringing to bear relevant, competing and complementary interests, function and viewpoints. More specifically, it is the means by which resources are apportioned, personnel selected and assigned, operations activated reviewed and modified."

**Span of Control**

Span of control is a sacrosanct principle of administration, or, it has been so till recently. Span of control is simply the number of subordinates or the units of work that an administrator can personally direct. In the words of Dimock, "The span of control is the number and range of direct, habitual communication contacts between the chief executive of an enterprise and his principal fellow-officers." This concept is related to the principle of "span of attention" so ably described by V.A. Graicunas? There are limits to human capacity; and if the span of supervision is extended too thinly, unsatisfactory results occur. The scholars, therefore, have been engaged in determining what should be the length of the span. There are some who limit it to 3 persons; others put it at 7; and still others restrict it to 20; and so on. There is no unanimity as to the exact number, but there does exist a general agreement that the shorter the span, the greater will be the contact, and consequently, more effective control. "On the other hand, there are dangers inherent in excessively limited span of control, such as, the risk of detailed supervision of the few reporting; the resultant failure to stimulate subordinates or to fully use the capacities of them. It is possible also that short spans of control mean long chains of commands." The fact of the matter is that there can be no rigid span of control. The exact length of span will depend on many variable factors like the personality of the supervisor, the diversification of the functions of the organisation, the age of the organisation, the traditions and environments of the organisation, and the caliber of the subordinates. The element of space may also affect the situation. Thus, the fact of all offices being located in one building or place or scattered over many buildings or places certainly influences the length of the span. In this connection, attention may be drawn to the distinction made by Urwick between "direct supervision" and "access" to the boss. In other words, while an officer can directly supervise only a limited number of persons, he can introduce some flexibility in the organisation by permitting larger number of subordinates to have "access" to him.

The whole idea of span of control has come under revision during recent years. The increasing use of automation in administration the information, revolution and the growing role of the specialists are some of the factors responsible for the change. Automation and mechanical processes are being used increasingly as means for simplifying and expediting communications, and ameliorating the volume and the delay problems of paper work. Recent technical advances have made it possible to introduce automation in offices as well Mechanisation has been applied to such activities as accounting tabulating, purchasing, sorting and computation work. The main function of these machines is to perform the ever-swelling volume of repetitive and routine tasks in the disposal of paper work. Inventory, record-keeping, billing and pay-roll book-keeping have become more efficient as a result of automation. Our own country, which is comparatively backward in this field, is fast taking to automation. There are more than 400 punch-card equipments in use in different organisations in India, governmental and private. Even computers are in use. According to the Committee on Automation, which submitted its Report in 1972, there were 140 computers in 1971, out of which 10 were in government departments, 39 in public undertakings, 55 in private sector undertakings and the remaining 36 were in different research institutions, institutes of Technology and universities. The ability of these machines to store information, to retrieve relevant facts to interpret them in terms of established criteria and to make decisions are the principal features of these developments. Automation render superfluous most of the clerical and routine jobs and reduces paper work. The electronic machines supply lot of relevant and accurate data to the administrator at a very fast rate with the result that he can control more work units, i.e., the work which required many more persons before the introduction of automation. The length of the span of control, therefore, has definitely increased, and it has become possible for the boss to control the work of more persons. Mechanisation has also affected the span of control in the area of headquarters field relationship by making communication and transport swift and easy, thus annihilating time and distance.

Another noteworthy phenomenon is the ever-growing number of specialists, professionals and technicians in public service. The specialists bring with them certain attitudes of mind. In the first place, they are experts in their fields and are conscious of it. Consequently, they do not tolerate interference in their own spheres of activities by the ignorant lazy men. Secondly, they mostly act as advisers and staff units, and as such are near the top. Thirdly, these specialists dislike vertical relationship in the organisation. The established pattern of organisation itself is, therefore, undergoing a change, and the familiar concept of superior-subordinate hierarchical relationship is under challenge. Each specialist compels recognition as an individual in his own right. For example, in a university or research organisation there are a number of specialists, who are recognised authorities in their respective fields. In such as organisation there is more of persuasion, consultation and discussion, and less of bossing and issuing commands. Decision tends to be group decisions. Decision making process gets decentralised and numerous decision-making centres crop up. The task of the chief executive in such an organisation, thus, becomes more of co-ordination than of supervision and control.

### Unity of Command

The principle, briefly and simply stated, means that "an employee should receive orders from one superior only."—Fayol.

In the words of Pfiffner and Presthus, "The concept of unity of command requires that every member of an organisation should report to one, and only one leader." Fayol is a great advocate of this principle. "Should it be violated, authority is undermined, discipline is in jeopardy, order disturbed and stability threatened.... As soon as two superiors wield their authority over the same person or department, uneasiness makes itself felt and should the cause persist, the disorder increases, the malady takes on the appearance of an animal organism troubled by a foreign body, and the following consequences are to be observed: either the dual command ends in disappearance or elimination of one of the superiors and organise well-being is restored, or else the organism continues to wither away. In no case is there adaptation of the social organism to dual command."

The above principle, like many others, is under fire. In the words of Seckler-Hudson,''..... the old concept of 'one single boss for each person is seldom found in fact in complex governmental situations. Many interrelationships exist outside the straight line of command which require working with, and reporting to, many persons for purposes of orderly and effective performance... the administrator in government has many bosses and he can neglect none of them. From, one he may receive policy orders; from another, personnel; from a third, budget; from a fourth, supplies and equipments."

Unity of command has been seriously affected by the increasing number and growing influence of staff and auxiliary agencies. The fact that the agencies are manned by experts has added to their growing significance. Ever since the end of the Second World War, there have been set up numerous Boards and Commissions, Advisory Bodies, Staff and Auxiliary Agencies, each one of which has started communicating directly to various hierarchicals so much so that the line officials has begun to wonder as to who is his boss, whose advice he should accept and whose orders he should obey. What we are having today, therefore, is not unity of command, not even duality of command, but multiplicity of command. The situation, in its worst form, exists at the level of the Collector or Deputy Commissioner of a district. There are

26 Heads of Departments in Uttar Pradesh who address the Collector, and 23 Departments which issue orders to him. In their turn each of these Departments is divided into a number of Sections, each of which issues orders to the Collector in its own right. Thus, one of the eight Sections in the Land Reforms Commissioner's Office in U.P. issued 716 circulars between 1954 and 1956 to the Collector. In short, no less than 116 authorities of this State Government in the Secretariat and outside, apart from Departments of the Central Government, issue orders and references to the Collector.

## Integration Versus Disintegration

In every modern State the ever-increasing role of administration has focused attention on the urgent need for unity in administrative process. The overloaded administrative machinery of the modern government is creaking and groaning under the ever-increasing weight of functions, and is in danger of becoming disjoined and put out of gear. Conflicts, bottlenecks, deadlocks and breakdowns in administrative mechanism are not infrequent. Integration and co-ordination have, therefore, become a *sine qua non* of a good administrative system today.

An administrative system is called integrated in which all the executive authority is conferred by law or constitution on one single person who thereupon becomes the Chief Executive. The reverse of it is a disintegrated system where executive authority is distributed by statute or constitution among a number of coeval bodies or agencies or persons. Closely allied to this concept is the idea of area administration versus functional administration. In the former system there obtains at any given level of administration an authority superior to all others with the power to co-ordinate their activities and resolve contradictions and conflicts. A good example of area administration was the District in the olden days with the Collector at the apex of the departmental officials at that level. District today has ceased to perform that role and the area administration has given place to functional administrations in which all departmental authorities at the district level have a coeval status and run along parallel lines resulting in a disintegrated and uncoordinated administrative system.

There is no administrative system in the world which is either completely integrated or disintegrated. What we have is varying degree of integration or disintegration. India offers a good example of an integrated administrative system. All the executive authority of the Union Government is vested by law in the President. Each Department of Government is under the charge of a Secretary or Additional/Special Secretary, and each Ministry has at its head a Minister. Above the Ministers stands the Cabinet of which the head is the Prime Minister. In practice, however, the system is not so neatly integrated. The Constitution itself has provided for authorities or agencies which are independent of executive control, for example Union Public Service Commission, Comptroller and Auditor-General and Election Commission. In addition, there exist a number of autonomous Commissions and Boards, Public Enterprises and Corporations which fall outside the regular administrative organisation. The more of such independent and autonomous agencies and bodies there are, the more difficult it becomes to tie up all the loose ends in a neatly integrated system.

The United States of America, on the other hand, offers a good example of a disintegrated administrative system. This country, with a federal form of governmental set-up and a strong deep-rooted tradition of local self-government, basing its government on the twin principle of separation of Powers and Checks and Balances, having a system of directly elected officers, and with a jungle of un-coordinated departments, commissions, bureaus, boards and other agencies, looks like a happy hunting-ground for the forces of dispersal and disintegration. The lack of unity is strikingly visible even at the national administrative headquarters. It is true that the Constitution has attempted to bring about administrative unity by vesting the entire executive authority in the. President, but it has done very little to help the President evolve a unified administrative structure. Unlike Britain and India, the American Cabinet need be an integrating and cohesive force. It is not a term; its members may belong to the same party or to different parties or to no parties; they do not "swim or sink together". Secondly, the Constitution has authorised the Congress to create administrative departments and agencies, as the need may arise. This provision has resulted in the creation of a medley (mostly within larger units) of Bureaus (Bureau of the Budget and Federal Bureau of Investigation), Commission (Civil Service Commission and Atomic Energy Commission), Boards (Planning Board, Social Security Board), and Agencies (Central Intelligence Agency), etc. These bodies are not neatly organised under the well-defined departments; they are rather parallel bodies free of departmental control. Some of these agencies, having powerful congressional support, tend to become substantially independent of executive direction. A good example is the civilian operations of the U.S. Corps of Engineers. Thirdly, at times these agencies may conflict and work at cross purposes. There is not infrequently inter-agency struggle for power until at times agencies, with congressional backing, can circumvent even the all-powerful Budget Bureau which, by being given the authority to clear all legislation from all agencies, is supposed in a way to create unity in administrative structure. The Federal Bureau of Investigation Retirement Bill, 1947, and the Foreign Service Act of 1946 are cases in point. Thus, the administrative agencies look two ways: every agency has to be concerned with the intention of its committees " on the Hill'' as well as with the directions it receives from the chief executive —a very unsatisfactory arrangement indeed! The position is much worse in the states and local governments. There are counties and cities which have a long-ballot system according to which most of the important officials are directly elected by the people, thus making co-ordination an improbable task.

Of the two systems, the integrated one has marked advantages which have been ably summarised by W.F. Willoughby as follows:

"It correlates the several operating services of the government into one highly integrated and unified piece of administrative mechanism ; it insures the establishment of an effective system of overhead administration and control ; it makes definite the line of administrative authority and responsibility ; it lays the basis for, if it does not automatically affect the elimination of duplication in organisation, plant, equipment, personnel, and activities ; it makes possible effective co-operative relations between services engaged in the same general field of activity that can be obtained in no other way; it furnishes the means by which overlapping and conflicts of jurisdictions may be avoided or readily adjusted: it facilitates greatly the standardisation of all administrative processes and procedures; it permits the centralisation of such general business operation as purchasing, the custody and issue of supplies, the recruitment and handling of personnel, the keeping of accounts, the maintenance of libraries, laboratories, blueprint-rooms etc., and finally, it furnishes the absolutely essential foundation for a properly organised and administered system."

**Centralisation and Decentralisation**

"...One of the important problems of organisation is to reconcile the administrator's natural desire for complete control, uniformity and certainty with the people's demand that governmental administration accommodate itself to local public sentiment.'' Similar dichotomy marks the posture and actions of our Government. To centralize or to decentralize seems to be the dilemma facing the Government today. On the one hand, the compulsions of a planned economy, the need for effective and strong defence and the urge for national integration pull in the direction of centralisation. On the other hand, the political commitment to take democracy to grass-roots and the growing demand for regional autonomy pull in the opposite direction of decentralisation. The Planning Commission symbolizes the trend towards centralisation, while Panchayati Raj epitomizes the trend towards decentralisation.

**Meaning**

Centralisation stands for concentration of authority at or near the top; decentralisation, on the other hand, denotes dispersal of authority among a number of individuals or units. In the words of White, "The progress of transfer of administrative authority from a lower to a higher level of government is called 'centralisation'; the converse, 'decentralisation'." The essential element in decentralisation is the delegation of decision-making functions. In the words of Charlesworth, "The significant question in any large administrative undertaking is whether or not any definitive actions are taken by the centre-head which can be taken at the periphery." The difference between the two concepts is well brought out by Fesler:

"Whether a given field service leans toward centralisation or toward decentralisation may be discerned from observation of the importance of matters on which field officials have decision-making authority, compared to matters wholly retained for headquarters decision; the extent of central consultation with field officials on matters that arise and are formally decided at headquarters, and the weight such field opinion carries; the frequency with which field officials must refer matters to headquarters for decision even though they arise at and are partially 'processed' in the field, the number and specificity of central regulations and orders governing decision-making in the field; the provision for citizen appeals to headquarters for overruling of field decisions; the degree to which all the agency's field activities within each geographic area are directed by a single field official; and the caliber of field officials. Neither the mere existence of a field service, nor its carrying of a heavy workload, nor its employment of ninetenths of the agency's personnel constitutes evidence of decentralisation."

Decentralisation should be distinguished from delegation. Decentralisation signifies the central authority diverting itself of certain powers which are given away to the local authorities, which, so to say, become autonomous in the field. Delegation, on the contrary, implies transfer of certain specified functions by the central to the local authority which thereupon acts as the agent of the former, which retains the right to issue directives or revise decisions. In brief, what is ceded is merely functions and not authority and responsibility.

Decentralisation may be political or administrative. Political decentralisation implies the setting-up of new levels of government. The creation of autonomous states within the Indian Union and of Panchayati Raj Institutions within the States is a good illustration of such decentralisation. Another dimension of it is the association of the public with administration, and this can be secured only by the dispersal of political and administrative authority. Administrative decentralisation may be vertical and territorial, or horizontal and functional. The former implies the superior authority setting up area administrations and vesting them with some sort of independent powers and functions. Districts and divisions are good examples of area administration. Various departments of government, both at the Union and State levels, have their own administrative areas known as circles, zones, districts, etc., vested with decision-making authority within prescribed limits. Territorial decentralisation, thus, involves the problem of relationship between the headquarters and numerous field agencies. Functional decentralisation signifies the central authority ceding certain areas of decision-making to technical or professional bodies of experts. Universities, All India Medical Council, Bar Associations, University Grants Commission, Central Social Welfare Board are examples of such bodies.

Decentralisation has many advantages. In the first place, it removes the danger of "apoplexy at the top and anemia at the extremities". The dispersal of authority, functions and responsibility, on the one hand, brings relief to the overburdened central authority, and strengthens field agencies and grass-root units, on the other. Secondly, the people immediately affected get an opportunity for adaptation and adjustment in the administrative programmes and operations which are brought closer to them. Thirdly, dispersal of authority encourages faster action, reduces delays and shortens the red-tape. Overall efficiency of administration, thus, increases. Fourthy, it gives an opportunity to develop resourcefulness and self-respect among subordinate administrators, who thus have to fend for themselves, to take their own decisions, and shoulder their own responsibilities. Fifthly, decentralisation facilitates experiments by various units by not committing the entire organisation to a particular course of action. It also permits healthy competition among units. Lastly, in the words of Charlesworth. "Decentralisation has a morc important justification that mere administrative efficiency. It bears directly upon the development of a sense of personal adequacy in the individual citizen; it has spiritual connotations."

## Demerits

Decentralisation, on the other hand, is not free from dangers. Too much of decentralisation may lead to anarchy. In any case, decentralisation makes co-ordination and integration of administrative operations difficult. Again, it is neither possible nor desirable to have complete decentralisation in personnel, budgeting, tax collection, accounting, planning, programming, etc. Moreover, increasingly rapid means of transport and communication, the needs of modern defence and the compulsions of economic planning are factors in favour of centralisation. Similarly, it is more economical and efficient to centralize house-keeping activities. Lastly, political commitment to common and uniform policies for the whole country, like raising the standard of living, free and compulsory education and prohibition, press in the direction of centralised administration.

Decentralisation, therefore, can be brought about only within limits. There have to be certain safeguards provided for in the administrative system. "Before divesting himself of functions, the centre-head must be sure of several things: (1) Local officers must report to no more than one central agency. (2) Jurisdictional lines must be meticulously drawn. (3) Procedures in the several field establishments must come up to a common standard, although they need not be uniform. (4) The local agency must have a sufficiently flexible physical and psychological structure to permit it to adjust to emergent local conditions. (5) The field unit must not make decisions affecting overall policy, although it should be encouraged to make its own decision to a point approaching that situation. (6) A system of ready appeals must be present. (7) Suggestions from the field to the centre must be freely channelled. (8) Adequate reporting and inspection methods must provide the centre-head with full and current knowledge of peripheral operations." After the centre-head has satisfied himself that these eight safeguards have been installed, he is free to tell his field supervisors that within those limits they are urged to run their organisations in their own way.

## Evaluation

Centralisation and decentralisation, however, are not *a priori* principles which can be universally applied at any time and at any place; they have a situational relevance. According to James W. Fesler, there are four kinds of factors which come into play in deciding for a centralised or a decentralised system. These are the factors of responsibility, administrative factors, functional factors, and external factors. One of the arguments against any kind of decentralisation is the principle of administrative responsibility. Authority and responsibility go hand in hand, and so long as the central authority is held responsible for any action, it is hesitant and even reluctant to cede discretionary authority to field officials? Among the administrative factors, mentioned by Fesler, are—"age of the agency, stability of its policies and methods, competence of its field personnel, pressure for speed and economy, and administrative sophistication." The main functional factors may be the variety of functions an agency performs, the technical nature of functions, and the need for nationwide uniformity. It is common experience that while certain types of functions like defence, planning, communication and transport requiring nationwide uniformity tend in the direction of centralisation, operating decisions can be easily decentralised at the appropriate lowest level. Long back, J.S. Mill recommended the vesting in the local agencies "not only the execution, but to a great degree the control of details." Among the external factors may be included the demand for popular participation in programmes and the pressure of political parties. The demand for "planning from blow" is a good illustration of this phenomenon. Grass-roots democracy implies a strong dose of decentralisation. Alexis de Tocqueville's views in this context are significant: "Indeed I cannot conceive that a nation can live and prosper without a powerful centralisation of government. But I am of opinion that a centralised administration is fit only to enervate the nation in which it exists by incessantly diminishing their local spirit, although such an administration can bring together at a given moment on a given point all the disposable resources. It may insure a victory in the hour of strife, but it gradually relaxes the sinews of strength. It may help admirably the transient greatness of man, but not the desirable prosperity of a nation."

# 4

# The Bureaucracy

## The Concept

A stylised (that is, Weberian ideal-type; see Weber, 1957) bureaucracy is an organisation purposefully adapted to attaining a single functional goal. It is organised hierarchically with a clear and strict chain of command from top to bottom. Moreover, the hierarchy is pyramidal in form, with several subordinates carrying out functionally related tasks under one superior at each level. Reflecting this, there is an elaborate division of labour throughout the organisation, with specialist tasks being assigned to appropriately skilled personnel, with the responsibilities becoming increasingly generalised and managerial up the hierarchy. All conduct in the pursuit of official duties is governed by a detailed set of rules and regulations, with 'precedent' being accorded almost mystical reverence. Recruitment into the service is on the basis of competence and specialised training rather than by birth or privilege. And office-holding in the organisation tends to be a life-long vocation; that is, a career.

The stylised version of a bureaucracy is open to the criticism that it overestimates the rationality and efficiency of standard operating procedures of standing organisations staffed by faceless experts. Conversely, it downplays the elements of 'red tapism', the petty conservatism of officials, and the insidious effects of such processes as exemplified in Parkinson's law that work expands to fill the time available for its completion. (There is also the related Peter principle that each person rises to her or his level of incompetence.) Such objections may well be valid, if to lesser and greater degrees in different bureaucracies. Yet they are also irrelevant to the point at hand. The essential argument is that, under modern conditions, few of the activities entrusted to bureaucracies could be carried out by non-bureaucratic organisations. In the Weberian philosophy, the decisive reason for the advance of bureaucratic organisation was its purely technical superiority over any other form of organisation. 'Bureaucracy-free' structures can indeed achieve collective goals, but only in small, decentralised local communities. That is, if we wish to pursue administrative and productive goals in a large and territorially extensive society, then we need a bureaucratic organisation. The Mughal emperors recognised this and established their own extensive bureaucracy to underpin their administrations; the British introduced the principles of European administration to the subcontinent.

A bureaucracy tenders expert advice to the government so that decisions can be made on the basis of the most informed choices. Once the decisions have been made, responsibility for implementing them is again vested in the bureaucracy. That is, even though a bureaucracy is part of the policy-making structure, bureaucrats are advisers and implementers of public choices made by the policy-makers and decision-makers. The permanence of the career civil servant brings stability and continuity to the task of administration. Moreover, when contrasted with the itinerant nature of many political 'masters' (that is, ministers), the very permanence of the civil servant confers an important measure of political influence over public policy. Information is power, and the bureaucracy is the repository of a vast store of information collected over the course of the years. The minister might call for all relevant information; but the choice of what is all the relevant information, and the retrieval and transmission of that information, is made by the civil servant. The information can be presented in such a manner as to skew the choices towards the option favoured by the bureaucracy. Similarly, civil servants can interpret policy directives in such a manner as to delay and thwart the implementation of government policy that is not to their liking. Bureaucracies act so as to maximise their own budget, for example by increased size of staff and enlarged scope of action. The bigger the bureaucracy, the more significant can be the factors of bureaucratic inertia and slippage.

The permanence of the bureaucracy requires that it be staffed by career civil servants. A person must have professional lifelong tenure, other than for unsatisfactory performance, in order to think of the civil service as a career. Furthermore, the theory of the permanence of the civil service is in contrast to the periodic turnover of politicians and the theory of governments being changed by the ballot box. Yet, in the discharge of official duties a civil servant cannot discriminate between individual politicians and political parties. Moreover, a civil servant is requried to tender advice in the formulation of public policy on the basis of an honest assessment of the best strategy for attaining the goals desired by means of the resources available to the state. Thereafter, once the policy is decided by the political executive (that is, the government), the civil servant is expected to implement it faithfully regardless of support for or opposition to the policy. It is all this which explains the condition of political neutrality of the civil servants and the civil service. A civil servant is not permitted to express personal ideological or party preferences other than in the privacy of the polling booth.

## The Public Service Commissions

The Indian constitution is distinctive for including provisions relating to the federal and state public services. The body responsible for the service conditions of civil servants in India is the public service commission: the Union Public Service Commission (UPSC) for the central and all-India services, and a state public service commission for the civil services of that state. Two or more states can be serviced by a joint PSC; a state may also choose to have the UPSC regulate its civil service. The requirement to have a PSC for the union government and for each state, or a Joint PSC for a group of states if so indicated by the legislatures of those states, is mandatory under the Indian constitution. The size, composition and conditions of service of the commissions is determined by governments and formally effected by the president and governors for the union and state PSCs respectively. In 1991 the UPSC comprised ten members plus the chairman. Members are appointed for six-year terms of service, but must retire at the ages of 65 and 62 respectively in the case of the union and state PSCs. Members may also resign or be removed from office on ground of insolvency, paid outside employment, infirmity of mind or body, or misbehaviour as established by the Supreme Court upon reference to it by the president. It is worth noting that even the members of state PSCs can be removed for misbehaviour only with a presidential reference to the Supreme Court. The governor is the formal appointing authority for state PSCs but cannot remove their members other than through the president.

The system of parliamentary government makes the political executive, namely the prime minister and cabinet, responsible to the parliament. In order to work in practice, this has to be buttressed by a permanent administrative executive answerable to, but also protected by, the political executive. The operational requirements of responsible government include (a) the existence of an independent and competent civil service (b) which is staffed by persons capable of giving advice to successive ministers based on long and continuous experience (c) who are secure in their positions as long they do not misbehave officially and (d) carry out the government's policy. In turn this necessitates the framing and administering of rules governing the recruitment and conduct of civil servants, commonly known as the conditions of service.

The Constitution of India contains four safeguards for the independence of the PSCs from the political executive:

- it specifies the manner and grounds for removal as noted above;
- it stipulates that the conditions of service cannot be altered to the disadvantage of an incumbent member of any PSC;
- it makes the expenses of the PSCs chargeable on the consolidated funds of the union and state governments as appropriate; and
- it debars commission members from accepting paid employment after their service on a PSC, except that

(a) ordinary members of the UPSC can be appointed as chairman of the UPSC or a state PSC, (b) the chairman of a state PSC can be appointed as chairman of another state PSC, or as a member or chairman of the UPSC, and (c) ordinary members of a state PSC can be appointed to the UPSC or to chair any state PSC or the UPSC. That is, in effect a member of any public service commission can be promoted within the PSC system but not take any employment outside the system either with the government or in the private sector.

In addition to performing advisory functions in the recruitment and service conditions of all state and union government employees, the union and state PSCs are requried by the constitution to submit annual reports to the president and governors respectively (Article 323). The advisory nature of the functions of the PSCs underlines the point that in parliamentary government, responsibility for the proper administration of the affairs of state vests in the cabinet through parliament. Parliamentary oversight is also ensured by requiring the annual reports of PSCs to be laid before each legislature as appropriate. On the administrative side, the relations of the UPSC with the government are under the formal coordination of the Ministry of Home Affairs. But the UPSC also has its own secretariat for conducting its daily business with the various departments.

Constitutional safeguards protect not just the public service commissions but also the civil servants. Rules made by parliament and state legislatures for regulating the conduct of civil servants are subject to judicial oversight vis-a-vis their constitutionality, and the courts have in fact annulled some rules for having contravened particular provisions of the constitution. Action against an official who violates 'good behaviour' can take one of three forms; dismissal, removal or reduction in rank. A dismissed employee is not eligible for re-employment as a civil servant; an officer who has merely been 'removed' is so eligible. The penalty for both categories includes disallowance of pension entitlements for past services. By contrast, 'compulsory retirement' does not entail loss of previously accumulated entitlements.

The constitution provides important procedural safeguards for the civil servant (but not for military personnel) against arbitrary disciplinary measures. A civil servant cannot be dismissed or removed by an authority subordinate to that by which the officer was appointed (Article 311.1). Moreover, no disciplinary action may be undertaken against an official without providing the officer with a 'reasonable opportunity' to rebut the charges (Article 311.2).

Originally, such opportunity had to be provided both at the point of initiating the inquiry into the charges of official misconduct, and at the point of imposing any penalty. The 42nd amendment of the constitution in 1976 took away the second right of an employee to make a representation against the proposed penalty. 'Reasonable opportunity' means that an official must be given the opportunity (a) to deny guilt and establish innocence by being informed of the charges against him and the basis of those charges, (b) for defence against the charges by means of cross-examination of witnesses offering evidence in support of the charges levelled against the employee and (c) for the presentation of evidence and witnesses that will help to establish the employee's innocence.

That is, the government is requried:

- to frame specific charges against an officer subject to disciplinary action;
- to inform the officer of those charges;
- to give the officer the opportunity to respond to the charges;
- to come to a decision on the charges only after taking into consideration the officer's response; and
- to follow the rules of natural justice in making any determination against the officer.

The 42nd amendment also took away the right of civil servants to take disputes over recruitment and conditions of service to the civil and high courts, restricting such a judicial recourse to the Supreme Court only (Article 323.A). The provision was implemented with the passage of a law by parliament in 1985 which set up a Central Administrative Tribunal for adjudicating all such disputes regarding all government employees other than defence personnel, officials of the Supreme Court and High Courts, and secretarial staff of parliament and the state legislatures.

**The Public Services**

There are three types of public service in India: the state services, whose officials are recruited, employed and dismissible by a state government; central services, whose officials are recruited, employed and dismissible by the union government for duties throughout the territory of India; and all-India services, whose officials are recruited and dismissible by the union government, but whose services are shared between the central government and that of any one state government. Examples of central services include the defence forces, the Indian Foreign Service (IFS), the Indian Railway Service, the Indian Audits and Account Service, the Indian Customs and Excise Service, the Postal Service and the Indian Revenue Service, Altogether there are more than fifty such services. Of lesser prestige, power and status than the all-India services, the central services are known collectively as the allied services. Of greatest exclusivity and glamour nevertheless is a central service, namely the IFS, the cream of the Indian diplomatic corps. Each of these separate services has a characteristic tendency to develop its own caste-like exclusiveness, with its own grades, salary and promotion structures. Cross-service transfer is very rare.

The Indian Administrative Service (IAS) and the Indian Police Service are the two all-India services listed in the constitution. Article 312 of the constitution empowered parliament to create additional all-India services common to the union and the states if requested by a two-thirds majority of the Rajya Sabha in a resolution stating that it is necessary and expedient in the national interest to do so. Only the Indian Forest Service has been created under this provision. States have resisted attempts to form still more all-India services. The stated reason for their opposition is the additional financial strain that would be imposed on them because of the higher pay scales of the all-India services. The unstated reasons include a reluctance to share the administration of any more services with the central government and to open up still more of the states' public services to non-state civil servants. The recruitment and conditions of service of the all-India services are regulated by rules framed under the All-India Services Act passed by parliament in 1951 under Article 312.

The modern IAS is the direct descendant of the Indian Civil Service (ICS) of the British Raj. The ICS was an administrative aristocracy. At a personal level, service in the colonies was sometimes the salvation for gentlemen condemned to mediocrity in their home countries. At the institutional level, the great strength of the ICS officers lay in their remarkable adaptability and dedication. While recruitment into the service placed a premium on liberal education and commonsense intelligence, in-service training emphasised administrative competence and managerial responsibility for a variety of tasks at senior levels of government. Debutante officers were assigned to subordinate offices in the districts and worked their passage up through senior district and divisional posts in states to the highest rungs of the state and central governments bureaucratic ladders. An explicit attempt was made to rotate officers from one place to another and from one function to another. ICS officers were the executive arm of the government. As senior executives, their administrative qualities were more important than their specialist skills.

The structure, recruitment, training and ethos of the ICS was retained in the case of the IAS. Like the ICS, the IAS is recruited from among the best and the brightest graduates, its officers trained and requried to discharge duties covering a wide range of functions across a number of postings. The 'sanctity' of these all-India services is protected by placing their recruitment, training and service conditions under the supervision of the UPSC as per Part IV of the constitution. The IAS is the only 'multifunctional' government service. The IAS officer is to be found in charge of running steel plants, electricity boards, food corporations, airlines, municipal corporations and even universities. The total number of public sector employees in India is more than 17 million, of whom IAS officers number fewer than 5000. They are recruited each year on the basis of competitive examinations followed by interviews of shortlisted candidates. Applicants must be 21-28 year old graduates of recognised universities. (The upper age restriction is relaxed to 31 in the case of scheduled castes and tribes.)

The selection procedure is designed to assess a candidate's overall ability, general knowledge and broad analytical skills. In the 1990s the number writing the examinations is approaching one lakh (the Indian unit of measurement for one hundred thousand). Of these almost one thousand (or 1 per cent of applicants) are taken into the central and all-India services, with the IAS intake numbering around 150 (or 0.15 per cent of the applicants). About one-fifth of the IAS recruits are women, and between one-quarter and one-third come from the scheduled castes and tribes. For a long time the examinations had to be written in English, but since 1978 candidates can choose to write in any of the recognised regional languages. Even so, English remains a compulsory paper, along with general knowledge and an essay composition designed to test powers of reasoning as well as qualities of writing and expression. Probationers are sent for training to the Lal Bahadur Shastri Academy of Administration in Mussoorie. The year in Mussoorie includes courses on the constitutional, economic and social framework of India today, and on public administration. At the end of the year, candidates are required to pass a written examination and qualifying examinations in Hindi and the language of the state to which they have been allotted. The requirement of a riding test has been discontinued. The year in Mussoorie is followed by up to two years of in-field training in the states before conformation of appointment.

The career of a fresh IAS officer begins with a posting as a Sub-Divisional Officer (SDO) within a district. The IAS officer is a central government employee; the district is the major administrative unit of the state inherited from the colonial system.

An IAS officer is normally assigned to one state cadre for his her entire professional life, and about 70 per cent of IAS offices are in fact under state postings at any given time. Where possible, the preferences of new recruits are accommodated when making the initial determinations on placements into state cadres. Thereafter, an officer may serve stints in the nation's capital, but will be considered to be on assignment to the centre from the state. In both

**Figure 4.1**
**Organisational Chart of Revenue Department, State of Maharashtra, 1993**

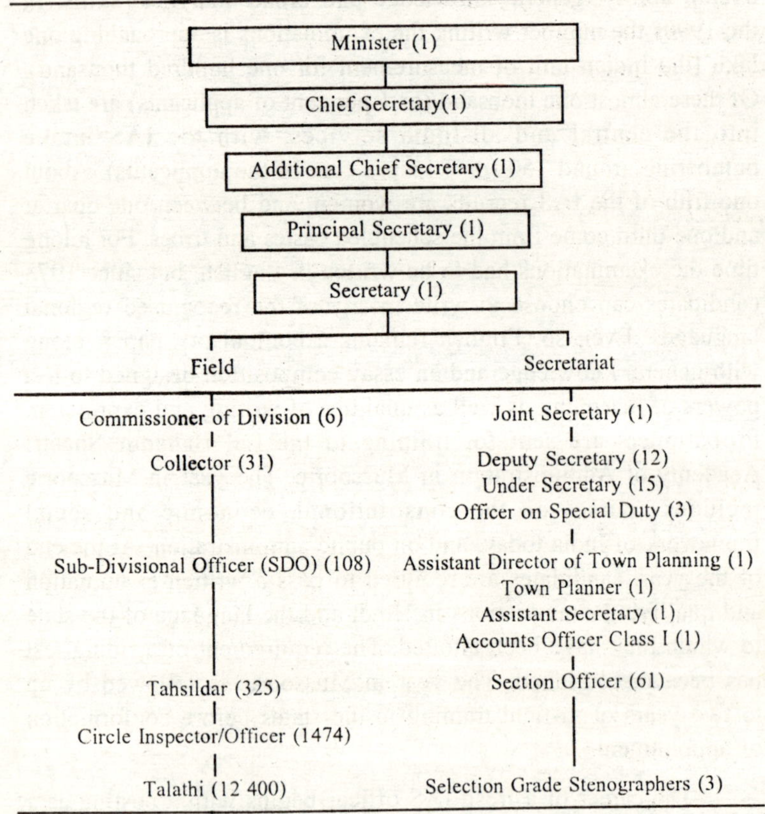


*Source:* Government of Maharashtra, *Karyakarm Andajpatrak (Programme Estimates) 1993-94: Revenue and Forests Department* (Nagpur: Government Publications, 1993), pp. 6, 157.

New Delhi and the state capitals, the apex of the bureaucracy is the secretariat. In both units of government, the chief executive of a department is the secretary, and the highest rank in the state civil service is the chief secretary (see Figure 4.1).

The state governments have their own public services which function under the supervision of provincial public service commissions. State officials serve throughout their careers within their state's territorial jurisdictions State administration is more demanding than central, since it is at this level that the tasks of development are executed, law and order is maintained and most of the interaction takcs place between citizens, politicians and civil servants. Yet state services are less prestigious, less well-paid and, therefore, less competently staffed. Their superficial resemblance with the central services is not matched in the quality of recruitment and training. There are also wide disparities between the different states, with Bihar and Maharashtra, for example, representing the poorer and better ends of the spectrum respectively. The latter has a sufficient depth of quality graduates to ensure an efficient state service even after its best are seduced by the central services. The former's pool of talent is so shallow that it is generally under-represented in the central services in proportion to its population.

The peculiar administrative burden-sharing between the union and state governments distinguishes India from other federal systems like the American, Australian and Canadian. Its advantage is that it confers a degree of uniformity of administrative structure and practice throughout the land that would be impossible otherwise. It is also one of the major integrative institutions in Indian policies. The all-India services have in fact been used consciously as a nation-building instrument. The mix of domicile and out-of-state staffing, for example, ensures a spread of talent all around the country and fosters the sense of belonging to one nation. At the same time, there is also an attempt to strike a balance between national integration and localism; at least one-fifth of IAS officers in any state must be recruited from within the state's own administrative service. But no more than half of any state's IAS cadre can be from within the state.

**Problems**

In the ideal-type bureaucracy that we discussed at the start of this chapter, the official's legal authority rests on technical expertise. In reality, the processional standards of the expert can collide with the administrative requirements of the managerial official (even if the two should be the same person). Organisations today tend to be both professionalised and bureaucratised. We need to distinguish between the two alternative sources of authority if we wish to clarify some of the core issues and conflicts in today's organisations.

Another problem concerns alternative principles of governance. The organising principle of social action can be rooted either in majority rule or in administrative efficiency. The first accepts the freedom to dissent from official decisions, the second demands unquestioning obedience of superiors. Because many organisations, for example political parties, have both principles, they can sometimes experience tension between the two contrary pulls. In pursuit of the second principle, the bureaucracy institutionalised by the British and bequeathed to independent India was designed for administration and stability. Its major requirement was to contain demands. By contrast, the major task of post-independence bureaucracy was to be responsive to citizen demands. The government of independent India faced the difficult task of conversion of a law-and-order and revenue collection apparatus into an instrument of national-building and development.

It is a cliche to say that independence changed the nature of the administrative tasks. It could be argued that the pre-and post-independence dichotomy is exaggerated. The concern of the British raj was not limited to the maintenance of law and order, but included some nation-building and development goals. Conversely, the requirements of maintaining law and order have if anything increased since independence, starting with the partition-related riots. Yet even while we should not exaggerate the change in the nature of bureaucratic tasks with independence, nor should we deny the substance of the underlying thesis. This is especially so in India because of the ambitious programme of planned economic development that was launched shortly after independence.

Democratisation of the civil services has another aspect to it. Article 335 of the constitution aims to break up the homogeneity of the administrative services by directing that the special claims of scheduled castes and tribes shall be taken into account in appointments to the central and state government services. We touched on the programmes of preferential policies earlier in Chapter 1. The letter and spirit of Article 335 have encountered two difficulties. As regards the letter, the same article stipulates that programmes of affirmative action shall be consistent with administrative efficiency. Possibly because of this rider, the elite services remain disproportionately 'Brahminised'. As regards the spirit, members of the scheduled castes and tribes who do make the transition to the prestigious all-India services are loath to continue to identify themselves with the backward and tribal communities. Instead, they assiduously cultivate the method of their new professional identity: which is still almost tangibly elitist.

The elitism of the service in composition and orientation had served the ICS well in ruling over a subject race. This is why, while many British had considered the ICS 'steel frame' one of the finest legacies bequeathed to independent India, many nationalists were contemptuous of an institution that was not Indian, nor civil, nor a service to the people. While democratisation has been attempted and to some extent achieved, by and large the premier administrative services remain elitist. They are narrowly recruited not simply in terms of social strata, but even in terms of educational background. The upper-class, urban families who send their children to the right schools and universities are over-represented; the poor, rural and backward communities are under-represented. In the 1960s, for example, about half of all IAS recruits came from just the four universities of Allahabad, Calcutta, Delhi and Madras. Some 70 per cent came from urban backgrounds, despite only 20 per cent of the population being urban. Only 20 per cent came from agricultural families, with 40 per cent being children of government officials.

We may conclude from this that recruitment on the basis of competitive examinations and interviews has a 'structural basis' in favour of the wealthy, urban and sophisticated graduate. By the mid-1970s, demonstrable progress had been achieved in democratising the services: the majority of IFS, IAS and allied services recruits were from the middle and lower classes (*Hindustan Times,* 6 February 1976). Recruits from a public school (in the English sense of the phrase) background had been pared down to about a fifth of the total intake. The fact remains however that an IAS officer who may be of humble origins quickly becomes elitist in orientation, helped by training, powers, and the perks and privileges of office.

A different kind of problem occurred at the lower rungs of the bureaucracy that were thoroughly bound by routine and precedent. To the lowly functionaries in the vast and labyrinthine bureaucracy of the British Raj, a government job was a comfortable livelihood which could best be safeguarded by pleasing superiors. Almost certainly Indian, the junior bureaucrat preferred regurgitation of his master's views to independent conceptual thinking, the safety of precedents to the frightening prospect of novel challenges. Success lay not in taking initiatives, but in the literal application of the formidable panoply of detailed regulations with which the steel frame had girded the subcontinent.

Another set of problems is generic to the Whitehall model of bureaucracy so well illustrated in the popular British television series *Yes Minister* and *Yes Prime Minister.* The permanence of the career civil servant and the transience of ministerial bosses leaves the latter open to manipulation by the former; there are jurisdictional wranglings between different departments concerning demarcation; and the cabinet, which should ensure coordination in a parliamentary system of government, can itself get entangled in 'turf warfare'. For example food production, which actually takes place within the territorial and legislative jurisdictions of states, is also covered by the Food and Agriculture Ministry, the Planning Commission, the Irrigation and Power Ministry and so on in New Delhi. The 'bureaucratic' rigidity has in some senses been hardened in India by the Whitehall model being transplanted to an entirely different social, economic and political environment. H.V. Kamath of the then-ruling Janata Party described the bureaucratic ethos thus in the Lok Sabha on 25 April 1979: 'If you can, don't move; if you must, move slowly; if pushed, move in circles; and if cornered, appoint a committee' (quoted in Gupta, 1982, p. 402).

India is not immune to the inter-service jealousies and interdepartmental rivalries that afflict all large bureaucracies. This means that officials are hypersensitive to the relativities of salary packages, status and powers of the various ministries. But it also means that any action requires multiple interdepartmental clearances. Part of the reason for this is once again the prevailing norm of safety first: extensive and repeated consultations ensure that responsibility for a mistake cannot easily be pinned on any one official. So no one is prepared to make a decision if it can somehow be passed on to someone else.

Under the regulatory regime established progressively after 1950, India fell victim to a relentless bureaucratic sprawl. Outside India at least, it was generally acknowledged that the country had a hugely bloated, inefficient and parasitically corrupt bureaucracy. A study conducted by the Federation of Indian Chambers of Commerce and Industry concluded that bureaucratic delays had cost the country a staggering Rs 1500 bn in thirty years since 1950. Each file awaiting government clearance for a billion rupee private sector project meant a loss of Rs 250000 per day to the company concerned, an annual production loss of Rs 2.7m and a revenue loss of Rs 1.6m to the government (OHT, 13 May 1982). By the mid-1990s there is widespread sentiment even in India that the country's bureaucracy has become an elephantine, amorphous lump. Its pervasive presence is felt everywhere, its effectiveness or usefulness are apparent almost nowhere.

The Congress government of P.V. Narasimha Rao (1991) decided to dismantle the heavily interventionist and regulatory state created by successive governments since independence. The dirigiste tendencies of the vast bureaucracy set up to administer the previous licence raj regime proved unsurprisingly resistant to change and demonstrated remarkable ingenuity in devising ways and means of thwarting reform. For example, the government decided on an 'open skies' policy that challenged the monopoly of the state-run domestic carrier, Indian Airlines (IA). Indian entrepreneurs took to the skies with characteristic verve. East West Airways, Jet Airways, Continental Aviation and Modiluft began to offer what IA had signally failed to: transporting passengers to their destinations on time and in comfort. Initial anti-competitive restrictions—IA was given the right to veto routing requests, private carriers were prohibited from charging fares less than 25 per cent below IA fares and from scheduling flights within one hour of IA flights—proved insufficient to dampen commuters' enthusiasm for the private air taxis. IA was compelled to improve its service to woo back customers: a textbook example of the virtues of competition. In addition, however, private airlines were told that they could not legally publish flight schedules and IA pilots were told that they could not switch jobs without a 'no objection certificate' from the IA: textbook examples of anti-competitive behaviour. Captured by the state sector employees, the bureaucracy was being driven by the interests of the people in it and not the public they were meant to serve. (For similar sentiments by a serving civil servant regarding Bangladesh, which emerged from the same British Raj culture, see Ahmed, 1994.)

## Civil-Political Relations

Tensions between the bureaucrat and the politician are endemic to all political systems. They are heightened in the case of former colonies because of the transformation of the bureaucracy from a coercive apparatus of the colonial state to a responsive instrument of the indigenous people. Paradoxically, they were particularly acute in India precisely because of the success in socialising Indians into the bureaucratic and parliamentary traditions of the Westminster style of government. Before independence, the civil servant was often the administrator-master confronting the politician as a threat to the colonial law and order. For regardless of personal predilections, the civil servant was an official agent of the colonial state. Independence brought about a reversal of roles, and both sets of people—politicians no less than bureaucrats—had to come to terms with the role reversal. The problems of psychological adjustments were helped by the qualities of both groups of people at the time of independence: the Indians in the pre-1947 ICS (almost half the ICS corps was Indian by then) and the leaders of nationalist movement were among the best and the brightest of their generation.

The same qualities were helpful also in another sense. On the one hand, Prime Minister Jawaharlal Nehru and his colleagues were confident enough of their own worth that they did not need to demonstrate their superiority by exacting retribution on those who had merely served in their lines of duty. On the other hand, they realised that India was fortunate to have inherited a proven framework of administration and a corps of experienced administrators. Being shrewd enough to recognise this, Nehru resisted calls from within the Congress Party to disband the ICS structure because of its elitist orientation and caste-like exclusivity. Instead, he stressed the ICS as a needed and welcome source of administrative competence and its potential as a nation-building and state-building instrument. He therefore retained it with a changed nomenclature.

Relative to 1947, as the quality of the civil servants and the politicians declined with the passage of time, suspicions between the two groups grew and tensions resurfaced. This was especially the case at the state level where the educational and intellectual caliber of the IAS officers was well above that of the political masters. The state of hostile coexistence spread upwards even to the central government with the propensity of cabinet ministers to shift responsibility for scandals to their departmental secretaries. Not surprisingly, this had a damaging effect on the morale and confidence of the civil servants. In the other direction, attempts at democratic decentralisation depend the political process down to the village level and exposed the civil servant to politics and politicians as rough and ready as they come. The net result was to politicize the bureaucracy from New Delhi to the villages. Those who were amenable to their master's wishers and biddings began to be rewarded with plum postings and promotions, while those who resisted unwarranted interference with the routines of administration discovered their political independence and professional integrity to be distinctly career-unfriendly. The existence of a thriving private sector and a tradition of lateral mobility between the public and private sectors reduces the costs of resignations and diversifies the sensitivities and loyalties of workers. Lacking this in India, civil servants dare not were their professional consciences on their dress shirts.

The carrot-and-stick approach gradually wore down the independence and integrity of the entire civil service, culminating in the complete capitulation of the bureaucracy to the excesses of the emergency during 1975-7: the bureaucrats honoured the venerable tradition of obeying orders lawfully issued. Tensions generated by the emergency excesses would have been partly ameliorated by the primacy given to the law-and-order function of the IAS officers, partly by the well-established habit by that date of political interference in bureaucratic affairs, and partly by the equally firmly established centralizing tendency of Mrs Indira Gandhi which was 'codified' by the emergency. The other item of interest in the emergency experience was that the quality of administration deteriorated with a centralized authoritarian regime. The lines of bureaucratic authority grew longer while the sensitivity to local needs, conditions and aspirations lessened (Heginbotham, 1976, pp. 88-9).

The emergency period was Mrs Gandhi's darkest hour, and the notion of a committed bureaucracy came to be associated with her reign. At the Congress Party meeting on 16 November 1969, she had attacked the administrative machinery for constituting a stumbling block in the path of progress. the left wing of the party took up the cause and mounted an offensive against the conservative and reactionary leadership of the bureaucracy whose upper-class prejudices were said to be out of tune with the imperatives of progressive social and economic change. They called instead for a new administrative cadre that would be committed to national objectives and responsive to social needs. The concept of a committed bureaucracy provided a cover for increasingly partisan interference by politicians—union and state ministers, MPs and MLA—in the affairs of administration. In 1993-4 stories circulated in the state of Bihar of an IAS officer having been slapped by a politician in the presence of other people and of having humbly accepted this very public insult. Still, he was more fortunate than Miss Chandralekha, a senior IAS officer in Tamil Nadu. On 19 May 1992, she was badly burnt and disfigured in an acid attack, purportedly for incurring the displeasure of Chief Minister Miss Jayalalitha (SW, 21 November 1992). The state government also recommended Chandralekha's suspension on trumped up charges, but the Union Minister of Personnel declined to oblige.

So the pursuit of a committed bureaucracy had succeeded in producing a class of bureaucrats that was instantly subservient to, if also simultaneously contemptuous of, the politicians. The increasing politicisation of the bureaucracy was only too clear with the attempts by the Janata Government (1977-9) to weed out those guilty of enthusiastically enforcing the emergency regulations, and Mrs Gandhi's follow-up action in punishing such officials as had vigorously helped the Janata Government in its campaign against her. Her son and successor Rajiv Gandhi took prime ministerial disdain of the civil servant still further. He announced the dismissal of Foreign Secretary A.P. Venkateswaran at a nationally televised press conference in February 1987. Venkateswaran, in attendance at the press conference, had received no advance warning of what was to come and was visibly stunned at the announcement.

In the end the civil servant's response to political encroachments was twofold. On the one hand, as a means of promoting self-interest, each officer began to cultivate political patrons, powerful local leaders at each level who could be counted on to return favours through the bureaucrat's career path. On the other hand, as a measure of self-protection, the malaise that had afflicted the lower rungs of the bureaucracy during the British Raj now spread to the top echelons, namely a literal application of the myriad of rules and regulations. For if it could be shown that proper procedures had been followed, then one could not be disciplined. There was a goal displacement from civil service to job security. By the 1990s IAS officers themselves in private conversations referred to their service as 'I Am Safe'. Despite all this, and even though the district officer might now come into contact more with the district and state politicians than with the ordinary folk, the

IAS district officer retains the mystical élan and predominance in the scheme of things.

**Corruption in the Bureaucracy**

The civil servant is to the businessman what the politician is to the bureaucrat. The plethora of controls introduced under the permitlicence raj have vested enormous powers in civil servants over business affairs. The system spawned an inefficient regulatory regime, cripplingly high compliance and transaction costs, a corrupt bureaucratic system and a rent-seeking political system. India's bureaucrats have only too often used red tape to suffocate the private sector. The goals of the Industries Development and Regulation Act of 1951 were help to small industries, prevention of capital concentration and dispersal of industrial expansion across the country. The regulatory regime created in pursuit of these goals discouraged successful firms from growing, encouraged them instead to lose money and, when they failed, forbade them to close. Setting up a new plant, relocating an existing one or expanding it in capacity or range of products could not be decided merely on commercial calculations, but were all subject to licence. They were also subject to the Monopolies and Trade Practices (MRTP) Act. Designed to guard the public interest against private monopolists, the MRTP protected the many public sector monopolies operated by bureaucrats against the public interest.

All of this against the backdrop of the wealth-consuming public servant treating the wealth-creating businessman with scorn and condescension. The prevailing bureaucratic attitude is that the businessman needs to be hemmed in by rules on all sides. Because the government's motive is egalitarian redistribution while that of the businessman is profit, the latter must be curbed by the former, argue the bureaucrats. In more recent times there has also been an element of envy. The official salaries of the civil servants ensure a total divorce between the status and income of bureaucrats. For the bright young person with drive, initiative and self-belief, the private sector offers more attractive salary packages and greater scope for rapid career advancement. Civil servants have suffered relative deprivation of material rewards since independence as business have prospered. Because they are in a position to affect private sector decisions worth millions of rupees, most give in to the temptation to transfer some of the freefloating money to their own pockets. In 1993, for example, a young District Magistrate in one of the metropolitan cities was asking and getting one hundred thousand rupees per approval for routine housing construction projects.

Political interference, reduced attractiveness of service and declining morale have all combined to whittle away the bureaucrat's will to remain honest. When politicians above (ministers) and below (party hacks) are both venal, then the IAS officer too gets sandwiched into corruption. India is notorious for its influence-peddling politicians, money-seeking bureaucrats and bribe-dispensing entrepreneurs. A permit-licence Raj creates recurring shortages and multiplies opportunities for illicit profit or 'rent'. Because action depends on bureaucratic and political discretion, the discretionary application of controls makes the rent part-property of the minister and the civil servant making the decision. Bribery is so thoroughly instituionalised that most people engaged in the transactions are aware of the scale of the charges and the lateral and upwards percentage shares in the illicit rent (See Wade, 1985). The market for public office can be quantified, for example, in the marriage market in Bihar: the dowry will reflect the illicit earning potential of the bridegroom's public sector job. Similarly, a state cabinet minister in Bihar will expect a kickback in proportion to the earning potential of the posting of an engineer to a construction project. In turn, squabbles between politicians for portfolios reflect the latter's earning potential rather than policy preferences. In Bihar at least the chief demand on a state cabinet minister is not to make policy but to exercise discretionary authority in exchange for due consideration. The culture of corruption has become deeply embedded in Indian public life.

It could be said that bribes serve to bring the costs of services in line with market prices. Bribery is an efficient mechanisms for rationing a good or service which is in short supply. Graft, it has been said often enough, lubricates the wheels of government in India. Yet even from the point of view of economic logic, public corruption is bad because it encourages inefficiency. Managers have built-in incentives to distort and disrupt markets because this increases their market power. It becomes something of a catch-22; rent-seeking is an efficient response to distortions, but distortions are also a logical response to the availability of rent. Special dispensation in order to circumvent bureaucratic or legal hurdles in return for material gain almost certainly occurs in every country. What makes the pervasiveness of corruption in India so distinctive is that graft is necessary to get lowliest officials to perform their *ordinary* duties for which they are receiving salaries from the public purse.

The biggest cost is political. Petty corruption is especially endemic at the lower, clerical levels of administration—precisely the point at which the ordinary citizen comes into daily contact with the bureaucracy. People are forced to pay bribes for securing virtually any service connected with the government, even that which is theirs by right and law. People naturally tend to judge the entire structure of government on the basis of direct experiences with the agents of government. It would be difficult to exaggerate the revulsion of ordinary Indians to the ubiquitous and institutionalised venality of public life (see Exhibit 4.1). More than any other factor, corruption of politicians and officials has eroded the legitimacy of dirigiste government at its core. Rajiv Gandhi's biggest political asset in 1984 was his image of being 'Mr. Clean'. Hence the importance of the Bofors scandal (involving the purchase of Swedish howitzers for the Indian army) which tainted him and contributed materially to his government's defeat in 1989. In March 1993 Prime Minister P.V. Narasimha Rao too was embarrassed by allegations of corruption. Harshad Mehta, a stockbroker facing changes arising from the $1.6 bn bank-securities scam of 1992, alleged that he paid Rs. 10m (about $390000) in cash to the prime minister at his residence on 4 November 1991 as a means of gaining political patronage. Because of the prevailing culture of corruption, not all Indians were convinced by Narasimha Rao's protestations of innocence.

## Reforms

Successive governments have made repeated attempts to reform the administrative structure of the country, but with little visible success. The structure of the all-India services would be

**EXHIBIT 4.1**

**The tale of the village headmaster, 1975**

Ram Pratap Shukla was a 44-year old headmaster in a school in the village of Khatwara in U.P. His salary had not been paid for 11 months. He had already gone thrice to Banda, the district headquarters, from his village before this story begins.

**2 June 1975**

Ram Pratap and his brother Shvi Pratap travelled from Khatwara to Banda, a distance of about 100 km. The bus fare cost him Rs. 15. Arrived in Banda, the two stayed in a dharamsala (charitable dormitory for indigent wayfarers). Because Ram Pratap was asthmatic and looked ill, the manager at first refused them admission but changed his mind when Shvi Pratap explained that they were in some distress.

**3 June 1975, 6.00 a.m.**

The brothers Pratap went to the offices of the Basic Shiksha Adhikari (Basic Education Officer). (Office hours in the summer are 6.00 a.m.-12.00 p.m.) They knocked on the doors of all, from the Adhikari to the clerks, to no avail. But at the cost of entertaining four clerks to tea, they learnt that the cheque for payment of the salary arrears was ready. The clerks said that money would have to be spent to get the cheque so that all sides gained in the transaction. The brothers returned dejected to the dharmsala, intending to revisit the education office the next morning.

**4 June 1975, 4.00 a.m.**

Ram Pratap Shukla suffered an asthma attack. By 6.00 a.m., when he was visibly dispersed, Shvi Pratap hurriedly summoned a rickshaw and took his brother to the Zila Parishad (District Board) office. Ram Pratap was dead on arrival. His body was placed under a tree outside the Zila Parishad office. Money for the funeral was donated by the local teachers's association and a jeep was arranged to take the body back to Khatwara.

The cheque for Rs. 3156.58 owing to Ram Pratap Shukla as accumulated salary was signed on 4 June 1975 after he was dead.

*Source:* The Statesman (New Delhi), 13 June 1975.

instantly recognisable to anyone familiar with their counterparts in British India, but not the quality of the services provided nor the working environment. As well as the Planning Commission, such eminent persons as Paul Appleby, Gopalaswami Ayyangar, A.D. Gorwala and V.T. Krishnamachari have submitted reports on restructuring the administrative services. Although discussion has been plentiful, action has been tardy. In January 1966, the government set up a 5-member Administrative Reforms Commission under the chairmanship of Deputy Prime Minister Morarji Desai to signal its elevated status and firmness of leadership. Its terms of reference included scrutiny of the machinery and procedures of the central government; the planning machinery at all levels; centre-state relations; financial, economic and personnel administration; and official machinery for the redress of public grievances. It submitted several reports, and the government responded by setting up a Department of Personnel and Administrative Reforms to process and study the reports. This was followed by the setting up of a Committee of Secretaries, and then a Committee of Ministers in 1973. In the meantime, life for the bureaucrats, the politicians and the people carried on as before.

There are several obstacles to substantive reforms of the administrative services, starting with the sheer weight of bureaucratic inerita. The administrative tradition may have been inheried from the British, but its scope and reach has expanded enormously under the impact of techlology and the explosion of government into economic and social activities. The structure of administration is therefore much more complicated and cumbersome than was the case before 1947. The inertia that is common to any organisation is given extra weight in India because of the size, diversity and federal nature of the country. The 'length of the line' (see Figure 4.1) had caused concern even during the British days. The concerns have become still more acute with the passage of time and the multiplication of tasks and taskmasters. There is a great physical distance between the deskbound and paper-pushing bureaucrat and the 'average Indian in the village'. This is reinforced by the social distance between the civil servants in the elitist services and the people they are supposed to serve. Together, the social and physical distances ensure that the higher bureaucracy is a self-contained and self-satisfied group.

The bureaucracy has a vested interest in preserving and perpetuating its stranglehold over the nation's affairs, while the bureaucrat has a vested interest in preserving a structure which provides a high-powered job for life to someone who might lack any specialist qualification suited to today's increasingly technocratic job market. The lack of specialist training also produces a dogged devotion to familiar routine. Inertia is encouraged and initiative discouraged by the strong sense of hierarchy and the automatic promotion system.

The need for public sector reform in India is as urgent as the continuing lack of it is surprising. It is possible that the series of economic reforms ushered in by Prime Minister Narasimha Rao and Finance Minister Manmohan Singh since mid-1991 will lead to a progressive retrenchment of the public sector from Indian society and economy and usher in major administrative reforms in its wake.

## Conclusion

The modern state is the professional state. Ministers lack both expertise and experience in administration. Professionalism in the art of government requires that policy formulation and policy implementation be placed in the hands of technocrats with the requisite specialist skills and knowledge of the principles of public administration. The total public payroll in India, including the higher state and central civil services as well as the multitude of clerks, peons and assorted hangers-on, has more than quadrupled from four million personnel in 1953 to seventeen million in 1993. The bureaucrats' tentacles reach into the farthest corners of the country and touch the most distant sphere of social activity in India. Their pay and emoluments is a major drain on the public exchequer. Nor is it productive expenditure: India's massive public service can almost be said to represent a vast reserve army of the underemployed. For the bureaucracy below the level of the IAS officers is inefficient and obstructionist rather than competent and facilitative. At the same time, the pervasiveness of government regulations matches the omnipresence of bureaucrats. Both are designed to ensure the delivery of services to the people; agricultural, educational, medical and other. In fact the combination has resulted in the growth of a bureaucratic underclass of 'fixers' and 'brokers' who serve as intermediaries between the people and the bureaucrats (Reddy and Haragopal, 1985). When not even the sound of pencils being sharpened and paper being pushed disturbs the somnolence of secretariat offices in the heat of an Indian summer, the bureaucratic favour-brokers are approached with the request *Jara pairavi kar dijiye* (idiomatically translated from Hindi, 'Please go and lobby on my behalf).

While the structure of the bureaucracy is recognisable as that inherited from the British, the pattern of interactions between the bureaucrat and the minister has been 'fundamentally transformed in the direction of a patrimonial regime in which the political leadership selects officers who are personally loyal, who serve their narrow political interests, and who expect reciprocal preferments in return; (Brass, 1990, p. 52). As this indicates, there is some slippage between the Weberian ideal of a rational-legal bureaucracy and the operational reality of the Indian bureaucracy. The civil servant in India is not guided solely by the formal roles and regulations. Rather, the operational environment is a complex and mutually reinforcing network of rules; personal kinship, caste and political ties; and financial considerations. Though all this, the principal beneficiaries of the system of patronage that has been established for the production and distribution of benefits and resources are the politicians and bureaucrats themselves. As with so much else in India, the steel of which the administrative frame is constructed has been adulterated with baser impurities.

## Note

1. Sometimes this creates interesting situations. In the late 1980s, there was a dispute between the governments of India and Bihar over the fair price for some land that the central government wished to acquire from the state. Intense negotiations were carried on between the two governments by an IAS officer of the Bihar cadre. As a representative of the state government, he would send a formal communication to the central government, and formally receive the same as a representative of the central government; and vice versa.

## References

Dwivedi and Jain (1985), Discusses the tension between the uses and abuses of bureaucratic power.

Heginbotham (1975). Using community development in the state of Tamil Nadu as a case study, explores the tensions created by the pressures of economic development and social change under the direction of a planning bureaucracy.

Jain (1983). A collection of essay examining the dilemmas of a politicised bureaucracy.

Maheshwari (1992). A good account of the recruitment, training and operation of the All-India Services.

Misra (1986). Lucid and well-documented exposition of a controversial thesis, that the 1950 constitution facilitated the emergence of a bureaucracy that is just as self-serving as its predecessor, but neither as honest nor efficient.

Wade (1985). A very good account of the institutionalisation of public corruption.

# 5

# Public Bureaucracies in Developing Countries

**Moises Naim**

Civil Service reform is one of many burning issues in development that are long on diagnostics and short on prescription. It is often quite easy to identify public bureaucracies that are not working and to note how such defective public sector organisations hinder development and perpetuate poverty. However, good ideas about how to upgrade devastated bureaucracies are much more scarce. Increasing salaries, recruiting better people, fighting corruption enhancing training, tightening controls, improving accountability, installing a merit system, de-centralising, streamlining procedures, privatising, or even "reinventing government" are some of the good ideas that, if effectively implemented, could improve performance in the public sector. Unfortunately, in many developing countries, such means of reaching utopia—that is, a more efficient government—are themselves utopian.

In most developing countries, public sector organisations have been so severely damaged by decades of abuse, neglect, congestion, and corruption that many have great difficulty performing the tasks for which they were created. In some cases, their "core" tasks tend to be simpler to perform than those that are commonly prescribed as solutions to their organisational problems. Upgrading the capacity of an institution often requires more skills and resources than those needed just to run it.

For example, establishing career plans, restructuring, or streamlining operations may indeed upgrade these institutions. But the impediments to the successful adoption of such means are so enormous that they make such solutions no less utopian than the ends at which they are aimed.

Writings on civil service reform in developing countries often suffer from this "utopian-means," offering prescriptions that, while obviously good ideas that merit attention, are typically very difficult to implement. A good idea that is very difficult to implement is, after all, not that good an idea. This should not be taken to mean that proposals about civil service reform should be confined to those few simple and relatively modest changes that public bureaucracies are capable of implementing. 'Outside pressures, resources, and change agents have often been powerful catalysts for positive reform. The point is that prescriptions about civil service reform have to be based on a deeper understanding of the determinants of public sector malfunction in developing countries than we seem to have today.

The performance problems of public bureaucracies result from a complex blend of political, economic, cultural, and organisational factors, thus limiting the effectiveness of solutions that are inspired by only one of these facets but ignore the others. For example, eliminating political influences in the recruitment and promotion practices of a public hospital may be a necessary condition for improving its performance. But without also changing the hospital's organisational culture, increasing its resources, and overhauling and modernising its standard operating procedures and managerial practices, depoliticisation alone is not enough. It may even lower performance.

Conversely, making more money available for a public hospital without making sure that the additional funds will not be appropriated to unions, private vendors, and the web of small groups that under the protection of politics manage to steer decision making in their favour, would also be useless. The same holds for managerial prescriptions that fail to take into account how the absurd and wasteful managerial practices often found in public bureaucracies are rational responses to the political cultural, and economic environment in which the organisation has to operate.

**Ten Paradoxes**

The search for novel and useful approaches to upgrade the public sector will have to incorporate explanations for some of the recurrent paradoxes that are common to almost all of Latin America's public bureaucracies. The following ten paradoxical characteristics of the region's public sector offer interesting avenues for further exploration into the nature of the problems.

The first paradox is the debilitating effect that expansion of the state has on state power. For decades, Latin American states sought to improve their performance and that of their public sector by expanding their scope of activities and through constant additions to the list of tasks for which they were directly responsible. Contrary to their intentions, this rapid and intense diversification effectively weakened the public sector. This phenomenon is now well documented. The social debacles that resulted from public sectors that were too busy managing steel mills, airlines, and hotels to pay adequate attention to health or education have been well analysed.

The second, closely related paradox is that, often, the more overstaffed an agency is, the more congested it tends to be. Many agencies seem to suffer from a chronic incapacity to offer timely and adequate responses to the needs of the public. Such congestion is frequently dealt with by increasing staff size. But adding staff seldom results in more operational slack. Such agencies are normally overwhelmed by requests to do things for which they lack the necessary resources and capacity.

The third paradox is that the more regulations, rules, and legal frameworks—*reglamentos,* in Latin America—there are, the less control there is, and the weaker that control tends to be. The system is, of course, more rigid, but at the same time, easier to undermine. In the quest to control corruption, the public sector has been burdened by so many controls and restrictions that its operating capacity has been severely impaired. At the same time, such excessive controls are rarely effective as tools to reduce corruption.

The fourth paradox is that the higher the responsibility of an individual, the less authority he or she has. The lack of proportion between responsibility and authority is often appalling. By authority I mean not only power, but the resources and tools that people need to perform their functions. This issue is related to congestion and to the increasingly inability of many of the region's public institutions to achieve the goals for which they were originally created. An audit of Latin American public agencies would probably reveal that a large number of them cannot, for a variety of reasons is more frequently found in agencies charged with delivering the public services more intensely utilised by the poor.

The fifth paradox is that, although governments have been findings the coordination of their activities increasingly difficult, throughout the 1970s and 1980s they enacted more and more policies whose implementation—and success—crucially depended on interagency coordination. The less governments are capable of coordination themselves, due to weak interagency coordination or almost nonexistent central coordination capacity, the more prone they seem to be to adopt policies that are dependent on interagency coordination-sharing information, closely monitoring each other's functions and effectively taking their interdependencies into account in their decision-making.

The sixth paradox is that the state seems better able to attract and assign talented public servants to the easier jobs than to the tough ones. It is easy to get a competent public administrator to manage a state-owned enterprise, for example, but difficult to get a competent person to work in the Ministry of Education or Ministry of Health. Thus, throughout Latin America there is a great contrast between the heads of the ministries of finance or economy, or the Chief of state-owned enterprises, and the people in charge of the most crucial and difficult task of providing education, health, and social services.

It is easier to be successful as the president of a state-owned company than as the head of a municipal garbage collection department. Again, this has a great deal to do with the lack of proportion between authority and responsibility. The president of the state-owned enterprise has more resources, people, tools, and institutional backing than the manager in charge of collecting garbage in a Latin American city.

The seventh paradox is that turnover rates seem to be inversely proportional to hierarchical levels. The higher in the hierarchy an individual is, the greater the probability that he or she will have a short tenure. There seems to be a dual system in which turnover is much higher at the upper and middle levels than at the lower levels.

The eighth paradox relates to the decentralisation that the Latin American and Caribbean region has been undertaking, along with the rest of the developing world and even the post-communist states. Decentralisation in Latin America is happening in different stages and is driven by two different forces—managerial and political. Managerial decentralisation occurs when, after analysing a public function, it is decided that the way to improve capacity and performance is to decentralize. Although this measure is often valid and effective, it is also frequently hampered by faulty implementation. Typically, a new organisational chart is drawn. Then the logo, institutional symbols, titles, and job descriptions of the organisation are changed. And the illusion of a new organisation is created. But out in the field and in daily operations, the organisational culture continues exactly as it was. It fact, altering patterns of behaviour and routines that people have been following for years, and for which in many cases there are powerful and implicit—political and economic motives, is very difficult.

As a consequence of the periodic attempts at decentralisation, the region has highly fragmented public sectors. Truncated decentralisation episodes have left organisations with organisational charts that blend old organisational forms with various changes implemented in successive decentralisation efforts—resulting in a hybrid that no one had planned. These organisations can be likened to an old house in which once you start peeling the paint off the wall, you discover several layers reflecting different attempts to remodel and modernise the house.

The results of different attempts, begun as new Governments and new managers came in, to give new life, new meaning, a new name to the organisation. Each attempt at reform is superimposed on the previous one. And many reform attempts are abandoned halfway through because conditions have changed or the person who initiated them has left his or her position. Normally, organisational changes take much longer than the tenure of those responsible for them.

The other force driving decentralisation—one that is more recent and much more intense and important is political. Many countries around the world, including Latin America, are moving toward a new federalism. Every region and city has constituencies seeking greater autonomy from the traditional centre. This movement toward decentralisation and regionalism has been rapid as a result of the deepening of democracy in the region. Democracy always increases participation and the need for people to have a greater say at the local level. As a result of these changes, the region is moving away from a highly centralised national and administrative organisation to one that is much more decentralised and in which power is in the hands of governors, mayors, councilmen, and city officials who have been directly elected by the citizens of that locality.

In the long run, decentralisation is bound to have a positive net effect, but there is increasing evidence that in the short run it is weakening the capacity of the state to deliver public services. There is increasing evidence, for example, that the decentralisation of educational services decreases their effectiveness in the short term. It is easy to imagine that this is also happening in other areas. Decentralisation does, of course, have consequences for the fiscal aspect of reform, the experience of Brazil in this respect is well known. The decentralisation of public finances there has made it difficult to bring the country's fiscal stance under control.

The point then is that although decentralisation may have positive political and administrative impacts, it is difficult to implement. In the short run countries may see the performance of their public bureaucracies decline as a result of badly implemented decentralisation programmes.

The ninth paradox is that despite ample opportunities to learn from past experiences, public organisations, overburdened with repetitious task and problems, tend to repeat mistakes. There is much evidence that public organisations in the region, and probably elsewhere as well, suffer from profound learning disabilities. In order to understand what causes the public organisation's impaired learning capacity it is important to to beyond denouncing it.

The tenth and last pardox is what I have referred to as the paradox of the forgotten price. One of the main goals of the macroeconomic reforms and attempts at economic liberalisation that are taking place around the world is getting the prices right. These reforms aim at setting an exchange rate to reflect market realities, getting the prices right for goods and services, and getting the interest rate right. But there is one price that people pay little attention to—the price paid to those in charge of getting the rest of the prices right.

The background materials for this conference provide useful statistics on wage compression in the civil service and the lagging salaries for higher-level public servants. Reforms have worsened salary conditions in the public sector. Historically, there has been a gap between public and private salaries, but reforms have wrenched open that gap. Economic reforms increase opportunities in the private sector and therefore increase the demand for managers, thus pushing up their salaries.

## Conclusion

As noted above, there general ways of tackling some of the problems implicit in these paradoxes. The first is the managerial technocratic approach: if there is salary compression analyse it, look at the statistics and the comparators, and develop an appropriate framework to correct the distortions. The second approach, which for lack of a better name can be called the economic approach, is driven both by fiscal considerations and a preoccupation with competitiveness, and the need to inject more competition into private and public sector salaries and labour markets. The third is the political approach, which essentially ask what the political determinants of the problems are and what determines whether there is the political will to achieve effective reform in the public sector.

To conclude, it is perhaps useful to note several issues that will concern us in the future. It is easy to predict that in the same way that mid and late 1980s and early 1990s became the era of macroeconomic reforms and economic shocks in Latin America, the late 1990s and beyond will be the era of institutional shocks and institutional reforms. As is often noted, the easy part has been accomplished. The decree driven reforms that have been carried out nearly everywhere were politically traumatic and socially painful, but administratively very easy; all that is needed to devalue the exchange rate or liberalise prices is the stroke of a pen.

To upgrade education of improve the delivery of health car services will require a much more complicated process of reform. We have hypotheses and some experience in this area, but we lack strong theoretical frameworks that can guide us through the maze of institutional reform. To undertake this kind of institutional reform—and here I will indulge in some "utopian means" prescriptions—it is important to begin to attract more talent to activities related to civil service reform, not to mention a desperate need to upgrade the quality of the agencies in charge of public sector human resources.

This approach will not be sufficient, however, if more and better knowledge does not become available. And more and better knowledge will not become available unless: (1) the managerial-technocratic approach, the economic approach, and the political approach to these problems are integrated; and (2) greater efforts are made to develop more comprehensive frameworks and more reliable inststruments to deal with these problems. This, in turn, will depend on a coherent, systematic, and sustained effort at consciousness raising—convincing our governments that investment of effort in macroeconomic reforms will be wasted if similar effort, talent, and funding are not invested in the institutional reform of the state. And this will require attracting and retaining the best talent available to deal with the complex tasks on which all the states in the region will embark in the coming years.

# 6

# Structure of Organisation—Chief Executive

## Two Types of Chief Executives

The chief executive is at the head of the administrative system of a country. Administration is like a pyramid, broadest at the base and tapering towards the top. At the vortex is the chief executive. There are, broadly speaking, two types of chief executives; (i) the Parliamentary, and (ii) the Presidential. In the former type, of which Britain and India are the outstanding examples, a distinction is drawn between the real chief executive and the titular (or, nominal) chief executive. The British Queen is, in theory, the repository of all executive authority, which, in practice, is exercised by the cabinet accountable to parliament. Thus, she is just the semblance of the chief executive, whereas the real chief executive is the cabinet. The Indian President is analogous to the British Monarch; the real chief executive is the Council of Ministers with the Prime Minister at the head. This distinction is absent in the presidential type of executive. The United States is the classical example of this type. In that country the President is vested with all executive powers, and it is he who exercises these powers himself and independently. Elected for a period of four years, he is unremovable from office—except through the difficult process of impeachment.

An analysis of the cabinet and presidential type of chief executive reveals many points of differences. To begin with, in countries where parliamentary system of government prevails, the real chief executive is the cabinet, which is a plural body. The Prime

Minister, who is the head of the cabinet, regards other members as his colleagues. Unlike this the chief executive in presidential system of government is a single individual, the President. The U.S. President has ten secretaries in charge of the ten administrative, departments; the latter are, however, his subordinates, not colleagues, and are removable by him. The second difference concerns executive-legislative relationship. In the parliamentary government, the members of the cabinet are also members of the parliament; in fact they provide legislative and fiscal leadership to it, initiating and piloting legislation and the budget. The cabinet is accountable to parliament, which has the ultimate power of removing it from office. There is, thus, a close, continuous and intimate executive-legislative relationship. In the presidential system, on the other hand, the President is neither a member of parliament nor accountable to, and removable by it, thanks to the separation of powers and a system of checks and balances. This position has made the Presidency and the Congress two separate coequal entities, independent of each other; and has even induced in the Congress a feeling of distrust towards the chief executive. A comparison of the two systems tips the scale in favour of the parliamentary system. Even in the United States some thinkers have favoured the modification of the presidency along the parliamentary lines.

Mention may also be made of the Swiss Executive which belongs to neither of the two types discussed above, though embodying features of both the types. This is the collegiate type of chief executive. The Swiss Executive is a plural body of seven members of equal status, thus implying absence of anyone like Prime Minister. These members have seats in the legislature to which they are accountable, but they have no right to vote. The Swiss Executive is elected for a fixed period during which it cannot be ousted from office. Nor can it dissolve the legislature. The collegiate type, thus, retains the principal merits of both the parliamentary and the presidential systems.

**Functions of the Chief Executive**

The chief executive has, broadly speaking, two types of functions to perform—political and administrative. The former function includes obtaining and retaining the legislative support for his policies and programmes, providing leadership to nation, etc. These are important functions which he can afford to neglect only at the risk of his losing office ere long. His administrative functions are summed up by Gulick in the word 'POSDCORB' which stands for the following activities:

*Planning*—that, is, working out in outline the things that need to be done and the methods for doing them to accomplish the purpose set for the enterprise.

*Organising*—that is, the establishment of the formal structure of authority through which work sub-divisions are arranged, defined and co-ordinated for the defined objective.

*Staffing*—that is, the whole personnel function of bringing in and training the staff and maintaining favourable conditions of work.

*Directing*—that is, the continuous task of making decisions and embodying them in specific and general orders and instructions, and serving as the leader of the enterprise.

*Co-ordaining*—that is, the all-important duty of interrelating the various parts of the work.

*Reporting*—that is, keeping those, to whom the executive is responsible, informed as to what is going on, which, thus, includes keeping himself and his subordinates informed through records, research and inspection.

*Budgeting*—with all that goes with budgeting in the form of planning, accounting and control.

The numerous administrative duties of the chief executive may now briefly be described. In the first place, he formulates administrative policy. The legislature enacts laws in general broad terms. It invests them with details to make them fit for application. While enacting laws the legislature only lays down general principles, leaving to the chief executive to provide necessary details to make the laws fit for application. Besides, a large number of statutes originate in the administration, which coming, as it does, in direct and constant contact with the population, can well assess people's needs and requirements. It is to be noted that official bills far outnumber the private members' bills in any legislative session.

Secondly, the chief executive authorizes the structure of the organisation through which administration functions. New activities necessitate the creation of new departments and agencies. Though in the presidential government, powers of the President are quite limited in the matter of organisation, he can create or abolish smaller agencies and transfer them from one department to another. In parliamentary government the chief executive has apparently a free hand in this respect. Generally speaking, internal structure of the departments is determined by him.

Thirdly, the chief executive wields power in personnel administration. He appoints and dismisses the public officials. He derives this power from the constitutional system of the land, and, thus, the scope of this power is not the same in all countries. However, even in countries where the merit system of recruitment normally prevails, key-appointments are made by him at his discretion. In India, for instance, governors, ambassadors, judges of the Supreme Courts and High Courts, etc., are appointed by him at his discretion. Though the Public Service Commission selects personnel for numerous posts in the government, technically speaking, it is he who appoints them, and may even remove them from service, subject to certain constitutional arrangements. In the presidential government of U.S.A., the President wields greater power in appointing personnel, though, in some cases, subject to senatorial confirmation.

Fourthly, the chief executive issues directives, proclamations, orders, etc., to make the administrative activities conform to the statutory provisions,. In carrying out a specific policy, numerous people, who usually do not know each other and are separated from one another, are engaged. Directives, circulars etc., help in inducing uniformity in their behaviour as well as providing necessary instructions and guidance. Indeed, the tone of administration is largely set by the quality and quantity of the directives, orders, etc., issued by the chief executive.

Fifthly, the chief executive orders investigations and enquiries; and by this general power he makes himself sure that the powers he delegates to numerous officials of varying ranks are not abused. Malpractices and defects of administration are brought to light by these periodically ordered enquiries and investigations. Further, this collection of information is vital to policy-formulation.

Sixthly, he has budgetary responsibilities. The chief executive prepares and submits the annual budget to the legislature, and, after the latter's approval, executes and implements it. The Indian financial codes, for example, enjoin upon the chief executive the responsibilities for the preparation of budget estimates. In the presidential government, on the other hand, the formal budgetary authority is vested in the Congress. In actual practice, however, it is the President, who through the Bureau of the Budget, submits budgetary proposals to the Legislature and has quite an effective veto power over the budget.

Seventhly, co-ordination is among his most important functions. In an administration, conflicts and differences are not unusual occurrences. Also, more than one department might be engaged in some single activity, leading, thus, to duplication and overlapping. The problems are, no doubt, tackled at all levels, but some of these do reach the chief executive for settlement. It is among his major functions to see that numerous activities currently undertaken by several departments in pursuance of a particular policy lead up to the realisation of the desired objective. One can scarcely over-emphasize this role of the chief executive; co-ordination is, indeed, the heart of administration.

The role of the chief executive is made up of all these functions. Obviously, no single individual can singly perform such a formidable conglomeration of functions. He has perforce to rely upon his subordinates among whom these functions are to be distributed. These subordinates, indeed, act as 'a filter and a funnel'. Only the more important issues and problems await his personal attention. It is to be remembered, however, that though he delegates his powers to his subordinates, he never abdicates them. The chief executive is always the chief executive; he is the administrator-in-chief. He has daily to take vital decision on numerous problems and issues. Only persons of extraordinary ability, can, thus, make good chief executives, C. Rajagopalachari, while delivering Patel Memorial Lectures, enumerated six requirements of a good administrator, namely, character capacity to judge upon relevant advice and to decide promptly and rightly; capacity to inspire confidence among subordinates; no vacillation after a decision is made; even temper and to bring into being a sense of social purpose.'

## Line and Staff

A look at the power and function of the chief executive convinces us that he cannot exercise his powers and perform his functions effectively, promptly and efficiently unaided and unassisted. He needs help. And, in practice, this help he receives from the organ, or organs, attached to him. Many of his functions are delegated to these organs. This delegation, however, does not interfere with his supreme responsibilities of supervision, direction and control over administration. Also, this organ, called by the generic term 'General Staff', reduces pressure upon the chief executive's time and energies by sifting analysing, and, in less important matters, even deciding things. Only the most important matters reach him for decision, and his decisions are conveyed to the concerned departments by the General Staff. Truly, the latter acts as a 'filter and a funnel'. The General Staff provides expert advice and assistance to the chief executive. Further, in a cabinet form of government, where members of the cabinet usually number more than a dozen, the need for the General Staff is easily conceded. There is an obvious need for a record of the general discussion and conclusions reached in the cabinet meeting. Otherwise, there may be room for uncertainty and dispute about what the cabinet had done at previous meetings. The need for the General Staff as an indispensable aid to the chief executive in the efficient and prompt discharge of his multifarious functions is apparent. L.D. White lays down the following functions as the objectives of the General Staff:

1. To ensure that the chief executive is adequately and currently informed.

2. To assist him in foreseeing problems and planning future programmes.

3. To ensure that matters for his decision reach his desk promptly, in condition to be settled intelligently and without delay, and to protect him against hasty or ill-considered judgements.

4. To exclude every matter that can be settled elsewhere in the system.

5. To protect his time.

6. To ensure means of ensuring compliance by subordinates with established policy and executive direction.

The general nature of the Staff Agency has been admirably set forth in the Report of the President's Committee on Administrative Management (1937). The Report observes:

"These aides would have no power to make decisions or issue instructions in their own right. They would not be interposed between the President and the heads of his departments. They would not be assistant presidents in any sense. Their functions would be, when any matter was presented to the President for action affecting any part of the Government, to assist him in obtaining quickly and without delay all pertinent information possessed by any of the executive departments so as to guide him in making his responsible decisions; and then, when decisions have been made, to assist him in seeing to it that every administrative department and agency affected is promptly informed. Their effectiveness in assisting the President will, we think, be directly proportional to their ability to discharge their functions with restraint. They would remain in the background, issue no orders, make no decisions, emit no public statements... They should be men in whom the President has personal confidence and whose character and attitude is such that they would not attempt to exercise power on their own account. They should be possessed of high competence, great physical vigour, and a passion for anonymity."

An important concept in the realm of organisation is that of Line and Staff. Both these terms are derived from the military vocabulary, but their meanings, when transplanted in the civil administration, are not yet free from confusion and even contradiction. As Harold Koontz and Cyril O' Donnell observe, "There is probably no other single area of management which, in practice, causes more difficulties, more friction, and more loss of time and effectiveness." A clear understanding of these terms is imperative because, firstly, the Line and Staff relationship emerge as an organisational way of life, and, secondly, these relationships inevitably affect a member's part in the coordination of group activity.

A government conducts its business with the help of a highly elaborate system of organisation held together by what may be termed 'chain of command'. The central hierarchy comprises the Line; assisting the Line are the Staff and the auxiliary agencies. Line works at the direct accomplishment of programme objectives, and is served by staff and auxiliary services. Staff provides specialised advice but does not command. Auxiliary provides common services.

Many writers have attempted to define these terms but not to the satisfaction of everyone. Writing in 1927, Willoughby divided the governmental activities into two parts—the primary or the functional and the institutional or house keeping activities. "Primary or functional activities are those which a service performs in order to accomplish the purpose for which it exists. Institutional or house-keeping activities, on the other hand, are those which it is necessary that a service shall perform in order that it may exist and operate as a service." Thus, the Ministry of Railways has, as its primary function, the task of running of railways between different points. In order that this primary function can be performed, it must build railway stations, employ persons, lay down rail-tracks, purchase rolling-stock and perform a host of other activities. These are all house-keeping or institutional activities. It is obvious that the primary activities are an end in themselves whereas the house-keeping activities are a means to an end. Willoughby did not mention Staff activities as a third category of activities. Subsequent writers distinguish the government agencies into Line, Auxiliary, and Staff. The second class of administrative agencies has not yet required a standard terminology—Willoughby terms them 'institutional' or 'house-keeping services'; Gaus calls them 'auxiliary, technical staff services': White names them 'auxiliary services'.

White writes: "The business of government...is transacted by means of an elaborate organisation, held together in a universal superior-subordinate relationship, and based on the principle of specialisation. The central hierarchy comprises the line; assisting the line are various units, some concerned with advisory and preparatory operations, known as staff, some concerned with house-keeping operations and described in the book, *Introduction to the Study of Public Administration* as the auxiliary agencies. The line comprises both the political command structure and permanent career rank... The line authorities are concerned with the substantive functions of government. They deal directly with people, providing services, regulating conduct, collecting taxes, and generally carrying forward the programmes authorised by legislative bodies. They are the central element of any administrative system; staff and auxiliary agencies are necessary in a large and complex organisation, but they are secondary. They serve the line; they serve the people." Pfiffner and Presthus observe: "In general ... the distinction between staff and line follows that between direct and indirect labour, 'the direct being line and the indirect being staff;" The term 'staff work' is preferred over 'staff agency' because it avoids doctrinaire controversy over whether a given person is 'staff' of 'line'. Pfiffner and Presthus classify staff into three types—general staff, technical staff, and auxiliary staff. "The general staff consists of those who assist the chief and whose time is spent for most part in strategic planning and deliberation on high policy. Departmental heads may spend a part of their time in general staff work, especially when the chief calls them into conferences to deliberate on policy. That is why it is often more accurate to refer to staff work rather than to staff agency. Some persons who do staff work, actually spend part of their time in performing, operating, line or production activities. The second type of staff activity, technical staff, consists of people and activities of a specialised nature, including laboratory research, engineering design, or functional supervision of direct workers... The third type of staff, auxiliary, is the one that gives students the most trouble, because it seems to contradict the saying that staff people should not command or give orders. Perhaps it would be better to call these 'auxiliary services'; the British use the term establishment services'. They include personnel, finance, supply, industrial engineering or administrative analysis. On a more pedestrian level one finds central mailing, maintenance of buildings and equipments, control of transportation, archives and record-keeping, real estate management and communication facilities."

## Line Agency

An administrative system is divided into agencies or departments principally on the basis of major substantive purpose. These agencies are, thus, concerned with the execution or fulfilment of the primary objects of the government, and deal directly with the people supplying services to people regulating their conduct, implementing programmes sanctioned by the legislature, collecting taxes and the like. It is with the Line agencies that the ordinary citizen comes into contact; and it is they which constitute the kernel of administration. The major 'Line' departments in the Government of India are those of Health, Defence, Education, Labour, Railways, Transport, Communications, Community Development, Commerce and Industry.

## Auxiliary Agency

The auxiliary function, or the 'house-keeping' function as Willoughby terms it, is undertaken to enable the Line agency to perform its primary function. This function is, thus, secondary. Nevertheless it is a necessary function, specially, in a complex and expanding organisation like government. The Department of Posts and Telegraphs has the primary duty of delivering letters and telegrams. This is the Line activity, and its performance depends upon the performance of numerous other functions like purchase of paper, printing of postcards and envelopes, acquiring of land, construction of post and telegraph offices, recruitment of personal, etc. All these functions serve the primary function, namely, delivery of letters and telegrams, and are, thus, auxiliary or house-keeping in nature.

In not too distant past each Line department strove for operating self-sufficiency, and made its own arrangement for performing its auxiliary functions. A characteristic of these auxiliary functions is that they are common to all Line departments. Therefore, significant economies could result, and benefits of specialisation and increased efficiency could accrue, if these functions are taken away from all the line departments, and are performed by separate agencies. Such a trend is already discernible, and separate auxiliary agencies exist in most governments. To cite the examples of the auxiliary agencies in the Government of India, the Central Public Works Department and the Directorate-General of Supply and Disposal may be mentioned. The former undertakes the construction of works for all Government departments through its engineers, and the latter looks after the processing of the machinery and equipment for the Government before purchasing these for the various Government departments. Necessary as the auxiliary functions are, utmost care, however, needs to be taken to ensure that these auxiliary functions are performed strictly according to time schedule, for delay impedes the performance of Line functions.

**Staff Agency**

Staff elements perform different kinds of roles. There is first the advisory and co-ordinating role in which the staff elements are essentially extensions of the chief executive himself, carrying on for him those functions which he would do himself if he had the time. They help plan, develop directives or coordinate actions of subordinates, all in the name of the executive's authority. Another role of staff is the provision of technical expertise. An operational research group might be considered as technical staff for the executive. A last role of a staff group is to provide services in such areas as personnel of finance not only to the executive but under his direction to the entire organisation. Here the major concern is to relieve subordinate Line and Staff groups of those specialised functions which are more effectively conducted from a central point. The word "staff" means a stick carried for support or defence, a prop. And, indeed, the Staff assists the Line by studying administrative problems, planning, communicating, advising, suggesting. It is, thus, an extension of the personality of the administrator, meaning "more eyes, more ears, and more hands to aid him in forming and carrying out his plans." It is his *alter ego*. Its distinguishing feature is that it cannot command, it has no operating responsibility. The indispensability of the staff agency is, thus, described by Henri Fayol:

"Whatever their ability and their capacity for work, the heads of great enterprises cannot fulfil alone all their obligations.... They are, thus, forced to have recourse to a group of men who have the strength, competence and time which the Head may lack. This group of men constitutes the Staff of the Management. It is a help, or reinforcement, a sort of extension of the manager's personality, to assist him in carrying out his duties. The Staff appears as a separate body only in large undertaking and its importance increases with the importance of the undertaking."

Though staff and auxiliary agencies asset the Line, the distinction between the two should not be forgotten. The staff has no operating responsibilities. Its work is of research and consultative type. The auxiliary agency does have operating responsibilities; it undertakes responsibilities for contacting, purchasing, recruiting, keeping of accounts, etc. Secondly, the auxiliary agency's concern is to maintain the Line agency. It is not bothered with the latter's improvement or reorganisation. The Staff, on the other hand, has a wider jurisdiction, which is identified with Gulick's 'POSDCORB' activities, though, it is true, its say is not final. It performs the following functions.

1. Advising, teaching, consultation.
2. Coordination, not merely through plans but also through human contacts, trouble-shooting and winning over opposition at all levels of organisation.
3. Fact-finding and research.
4. Planning.
5. Contact with other organisations and individuals to know what is going on.

6. Assisting the Line without infringing its authority.
7. Sometimes exercising delegated authority from the Line commander.

The ultimate object of Staff is an improvement of both the product and the production methods.

Staff is, thus, indispensable to the chief executive in the performance of his multifarious tasks. It is thus, obvious that the staff agency personel must be intellectually virile and possess a sense of evaluating a problem in the context of the total needs of administration. They must not be uncompromising idealists. They are to be recruited from amongst persons who also know the art of getting along with others. They must be endowed with persuasive gift and have a capacity to express their ideas clearly and cogently. They must never let the Line feel that they are a superior lot. Above all, they must have, in the words of the Brownlow Committee, a 'passion' for anonymity'.

It has been mentioned above that Staff is only advisory in character, and Line has the monopoly of execution. A pertinent question now is: Can a hard and fast line be drawn between Line and Staff functions? The proper relationship between these two has been subject of lively debate, so much so that, in the words of Dimock, Dimock and Koeing, "The right adjustment between line and staff constitutes one of the most difficult areas of management."

The earlier writers conceived the Line and staff relationship as an aspect of formal organisation. Indicative of this trend is Sheldon's observation that "the Staff organisation may be described as a deliberate organisation for thought just as the Line organisation is the organisation for execution." This watertight division between the two has been questioned and has undergone modification in subsequent writings. Suggestive of this new concept is Albert Lepawsky's observation that "Staff and Line are Co-ordinates, operating not in a hierarchical relation to Staff over Line, but on a horizontal plane of authority and responsibility under the chief executive." He further points out: "A Staff, man who does not give commands to the Line is ineffectual, and a Line man who does understand and exercise a modicum of staff function is a failure." The growing unreality of identifying Staff with counsel, and Line with execution and command may be explained by two factors. The expansion of the governmental organisation is followed by a more minute division of labour and resultant speculation, which makes staff work a matter of increasing necessity. "Given a programme characterised by specialisation and variety, staff work becomes the indispensable ingredient of a unified and balanced administration. As the number of staff official multiplies, therefore, along with the varieties of staff work, some of this work shades off into the type of function traditionally reserved to Line officials. When this point is reached, staff work becomes in some degree a combination of both direct and indirect activities, including advice as well as directions to Line official. In practice, a function is seldom pure; more often it is an interesting and frequently a troublesome blend." Secondly, the writings of Simon and others have made the watertight division between Staff and Line look unreal. Authority is now believed to be more a matter of influence, rather than of command. It is clear, then, that staff exercises authority, it controls and commands. Unreality of this watertight division becomes all the more striking when one realizes that the staff work has not been clearly segregated. Heads of 'Line' department spend a chunk of their time in general staff work. Similarly, persons doing staff work set aside a part of their time for performing 'Line' functions. Line and Staff are not types of organisations or groupings of activities. The concept of Line and Staff must be looked at from the standpoint of authority relationships. The Line authority is a kind of relationship in which a superior exercises direct command over a subordinate. Line is synonymous with scalar chain; it is an authority relationship in direct Line or steps. Staff is likewise a relationship but is advisory in nature; the flow of staff authority is upward. Although it is true that certain departments may stand in a predominantly Line or Staff position with respect to other departments, Line and Staff are authority relationships. It is true that the Planning Commission in the Central government, for example, being primarily advisory to the top executive, may be thought of as a staff organisation. But within the organisation one will find Line relationship. The chairman of the Commission stand in a Line authority position with respect to his immediate subordinates. Similarly, in a Line department one may find many subordinates who have an advisory role and who, therefore have a staff relationship to that department.

When one looks at an organisational structure as a whole, the general character of Line and Staff relationship for the total organisation emerges. Certain departments are predominantly Staff in their relationship to the entire organisation. Other departments are primarily Line.

Although one may refer to one department as a Line department and another as a Staff department, grouping of activities does not give these various departments such characteristics. "Line and Staff are characterisations of authority relationship and not departmental activities." The activities of the director of training in, say, Heavy Electricals Ltd., are likely to primarily, be advisory to the main stream of that company's operations, and may, consequently, be referred to as a Staff function. But in a training institute, its department of training will stand in a Line relationship to the organisation as a whole.

Indeed, one can go to the extent of even asserting that the Staff controls the Line, at least in certain fields. Staff agencies like personnel, budget and finance, organisation and methods, planning, etc., have emerged to wield 'coercive' power over the Line agencies. The gradual ascendancy of Staff over Line has nevertheless engendered tension between the two, and invited criticism as well. Inflated staff work has inherent dangers. According to Willard N. Hogan, preoccupation with budgets and controls of different types 'puts a premium on negativism in public administration'. Planning coordination, it is accordingly argued, should be entrusted to Line departments in accordance with the management principle of combining functional responsibility with corresponding authority. "Centralised services and budgetary and personnel controls are giving us a bad case of organisational schizophrenia as the control of mechanics becomes dissociated from the builds up competing interests with, policy direction." Staff and Line are, generally speaking, not friendly to one another. They are found in a state of conflict. The staff work must be performed by persons of high intellectual attainments and specialised training. The fact that they are near the chief executive naturally makes them 'the king's most trusted counsellors', relegating their Line counterparts to a modest position in the power hierarchy. In certain matters like finance and personnel, the Staff even exercises 'coercive' power over Line.

This conflict may be lessened if the Staff becomes more tactful, persuasive, and friendly in its dealing with the Line. Efficient staff work requires the staff to seek the advice of responsible Line officers and to have them, if possible, agreeable to his recommendation before it goes to the chief executive. A Line officer is more likely to follow a recommendation if it can be shown that the advice meets with the approval of these officers who must implement the requried decision. A well-told recommendation is likely to be accepted. It would be better if persons with Line experience are appointed on Staff positions. This is a feasible proposition in the context of the generalist civil service that we have in India. In fact, as far as is found feasible, there should be periodic transfer between Line and Staff.

The basic nature of staff as an advisory relationship characterizes the nature of staff authority. Although the Staff officer may exercise Line authority over the subordinate in *his* department to the extent that his position is purely staff, he has no Line authority. His advice flows *upward* to his superior. If it is to be transformed into Line action, it is the function of the Line superior so to decide.

Staff is sometimes prone to step into the position of directing the lower Line elements without following down the full chain of command. Confusion then arises as to whose direction to follow. The resolution of such conflicts is the subject of such organisational bickering. Some organisations have been known to be uncertain whether a given function in truly Staff or Line even whether this distinction is realistic. The point at issue is whether certain functions traditionally thought to be Staff are too crucial to Line operations to be so considered any longer. Engineering, purchasing and finance, for example, are sometimes spoken of as bearing heavily on Line activities, and, therefore, should be in the Line. The tendency appears to be in the direction of placing such elements in the Line rather than the Staff.

*The functional organisation* tries to resolve this divergence between theory and actual practice. This form recognizes that the specialists have authority over Line officials at lower levels. The problems of this function arrangement are obvious. Unity of command is not clearly enforced, and there may be placed upon the lowest levels of the organisation the undesirable burden of deciding who the boss is at any given time. While a completely functional organisation cannot be expected to succeed, various mixtures with Line and Staff organisational principles can prove to be valuable in management.

**Staff Agencies in India**

Staff Agencies in India include the Cabinet Secretariat, the Prime Minister's Office (known as Prime Minister's Secretariat till June 1977), the Cabinet Committees, the Planning Commission, the Budget and Economic Affairs Department in the Finance ministry, the Administrative Vigilance Division in the Home Affairs Ministry, and the Staff Inspection Unit (S.I.U.) in the Finance Ministry.

**Cabinet Secretariat**

The Cabinet Secretariat which replaced the Secretariat of the Governor-General's Executive Council in August 1947, performs staff functions, serving the Cabinet as well as the standing committees of the Cabinet. It performs the necessary secretariat work pertaining to the meetings of the Cabinet and its Committees. Its functions include preparation of agenda for the meetings of the Cabinet, keeping record of discussion in the Cabinet, and of decision taken there, circulation of memoranda on issues awaiting the Cabinet's approval, circulation of the decision to each Ministry, preparation and submission of monthly summaries on a large number of specified subjects to the Cabinet.

A head is given a list of the subjects that are brought before the Cabinet, and with which, therefore, the Cabinet Secretariat has do deal:

1. Cases involving legislation including the issue of Ordinances.
2. Addresses and messages of the President to Parliament.
3. Proposals to summon or prorogue the Parliament or to dissolve the Lok Sabha.
4. Cases involving negotiations with foreign countries on treaties, agreements, etc.
5. Proposals for sending abroad delegations of persons in any capacity.
6. Proposals to appoint public committees of enquiry and consideration of reports of such committees.
7. Cases involving financial implications.
8. Cases which a Ministry puts to Cabinet for decision or direction.
9. Cases of disagreements between Ministries.
10. Proposals to vary or reverse a decision previously taken by the Cabinet.
11. Cases which the President or the Prime Minister may require to be put to Cabinet.
12. Proposals to withdraw a prosecution instituted by the Government.

The Cabinet Secretariat functions under the direct charge of the Prime Minister and is headed by a functionary called the Cabinet Secretary. The Cabinet Secretary is the seniormost civil servant and is the principal adviser to the Prime Minister. He is the Chairman of the Committees of Secretaries as well as of the Senior Selection Board.

Till May 1977 the Cabinet Secretariat had under it the Department of Personnel and Administrative Reforms. This Department was transferred to the Ministry of Home Affairs in that month.

**Prime Minister's Office**

The Prime Minister's Office, known as the Prime Minister's Secretariat till June 1977, came into existence on 15th August 1947, when India became a Dominion. The Secretariat was created for the immediate purpose of taking over the functions performed until then by the Secretary to Governor-General (Personal), as the Prime Minister took over all functions which the Governor-General prior to 15th August 1947, performed as the executive head of the Government. Under Indira Gandhi's prime ministership, it acquired towering importance as the real seat of top decision-making in the government. The dangers of such a position were fully revealed during internal emergency (26th June 1975—23 March 1977). Indeed, it functioned as the Government of India, pushing all the ministries into a position of political insignificance. The Janata Party Government, under Morarji Desai, swiftly acted to reduce its exaggerated importance, and in 1977, designated it as the Prime Minister's Office.

The Prime Minister's office assists the Prime Minister in his public activities in that capacity and in his functions as Head of Government within the general framework of established government procedure. Generally speaking, the status of the officers of the Prime Minister's Secretariat can be taken to be the same as a status of officers of the corresponding rank in the Ministries of the Government.

**Cabinet Committees**

As in Britain, the Cabinet Committees have played an effective role in India except during the later part of Indira Gandhi's prime ministership (1971—March 1977). The Cabinet carries on much of its work through its Committees which generally have the authority to give binding decisions on matters assigned to them.

Any decision of a committee may, however, be reviewed by the Cabinet. The decisions arrived at by the committees are reported to the Cabinet for information. Ordinarily, no matter comes before the Cabinet unless it has first been considered by the concerned committee of the Cabinet.

These committees facilitate effective coordination and quick decisions in addition to relieving the Cabinet of considerable amount of preliminary work, leaving it free to concentrate upon more important matters. They are of two types—standing ones and *ad hoc* ones. An *ad hoc* committee may be appointed by the Cabinet or the Prime Minister for investigating and reporting to the Cabinet on such matters as may be specified and, if so authorised, to give even binding decisions on such matters. The names, composition and functions of Cabinet Committees are kept confidential by the Government and thus we do not ordinarily know much about them. But the Janata Government (1977-79) had set up six Cabinet Committees.

## Cabinet Committees

| | *Name of the Cabinet Committee* | | *Membership* | *Functions* |
|---|---|---|---|---|
| 1. | Political Affairs | (i) | Prime Minister (Chairman) | All important matters relating to both internal developments and foreign relations. |
| | | (ii) | Home Minister | |
| | | (iii) | Defence Minister | |
| | | (iv) | External Affairs Minister | |
| | | (v) | Finance Minister | |
| 2. | Economic Affairs Committee | (i) | Prime Minister (Chairman) | To direct and coordinate governmental activities in the economic field and generally to regulate the working of the national economy. |
| | | (ii) | Home Minister | |
| | | (iii) | Defence Minister | |
| | | (iv) | Finance Minister | |
| | | (v) | Food and Agriculture Minister | |
| | | (vi) | Commerce Minister | |

| | | |
|---|---|---|
| | (vii) Industry Minister<br>(viii) Labour Minister | |
| 3. Committee on Parliamentary Affairs | (i) Home Minister (Chairman)<br>(ii) Information and Broadcasting Minister<br>(iii) Minister for Labour & Parliamentary Affairs<br>(iv) Law Minister | Looks after the progress of Government business in Parliament to secure the smooth passage of legislation and determines the Government's attitude to non-official bills and resolutions coming up before Parliament. |
| 4. Appointments Committee | (i) Prime Minister (Chairman)<br>(ii) Home Minister<br>(iii) The Minister concerned | (i) To take decision in respect of:<br>(a) Secretariat appointment of the rank of the Deputy Secretary and above;<br>(b) Chairman, managing directors and general managers of state-owned public corporations, compancies and enterprises including Governors of Reserve Bank;<br>(c) Other appointments which are made by the Government or which require the approval of the Government of India, and which carry a salary of Rs. 2,000/- per month and above;<br>(d) Certain specified senior appointments under the ministries of Railways, External Affairs, and Defence. |

| | | |
|---|---|---|
| | | (ii) To decide all cases of disagreement between the Union Public Service Commission and the Department concerned in regard to any appointment |
| 5. Committee on Accommodation | (i) Home Minister (Chairman)<br>(ii) Finance Minister<br>(iii) Works & Housing Minister<br>(iv) Minister for Labour and Parliamentary Affairs | Deals with matters relating to accommodation. |
| 6. Informal Group of Ministers on Prime Situation | (i) Home Minister (Chairman)<br>(ii) Commerce Minister<br>(iii) Railway Minister | Keeps a close watch on the prime-situation in the country. |

The Political Affairs Committee functions even under the present Government. So does the Appointments Committee. Of these committees the most powerful is the Political Affairs Committee. Consisting as it does of the senior ministers in terms of their political stature or the importance of the portfolios held by them, it functions as a "Super-Cabinet" in providing higher direction to the Government.

As would be seen from the above Table, the membership of the Cabinet Committee varies from three to eight. The chairmanship of the cabinet committee is shared between the Prime Minister and the Home Minister.

**Planning Commission**

Established by a Government resolution in March 1950, the Planning Commission, with the Prime Minister as the Chairman, soon emerged as a powerful and effective staff agency in India, though its power has dwindled considerably since seventies. The functions of the Commission are as follows:

1. To make an assessment of the material, capital and human resources of the country, including technical personnel, and to investigate the possibilities of augmenting such of these resources as are found to be deficient in relation to the nation's requirements.

2. To formulate a plan for the most effective and balanced utilisation of the country's resources.

3. To determine priorities as between projects and programmes accepted in the plan.

4. To indicate the factors that retard economic development, and to determine conditions which should be established for the success of the plan.

5. To determine the nature of the machinery to secure the successful implementation of the plan.

6. To appraise from time to time the progress of the plan and to recommend the necessary adjustments of policies and measures.

7. To make recommendations on a consideration of the prevailing economic conditions, current policies, measures and development programmes, or on an examination of problems referred to it for advice by Central or State Governments or for facilitating the discharge of the duties assigned to it.

The Planning Commission at present (1977) consists of chairman, deputy chairman and six members. The Prime Minister is its chairman. The deputy chairman is the full time functional head of the Commission. Of the six members three are ministers in the Central Government—the Finance Minister, the Home Minister and the Defence Minister. The remaining three ones are all full-item members. Each member looks after one or more subjects and directs the study of problems in his field, but all the members function as a body. All cases involving policy are considered by the Commission as a whole. The formulation of plans, adjustments in the plans matter involving departure from the plan-policies, important cases involving disagreement with a Central Ministry or a State Government, and difference of opinion between two members are some of such cases.

The Commission grew to be a factor of key importance in the Indian administration during the Prime Ministership of Jawaharlal Nehru, Books written during this period describe the awesome powers exercised by the Planning Commission. Asok Chanda calls it "the Economic Cabinet, not merely for the Union but also for the States." Similarly, P.P. Agarwal writes: "Though the Planning Commission is an advisory organ of the government, it has come to exercise significant influence over the formation of public policies even in matters other than of development, and its advisory role, in a way, extends over the entire administration." The presence of the Prime Minister and Ministers of the Cabinet rank in the Commission naturally invests it with extraordinary significance. Indeed, this formal association of the Prime Minister and other Ministers with the Commission evoked concern of the Estimates Committee of the Lok Sabha, which made a plea for a "review of the entire position regarding the formal association of Cabinet Ministers of the Central Government with the Planning Commission." Further, the deputy chairman of the Commission has been accorded the status of a Cabinet minister and other full-time members enjoy the rank of ministers of state; they are invited to the Cabinet meetings as and when necessary. Economic issues that arise in the Ministries are first discussed in the Commission before they are considered in the Cabinet. It is, thus, evident that it participates through meetings in the Commission and joint meetings with the Cabinet in the formulation of policies and programmes.

The participation of the Planning Commission in policy-formation has come in for criticism. Asok Chanda argues that "the position of pre-eminence accorded to the Planning Commission is inconsistent with the conception of a cabinet form of Government"— the determinant of policies and objectives is the primary function of the Cabinet accountable to Parliament. It is interesting to note that D.R. Gadgil, who later became the Deputy Chairman of the Planning Commission, was also critical of the

Planning Commission. Arguing that the Commission had failed, he observed: "The root of the failure lies in the process by which the Planning Commission, essentially only an advisory body, has come to mix itself with the actual process of the formation of public policies even in matters other than of development." He continues: "It was, perhaps, the composition of the Planning Commission which made it inevitable that this should happen . . . . . The case with which not only the senior officials of the Commission, but also experts changed from Government department to the Planning Commission and *vice versa,* or combined duties in both the organisations, emphasised the basic similarity in the activities of the Ministers, and (it) . . . . . . is the power complex of Planning Commission or its members, their natural desire to exercise power and patronage like Ministers that are chiefly responsible for the neglect by the Commission of its main function and for a needless extension of is activities over many irrelevant fields. The misdirection has been helped largely by membership of the Prime Minister and the Finance Minister of the Planning Commission which appears to have vested the Planning Commission and its decisions with an unnatural kind of prestige and importance." He suggests the Commission to shed its role of direct participation in policy-making.

It is to be noted that the Estimates Committee, in its twenty-first report, felt that "the time has come when a review of entire position regarding the formal association of Cabinet Ministers of the Central Government with the Planning Commission should be made." The Committee, in the same report, recommended abolition of the post of the *de facto* member of the Commission, and the setting up of a body corresponding to the Planning Commission in each State. The latter step, it argued, "would go far to secure the success of planning in the country".

The dizzy heights of the Planning Commission could not be maintained for long. Since the advent of Indira Gandhi, as Prime Minister in 1967, the Planning Commission suffered both in prestige and authority. It does not enjoy any exalted measure of political support. It epitomises centralisation of power and authority, which is now resented by the stage governments, especially those like West Bengal, Andhra Pradesh, Tamil Nadu etc. Ruled by the non-Congress parties. Of late, the Planning Commission has been on way to becoming that organisation which has 'perks' but not much power!

Other staff agencies in India are the Budget and Economic Affairs Department in the Ministry of Finance, Vigilance Division in the Ministry of Home Affairs, and the Staff Inspection Unit in the Ministry of Finance. The Department of Economic Affairs, primarily concerned with the formulation of the financial policy of the Central Government, looks after a diversified group of subjects, like banking, currency, capital issues, public debt, foreign exchange, balance of payments, consolidation and preparation of central budgets, review of state budgets, technical assistance programmes, etc. The Administrative Vigilance Division provides a centralised drive, direction and co-ordination in regard to the battle against corruption in the public services. Each Ministry and Department has a Vigilance Officer, and the Director, Administrative Vigilance Division, acts as the chief guide and coordinator of the combined operations. The former is responsible for:

*(a)* examining all aspects of the work with a view to locating points where opportunity for corruption is likely to arise; for organising regular and surprise inspections and devising other ways and means for minimising the scope for corruption; and

*(b)* for initiating prompt action and pursuing it with speed and vigour when there appear to be reasonable grounds for suspicion of corruption or malpractices against individual officers.

The Staff Inspection Unit, constituted in April 1964, replaced the Special Reorganisation Unit which had been in existence since 1953. The Staff Inspection Unit is located in the Department of Expenditure (Ministry of Finance), and is charged with (i) securing economy in staff consistent with administrative efficiency, and

(ii) evolving performance standards and work norms. The functions of the Staff Inspection Unit is to keep the staffing position in Ministries/offices under the Central Government under constant review in accordance with predetermined programmes of work-measurement studies. It also undertakes *ad hoc* reviews, on special requests of Ministries/Offices not included in the programme as well as of public sector undertakings.

**Staff Agencies in Britain**

The Cabinet Secretariat is an important element in the organisation of the British Government. Established in 1916 under the stress of the First World War, it has steadily grown in importance, is now considered indispensable. S.E. Finer rightly points out that it is "a single device but its enormous effectiveness is only grasped in its absence". This body serves not only the cabinet but also the cabinet committees, and, at times, the *ad hoc* meetings of some ministers to resolve interdepartmental conflicts and disagreements. Its functions include compilation of its agenda, as well as of the subcommittees, circulation of memoranda and of periodical reports on the implementation of decisions, etc. It keeps the non-cabinet ministers informed of the results of the discussion that affect them. It acts as a memory of the cabinet; it is in a position to point out when was a topic discussed in the past and what was the decision then taken. When all is said, however, its function is not one of policy-making; it is, par excellence, a recording body. "Unit the establishment of the Cabinet Secretariat, there was no record of conclusions other than the Report which the Prime Minister sent to the sovereign. . . . . There must have been plenty of room for uncertainty and dispute about what the cabinet had done. No doubt, at the end of the meeting ministers dispersed hoping that everybody knew and would remember what had been agreed upon. With all the complexities of modern government, this way of transacting business would be quite impossible, or would, at any rate, lead to much confusion."

Another innovation to relieve the cabinet of some burden of work has been the emergence of cabinet committees, though "it is undesirable during the life-time of a government to reveal the existence of cabinet committees, their terms of reference, or the names of their chairman." These committees consist of the cabinet ministers but may also include non-cabinet ministers, civil servants, chief of staff, etc., in some of them. This device enables interested ministers to bargain and compromise with one another, and, thus, reduce pressure of work upon the cabinet. Consequently, the cabinet is left free to devote itself to more important matters. The importance of this device becomes apparent when we remember that the cabinet is today confronted with an increasing amount of work. Secondly, these committees, which include non-cabinet ministers as well, provide them (non-cabinet ministers) an opportunity of expressing their views, freely on matters in which they are interested. Thirdly, this system promotes continuous co-ordination. With the enormous extension of governmental field, "the amount of business requiring collective deliberation and decision in excess of what can properly be handled by the cabinet. But it is not necessary that the cabinet should deal with all these matters. Just as some questions are appropriate to the cabinet, so some can go to committees of the cabinet for final decision, or at least can go there in the first place so that the issue can be sorted out before cabinet consideration." Nevertheless, it must be borne in mind that these committees and subordinate to the cabinet which must confirm the decisions taken in a committee.

The Cabinet Committees are of two types—the standing, and the *ad hoc*. In 1976, there were about 25 cabinet committees in Great Britain. The more important of them are the following:

1. The Overseas Policy and Defence Committee, chaired by the Prime Minister.
2. The Committee on Macroeconomics, chaired by the Prime Minister.
3. The Committee on Industrial Development, chaired by the Chancellor of the Exchequer.
4. The Home Affairs Committee.

5. The Social Services Committee, chaired by the Secretary of State for Health and Social Services.
6. The Legislation Committee.
7. The Public Expenditure Scrutiny Committee.
8. The Energy Committee.
9. The Queen's Speeches Committee.
10. The Devolution Committee.
11. The Northern Ireland Committee.
12. The Agriculture Committee.
13. The Transport Committee.
14. The Urban Aid Committee, chaired by the Minister of the Environment.

The cabinet committees are quite important bodies in governmental decision-making. One is only to remember that the decision to make the atomic bomb and to invade the Suez was taken by cabinet committees, not by the full cabinet. Indeed, today the ministers seem to spend more time in cabinet committees than in cabinet itself.

**The Executive Office of the President of United States**

It is only recently that the President of the United States could come to posses a well-equipped office to effectively aid and assist him to coping with the heavy burden of his work. Until 1857, he had to hire his own secretary. In that year he was provided with a private secretary, a steward and a messenger. In 1928, the number of secretaries rose to three. It is obvious, the President received meagre help in discharging his duties. The situation got ample confirmation in the Reports of the President' Committee on Administrative Management (1937), and of the Hoover Commission on Organisation of the Executive Branch of the Government (1949), though it must be recalled that the Budget and

Accounting Act 1921, had created the Bureau of the Budget to act as a great arm of overhead management.

The recommendations of the Brownlow Committee were enshrined in the Reorganisation Act of 1939, which laid the legal foundation for the establishment of the executive office of the President—"perhaps the most significant step forward since the Budget and Accounting Act of 1921." The executive office of the President is made up of the While House Office, the Office of Defence Mobilisation, the Council of Economic Advisers, and some other agencies like the General Accounting Office, the Office of Economic Stabilisation etc.

**White House Office**

The White House Office covers the entire range of the Presidency Consisting of personal assistants, appointed by the President, this office performs all those functions that assist him in the day-to-day running of his office. The office analyses the problems confronting him and assists him in taking decisions. It transmits his decisions and orders to the departments, thus becoming an essential link between the latter and the President. Also, it is this office which, as the representative of the President, deals with the party-men, members of Congress, and private groups. Under President Eisenhowever, the White House staff consisted of about 250 persons.

**Office of Budget and Management**

The Office of Budget and Management, known until recently as the Bureau of the Budget, created by the Budget Accounting Act of 1921, has become an arm of overhead management; indeed to quote Arthur Macmahon, it is the "embodiment of the Presidency" in the administration. Its primary duty is to assist the President in the preparation and execution of the annual budget. In addition, it subjects all the executive orders, proposals for legislation, originating from the executive branch, and bills coming from Congress for review and analysis. It suggests the schemes for better organisation and management of agencies and departments of the executive branch. It also co-ordinates the federal statistical activities. The Office of Budget and Management works through offices for budget review, legislative reference, management and organisation, and statistical standards.

**National Security Council**

Set up by the National Security Act of 1947, the National Security Council advises the President on the integration of military, foreign and domestic policies pertaining to national security; assesses and appraises the objectives, commitments and risks of the United States in relation to the country's military power, and considers policies on matters of common interest to the departments and agencies of the government. The Council only studies and advises; the President takes the decision.

The Office of the Defence Mobilisation, dealing with national security, engages in mobilisation planning and executes the plans in times of emergency. The Council of Economic Advisers, established in 1946, assists the President in preparing his annual economic report to the Congress, and submits to him information on economic matters.

It is to be seen, thus, the President is today receiving aid and assistance from a number of organs. His staff is constantly growing in size and power. President Kennedy had added a few more agencies to the list. This proliferation of the staff agencies has posed new problems and has, of late, come in for considerable criticism. L.D. White writes: "This build-up of organisational structure leads inevitably to the questions put by Marshall Dimock, 'Where does this process stop? Is the President doomed to suffocate within the confines of a large and complex staff, without the assistance of which he is paralysed'?" The dilemma has led some to the conclusion that the business of the federal government has now become so vast that it is impossible to bring all of it under the responsibility of any single executive, and that some kind of collective responsibility such as is found in the British cabinet, or some radical splitting off of large blocks of business into autonomous corporations, or the devolution of functions to the states must be the source of relief." Some have suggested the greater utilisation of the Vice-Presidency and the Cabinet. Under

President Eisenhower, Vice-Presidency emerged as an office of considerable significance, and President Johnson added new dimension to this office by entrusting its incumbent with important functions and assignments.

# Structure of Organisation—Departments

## Fundamental Unit of Administration

Line Agencies in the Government, broadly speaking, include Departments, Public Corporations, and Commissions. A department is the fundamental organisation unit of administration on which rests the obligation of carrying on governmental operations. This unit is the highest one in the administrative hierarchy, immediately below the Chief Executive and responsible and subordinate to the latter. These are the two tests of determining whether a particular unit is a department or not. Department is the traditional and most important form of dividing and conducting governmental operations. "The departmental system is the natural out-growth of the need for the division of labour in administrations, and becomes acute when the functions of an enterprise multiply over and over as in the case of a modern government and especially the federal government."

Departments are immediately below the Chief Executive but not necessarily has he is free hand in organising and reorganising them. Authority to organise departments may be vested in the Constitution, the Parliament, or the Executive. In the U.S.A., the Congress regulates the details of governmental organisation; the President is not free to reorganise the executive branch of the government. These restrictions, however, do not confront the British Executive. The Ministers of Crown (Tansfer of Functions) Act 1946, conferred on the British Executive the power to organise and reorganise departments in the manner it thought necessary. In India, the formation and dissolution of ministries and departments is an executive function shereas in the Soviet Union there is the constitutional sanction behind the ministries which can be abolished only after an amendment of the Constitution.

**Integrated Versus Uncorrelated Organisation**

According to Willoughby, governmental operations may be organised, in accordance with two principles—(i) independent or uncorrelated, and (ii) integrated or departmental. The uncorrelated system is characterised by the treatment of each service or agency as an independent unit not related to other services, and the Line of authority running direct from it to the chief executive or the legislature. In the departmental system, on the other hand, related activities operating in the same general field, are grouped together into departments maintaining, thus, close relations with each other, and consequently, the line of authority runs from the service to the department, and from the department to the chief executive.

It is now agreed that the departmental system "is, from almost every point of view, far superior." The departmental system leads to simplification of governmental operations. It is common knowledge that the functions of a modern government are vast, varied and complicated. One cannot have a conception of the scope of governmental work and the agencies performing it in the absence of an integration of related activities, falling within the same general field. Simplification is, therefore, a vital need. Moreover, this integration will facilitate intelligent legislation as well. Secondly, the proper grouping of services operating in the same general field facilitates the formulation and implementation of a proper work programme. The chief executive can evolve a proper work programme only when he has to deal with a few chief subordinates, each of whom is made in charge of services falling in the general field. Similarly, the legislature too, can give intelligent consideration only if related operations are grouped together. It also saves the time of the legislature in so far as the latter has not to devote itself to separate budgets of the agencies. Thirdly, it helps the chief executive in exercising better control over administration, his attention now being confined to a few departments. Fourthly, under the departmental system, "conflicts of jurisdiction, overlapping of functions, and duplications of organisation, plant and activities" may be avoided. Fifthly, the departmental system leads to a better utilisation of technical plant, such as libraries and laboratories. Under the uncorrelated system, each agency has to maintain its own complete organisation and installations. If several services, whose operations fall in the same field, are grouped in a department, they all can avail of the services of the single agency, which can now be better equipped. Sixthly, the grouping of related services departmentally brings about economy and efficiency in the performance of what are called institutional or house-keeping activities. The general character of the latter is the same for all services. Hence, performance by central agencies, of the house-keeping activities results in economy and efficiency, and promotes standardisation and uniformity of administrative processes.

We are, thus, left in no doubt as regards the superiority of the departmental system to the uncorrelated one. However, "many if not all of the advantages inhering in the integrated system can be neutralised if not wholly lost by a failure to meet the requirements of this system." The most important requirement of the system is that all those services, and those services only, which perform the same general function and operate in the same general field should be grouped together under a separate department. This implies that the department should be uni-functional, i.e. (a) all those services whose operations fall within the same field should be grouped under a separate department; and (b) no other services should behaviour included in that department. W.F. Willoughby cites the following disadvantages resulting from the non-observance of (b):

*(i)* It interjects discordant and disturbing elements, which complicate and render difficult the proper co-ordination of the services having to do with department's essential function and the standardisation of their administrative practices and procedures.

*(ii)* It makes a demand upon the attention and time of the head of the department, which should be devoted

exclusively to his primary duties and it places upon him a responsibility which he should not have and which he is sure to meet only in a perfunctory manner.

*(iii)* It subjects the administrative agency to the control of a head who does nothing towards its effective operation, though he causes delay in the work.

It need, therefore, be stressed that departments should be uni-functional. L.D. White rightly points out that "the goal of uni-functional departments is now generally accepted, however, difficult to achieve, and the objective is conductive to departmental unity." The difficulty arises from the marginal cases in which more than one department may put forward valid claims.

**Bases of Organisation**

Aristotle had suggested two alternatives, namely:

*(i)* division of work according to persons or classes, and

*(ii)* division of work according to the services to be rendered.

These alternatives were also adopted by the Haldane Committee on the Machinery of Government (1918). It would be better to quote from the Report itself;

"Upon what principles are the functions of Departments to be determined and allocated? There appear to be only two alternative which may be briefly described as distribution according to persons or classes to be dealt with and distribution according to the service to the performed. Under the former method each minister... would be responsible to Parliament for those activities of the Government which would affect the sectional interests of the particular class of persons and there might be, for example, a ministry for paupers.... Now, the inevitable outcome of this method of organisation is a tendency to Lilliputian administration. It is impossible that the specialised service which each Department has to render to the community, can be of as high a standard when its work is at the same time limited to a particular class of persons and extended to every variety of provision for him, as when the Department concentrates itself on the provision of one particular service only by whomsoever required, and looks beyond the interests of comparatively small classes.

"The other method and the one which we recommend for the adoption is that of defining of the field of activity in case of each Department according to the particular service which it renders to the community as a whole.... The method cannot, of course, be applied with absolute rigidity. The work of the Education Department, for example, may incidentally trench on the sphere of health as in the arrangement of school-houses and care for the health of the scholars. Such incidental overlapping is inevitable, and any difficulties to which it may give rise must be met by systematic arrangements for the collaboration of Departments jointly interested.... But notwithstanding such necessary qualifications, we think that much would be gained if the distribution of departmental activities were guided by a general principle; and we have come to the conclusion that distribution according to the nature of the service to be rendered to the community as a whole is the principle which is likely to lead to the minimum amount of confusion and overlapping".

Though the Haldane Committee Report recognised two principles for allocation of work, a study of organisation reveals four different bases for organisation: (i) function or purpose, (ii) process, (iii) clientele, and (iv) area. Luther Gulick calls these purpose, process, person and place—the four P's—as the bases of organisation.

*(i)* *Purpose.* By purpose is meant the major objective to behaviour aimed at or major service to be performed. Functional division of work is very common, and is regarded by many as the only efficient method. Ministers of Defence, Education, Transport and Communications and Railways in the Government of India have been formed on this basis.

*(ii)* *Process.* Process is identified with a technique, profession, or skill of a somewhat specialised type.

though it is to be admitted that it is not quite easy to differentiate between process and function. Ministry of Law in India manifests this principle. Generally speaking, process or profession is found as basis of staff organisation rather than of link organisation.

(iii) *Clientele.* Sometimes clientele, too becomes the basis of organisation. The Department of Rehabilitation at the Centre and the Department of Tribal Welfare in some States in India have been formed on this principle. Similarly, the office of Indian affairs, and Veterans' Administration in the U.S.A. are the examples of clientele being the basis of organisation. There is a possible justification for creating client-based organisations. Some groups in the community have distinctive problems, so special as to differentiate them from the rest of the community. They need to be differently dealt with, hence, separate departments for them. The problems confronting the persons migrating from Pakistan in the wake of Independence were of a quite distinct character, necessitating a different treatment. Hence, a separate Ministry of Rehabilitation was formed. A clientele organisation, generally, caters to all or most of the needs of the group served.

(iv) *Area of Territory.* Finally, area, i.e., the place where a job is done, may be the basis of organisation. Underlying this principle is the belief that a region may have problems peculiar to itself, lending it a distinctive character, and thereby favouring a separate handling or treatment. The now-defunct North-East Frontier Agency (N.E.F.A.) in India, and the office of the Secretary of State for Scotland in Britain indicate the adoption of this basis of organisation. Also, at one level or another, most departments have their operating units organised on the area or territorial basis. The Ministry of Railways, thus, has nine territorial zones—Eastern, North-Eastern, North-East Frontier, South-Eastern, South Central, Northern, Western, Central and Southern. Zonal Councils, too, have been organised on this principle.

## Bases of Departmental Organisation

The work of Government is, thus, distributed among departments according to four possible bases, namely, function, process, clientele, and area. These bases are not alternative bases of organisation. All the four bases or principles are pressed into service while dividing the work of Government into departments. No single base, however admirable it may theoretically be, can be be made the sole criterion of dividing the work. This point can be illustrated by showing how the four bases have been employed for departmentalisation in the Government of India:

| | | | *Ministries* |
|---|---|---|---|
| 1. | Function | *(i)* | Health and Faily Welfare, |
| | | *(ii)* | Education and Culture. |
| | | *(iii)* | Labour, |
| | | *(iv)* | Shipping and Transport, |
| | | *(v)* | Defence. |
| 2. | Process | *(i)* | Law |
| | | *(ii)* | Works and Housing |
| | | *(iii)* | Steel and Mines, |
| 3. | Clientele | *(i)* | Department of Rehabilitation, |
| | | *(ii)* | Ministry of Agriculture, |
| 4. | Area | *(i)* | External Affairs, |
| | | *(ii)* | Indian Missions Abroad |
| | | *(iii)* | Regional Offices of the Director of Supply and Disposal. |

The following Table shows that the selection of the proper mode of division must be guided by the circumstances of the case as well as the objective aimed at. If objective be the provision of service to the people, functional method is broadly speaking, the best; if economy in technical staff is the aim, choice should be for the process method; if the aim is to help a certain segment or class

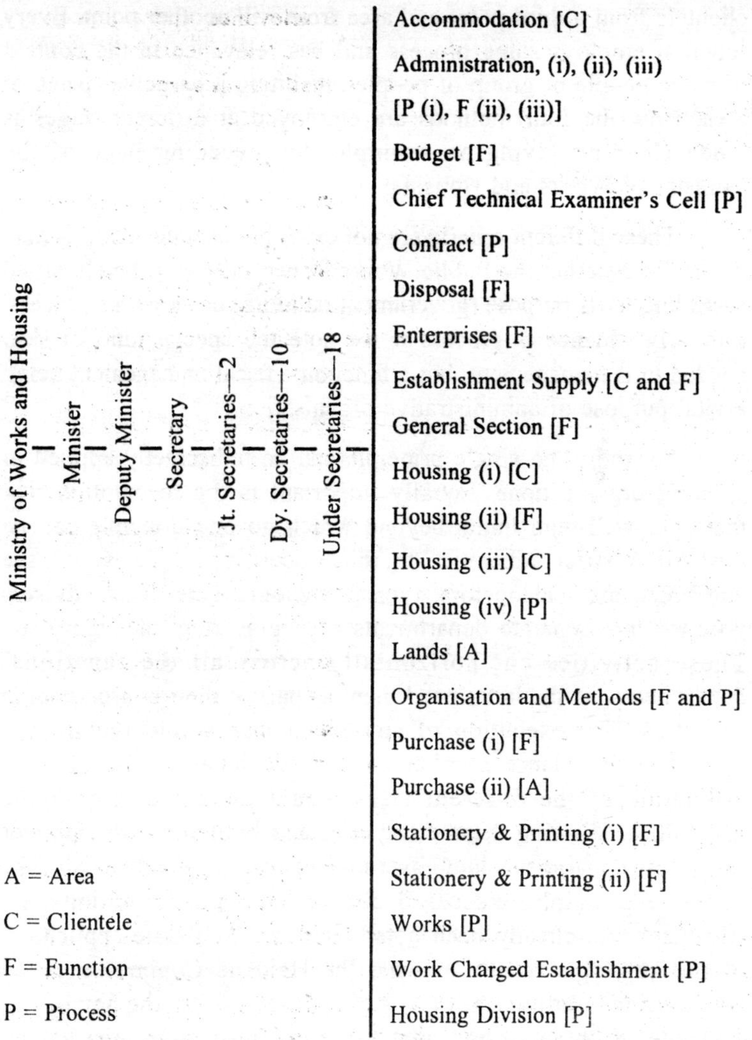


of people, recourse better be had to the clientele method; and lastly, the area method may be recommended if certain regions are affected with peculiar problems, or if a service is to be extended to a specified area only. In practice, however, four methods overlap each other, and are inter-penetrated. This basis of division may appear to be functional from one point, process from another point, clientele from a third point and area from still another point. Every function employs some process and has relevance in the context of some people or group of people inhabiting a particular place or area. How the four methods are employed at different stages is made clear by giving an example the preceding page of the Ministry of Works and Housing.

These different criteria are not exact or absolute. Thus, it may be argued whether the Public Works Department is to be classified according to its purpose (government building) or its works process. Similarly, finance is process if we note the special kind of skill needed in is management, but a function—fiscal management being a vital purpose of administrative organisation.

Secondly, no single principle can be indiscreetly applied in creating organisations. Equally important is the recognition that there are well-nigh limits beyond which no one principle can be pushed. A strict adherence to the process principle would see engineers, medical doctors, typists, stenographers, legal advisers grouped into separate departments of engineering, medicine, etc. These activities cut horizontally across all the functional departments, as the latter need them as part of their house-keeping activities. The execution of any given task would require co-operation of a large number of process departments. The co-ordination of the different tasks would place insurmountable difficulties. Viewing these difficulties and limitations, the number of process departments in a government is comparatively small. The clientele principle, discussed above, has rigid limitations. Its advantage has already been noted. But any wholesale application of this principle results in what the Haldane Committee called 'Lilliputian administration'. Again, the use of the territorial principle of organisation ought to be confined to regions having problems so special or distinct that they (problems) need separate handling. To carry this to its logical conclusion could be to recreate Heptarchy." Finally, the limitations of the functional principle, too need be noted. It does not entirely eliminate overlapping "any more than any filing system of library classification system eliminates cross-references". Again a given task is usually shared by many departments, as the primary responsibility of one department may be the secondary responsibility of another department. Thus, the Ministry of Education shares social education with the Ministry of Community Development and Co-operation.

Thirdly, the different bases of organisation are not mutually exclusive; these, in fact, supplement one another. The division of work at the departmental level may take place according to one principle; but, as we come down to the levels of divisions and sections, recourse has necessarily to be made to other principles. This is for the sake of convenience and efficient execution of the task.

Nevertheless,—and, this is our fourth observation—functional basis is the most commended one. It minizes confusion, overlapping and duplication of function. It is most conducive to acquisition of knowledge and development of skill. It permits the entire range of closely related problems to be viewed as a whole and in right perspective. And lastly, the purpose of the department is clear to the people. The first Hoover Commission, too, commended organisation by major purpose. It recommended; "The numerous agencies of the executive branch must be grouped into departments as nearly as possible by major purposes in order to give a coherent mission to each department." This, is the view of the Commission, would eliminate overlaps and facilitate development of co-ordinated policies. The Study Team of the Administrative Reforms Commission (1966-1970) called it the principle of rationality. It observed; "Two broad criteria usually determining any grouping exercise—these are rationality and manageability. The criterion of rationality is not applicable everywhere, but where it is, the grouping of subjects according to this principle can lead to the most effective type of co-ordination. Where this principle is not applicable, the only course to adopt is to have heterogeneous grouping subject to manageability of individual charges. The exercise of grouping, thus, involves two levels of thought. The identification of areas where the rationality principle should operate and the arrangement of subjects according to this principle is one level. For the rest, the exercise is not much better than a kind of jigsaw puzzle because what is required is to put the pieces together keeping in mind only broad common sense considerations about.

optimum sizes of ministries and departments. But there is a third criterion also, which is in some way more important than the above two. This is the criterion of stability. Administration not being a precise science there could be several views about how things should be done depending on what is desired to be stressed. However, whatever emerges as the eventual view should be capable of being maintained for some years to come. And if the consideration of stability is important for the future, it is also important now. Changes in allocation of business should, in other words, be made only if there is compelling reason for doing so."

It would appear from the preceding paragraphs that departmentalisation is just and exercise in rational analysis. Far from it, it is beset with political issues. A scheme of reorganisation meets with vigorous opposition from the pressure groups and vested interests. And, official of a department, which is likely to be adversely affected, are found, if the attempted reform is carried out mustering persuasive arguments in favour of retaining the *status quo*. "Usually the noise alone is enough to intimidate reform."

**Location of Authority**

The topmost point in a department is of extraordinary importance, all directions flow from it, and overall control is exercised by it. In fact, it is not incorrect to assume that the head sets tone and temper for the entire department. It is, therefore, of fundamental importance to decide whether the administrative responsibility should vest in a single individual or in a plural body. The former system is called the Bureau System, and the latter is known as the Board or Commission System.

In practice, we find government adopting both the systems. In India, most of the Central Government Departments have a single individual at the top, namely, the Secretary to the Government. The notable examples of the Board or Commission type of headship are the Railway Board, which heads the railway department, and the Posts and Telegraphs Board. The Department of Atomic Energy, the Department of Electronics and the Department of Space have each a commission form of organisation at its head. Also, the Departments of Income-tax, Central Excise and Customs are headed by the Central Board of Revenue. Similarly, in Britain Departments of Inland Revenue, Trade, Industry and Transport, etc. have boards at their heads. Despite the presence of the plural headship in certain spheres, however, it is, by and large, the bureau system which is prevalent. Indeed, as we shall see subsequently, the bureau system of headship is the norm, and the board or commission system is an exception.

It is appropriate here to drew a distinction between an administrative board at the head of a department, and an advisory board attached to a department for offering advice on certain specific points or in a general way. As the word 'advisory' indicates, the latter is bereft of administrative responsibilities of the department. There may also be an administrative board, not heading a department, but forming part of the departmental hierarchy at some lower level and endowed with functions which may be quasi-legislative and quasi-judicial in nature. An obvious example is the Board of High School and Intermediate Education, Uttar Pradesh.

**Departmental Organisation in the Central Governmental**

The powers and functions of the Government of India are divided into Ministries. Allocation of Government business is regulated by Rules of Business formed under Article 77 (3) of the Constitution. The allocation is made by the President on the advice of the Prime Minister by specifying the items of business allocated to each Minister, and by assigning a Ministry or a part of a Ministry or more than one Ministry to the charge of a Minister. A ministry may comprise only one department, or more than one. A typical Ministry of the Central Government is a three-tier structure, comprising—(i) the political head, that is, the Minister, who may be assisted by one or more ministers of state, deputy ministers, or parliamentary secretaries; (ii) the secretariat organisation of the ministry, with the Secretary, who is a permanent official, as the head; and (iii) the executive organisation of the departments comprising a ministry, the official head bearing the designation of Director-General, Inspector-General, etc.

Where the execution of the policies of Government requires decentralisation of executive direction and the establishment of field agencies, a Ministry has under it subsidiary organisations which are called Attached and Subordinate offices. The Attached Offices are responsible for providing executive direction required in the implementation of the policies laid down by the Ministry to whom they are attached. They also serve as respsitory of technical information and advice to the Ministry on technical aspects of questions dealt with by them. The subordinate offices function as field establishments or as agencies responsible for the detailed execution of the decision of Government. They, generally, function under the direction of an attached office, or in cases where the volume of executive direction involved is not considerable, directly under a Ministry.

The political element in a Ministry consists of the Minister, who, if work so demands, may be assisted by ministers of state, deputy ministers and parliamentary secretaries. These political officers change with a change in the ministry, and, thus, do not have permanent tenure. The fate of this political element is inevitably linked up with the fate of the political party to which they belong; the ousting of the party in power means the exit of this political element. Also, as the ministers are appointed on the advice of the Prime Minister, they may have to quit when the latter so desires. The Minister is the political head of the department. He lays down the broad policy of the department and also decides the major policy issues cropping up in the department. Of course, this vital function he cannot perform without the expert assistance of the permanent civil servants. The latter supply essential material, statistical and otherwise, without which policy-formulation is neither feasible nor possible. It is interesting here to quote Earl Attlee: "The first thing a Minister finds on entering office is that he can depend absolutely on the loyalty of his staff, and on leaving office, he will seldom be able to say what the private political views are even of those with whom he has worked mostly closely. The second thing that he will discover is that the civil servant is prepared to put up every possible objection to his policy, not from a desire to thwart him, but because it is his duty to see that the minister understands all the difficulties and dangers of the course which he wishes to adopt." Besides laying down the broad policy of the department, the minister also keeps a general watch over the execution of agreed policy. It is also imperative that he should supply dynamism to the administration under him. This aspect of his duty assumes considerable importance in view of a certain inherent static character of the administrative setup. As the late Prime Minister, Jawaharlal Nehru put it, "Where the whole social structure is changing rapidly, it requires dynamism at the top (of the administrative setup) and the Minister must supply it." Lastly, he is accountable to Parliament for the policies and activities of his department. One of the tenets of parliamentary democracy is the ministerial responsibility, constitutionally speaking. Quite revealing in this connection is the debate in the British House of Commons in July 1954, on the Crichel Down Affairs culminating in the resignation of the Minister of Agriculture Sir David Moxwell-Fyfe the Home Secretary, observed:

> "Where action-has been taken by a civil servant of which the Minister disapproves and has no prior knowledge, and the conduct of the official is reprehensible, then there is no obligation on the part of the Minister to endorse what he believes to be wrong or to defend what are clearly shown to be the errors of his officers. The Minister is not bound to defend action of which he did not know or which he does oppose but, of course, he remains constitutionally responsible to Parliament for the fact that something has gone wrong and he alone can tell Parliament what has occurred and render an account of his stewardship."

In India the ministerial responsibility was upheld, for the first time, in 1958, when T.T. Krishnamachari, the Finance Minister, resigned over what has generally come to be called the Life Insurance Corporation Affair. The Prime Minister, while accepting the resignation of the Finance Minister remarked: "Whoever might behaviour responsible for this, you (*i.e.*, the Finance Minister) very rightly say that, according to our convention, the Minister has to assume responsibility even though he might have had little knowledge of what others did and was not directly responsible for any of these steps." The ministerial responsibility is, thus, a firmly established concept in Indian policy. The Minister represents the department under him before Parliament as well as the general public. He initiates necessary legislation in Parliament, and answers questions put by members of that august body.

The Minister, as said earlier, may be assisted by the ministers of State, deputy ministers and parliamentary secretaries. A Minister of State usually works under the general supervision and guidance of the Minister who assigns the former some specific items of work. In some cases, however, the Minister of State may be in sole charge of the Ministry.

The deputy minister usually has no specific administrative responsibility for the conduct of work of the department. His duties "should be to answer questions in Parliament on behalf of ministers concerned, to assist them in piloting Bills; to explain policies and programmes to the general public and constituencies, and maintain liaison with Members of Parliament, political parties and the Press: and to undertake a special study or investigation of particular problems which were entrusted.... by the ministers concerned." The parliamentary secretary assists the Minister in the discharge of his parliamentary functions.

The Minister is in charge of the department, but it is the Secretary who is the head of the department. Under the political head sprawls the secretariat organisation of the department. The head of this secretariat set up is the Secretary, who is the principal advisor of Minister on the whole gamut of policies and administrative activities of the department. The secretariat is the office of the Secretary. The term seems to have been derived from the word 'secret', this meaning, however, does not fully explain the role that it plays in a democratic setup with the Minister held accountable to Parliament. The policymaking level is the secretariat which also provides general guidance to, and exercises overall control over the executive agencies, and acts as a necessary link between the executive agencies and the cabinet. As said earlier, the Secretary brings all the relevant facts of the case before the Minister so that an informal decision can be taken by the latter. He must keep his Minister fully informed and must be fearless in expressing what Sir Edward Bridges has called "the Departmental Philosophy". It is his right and duty to advise, to warn, to encourage, and to explain. Secondly, the Secretary has the responsibility of conducting the administration of his department in an efficient and economical way. And lastly, it is he who represents his department before the Public Accounts Committee of Parliament.

The secretariat organisation of the department is staffed by two categories of personnel, namely—(i) the officer class, and (ii) the subordinate class. The former includes the secretary, the deputy secretary and the under-secretary. If, however, the department is a big one, there may be joint or additional secretaries, who are made in charge of a wing of the department and who deal directly with the Minister about matter falling without the allotted sphere. With their status more on less equal to that of the secretary, the Joint or Additional secretaries provide relief to the over-burdened secretary, though, to be sure, the former as a rule consult him on important matters.

The officer class usually belongs to the Indian Administrative Service (or, the former Indian Civil Service) and is recruited by the Central Government from the I.A.S. cadres of several States under what has come to be called the tenure system, first introduced in 1905 by Lord Curzon. The principal features of the tenure system are: "first, that the Government of India Secretariat should be staffed not by direct recruitment but by the importation of officers already serving in the provinces; and secondly, that there should be regular alternation between a tenure of office in the central secretariat and a tenure of office in a post in the provinces." Under this system, the officers who are engaged in policy-formulation have had first-hand knowledge of the conditions under which implementation of policies takes place. As a result, policy formulation tends to become realistic. This tenure system, however, is restricted in scope, as some of the departments have their separate services. For example, the Ministry of External Affairs draws its officers from the Indian Foreign Service. Another source of recruitment of this class is the Central Secretariat Service, set up in 1950.

The subordinate staff of the secretariat consists of the clerical staff arranged into upper and lower division clerks. The lower division clerks are recruited by a competitive examination whereas the upper division clerks are recruited partly by promotion from the lower rung, i.e., the lower division clerks, and partly by competitive examinations.

The secretariat is the advisor of the Minister, assisting the Minister in policy formulation. In a very real sense, thus, the secretariat is 'staff' rather than 'line'. Execution of policy rests with the executive organisation having its own head, which is just below the secretariat. The Secretary, who heads the secretariat is the principal advisor of the Minister in policy-formulation. The executive machinery of the department is a separate organisation, which, too, is called department, with its own presiding officer, styled as the head of department. The head of departments are engaged in the task of implementation of the policy and programme approved by the Minister. Besides this, they conduct the administration of the departments and render technical advice to the secretariat on matters pertaining to their sphere. It is vital, therefore, that perfect harmony should prevail between them and the secretariat. But, in practice, there appears to be lack of harmony as a result of extreme centralisation of authority in the hands of the secretariat as well as excessive interference of the secretariat in the functioning of the department. A.D. Gorwala has sharply commented upon this point. He observed:

> "One of the best examples of an organisational defect in which one branch of the administration encroaches on the functions of the other, is furnished by the relationship between the Secretariat, that is, the Ministry, and the head of the department working under it. Here, although this limits of actions of both are very well known, the Ministry being responsible for the formulation of policy, and the department for its implementation, yet often so great is the anxiety of the Ministry to see the work carried out that it continuously interferes. The result is that the head of the department is deprived of all initiatives and instead of being allowed to attend to make progress with his own work, has to spend a great deal of time submitting unnecessary reports, explaining the position in individual matters to the Ministry and getting

> its orders on points which lie well within his own sphere of authority. The attempt by a Ministry to do the work of the head of a department invariably ends in inefficiency and failure. The work is delayed, it gets badly done, and when things go wrong, there is no single person who can behaviour held responsible. The departmental chief and other officers lose heart and all that occurs is waste of time, men and material, ending in lack of success of policy."

Similarly, the Third Five Year Plan observed "..... Central Ministries and perhaps Secretariat Departments in the States have tended to assume responsibility for an increasing amount of original work. This has reduced the initiative of the Executive Departments and their ability to function on their own. The main preoccupation of Ministries and Secretariat Departments should be with matters of policy, general supervision and enforcement of standards, and executive task should be left to be carried out by department and authorities specially designated for the purpose."

As pointed out earlier, the powers and functions of the Central Government are divided into Ministries/Departments numbering fifty seven in 1985. The number stood at fifty-six in 1983, fifty-three in 1979, thirty-five in 1962, forty-one in 1966, forty-six in 1969, forty-seven in 1970, fifty in 1972, and fifty-three in 1979.

**Ministries and Departments in the Central Government in 1985**

1-3. Ministry of Agriculture and Rural Development
- Department of Agriculture & Co-operation
- Department of Agriculture Research & Education
- Department of Rural Development

4-6. Ministry of Commerce and Supply
- Department of Textiles
- Department of Supply

7. Ministry of Chemicals and Fertilizers

8-9. Ministry of Communications
- Department of Posts
- Department of Tele Communications

10-13. Ministry of Defence
- Department of Defence
- Department of Defence Production
- Department of Defence Research & Development

14. Ministry of Education
15. Ministry of Environment and Forests
16. Ministry of External Affairs

17-20. Ministry of Finance
- Department of Expenditure
- Department of Economic Affairs
- Department of Revenue

21-22. Ministry of Food and Civil Supplies
- Department of Food
- Department of Civil Supplies

23-24. Ministry of Health and Family Planning
- Department of Health
- Department of Family Welfare

25-26. Ministry of Home Affairs
- Department of Official Language

27-28. Ministry of Industry and Company Affairs
- Department of Industry
- Department of Company Affairs

29. Ministry of Information and Broadcasting

30-31. Ministry of Irrigation and Power
- Department of Irrigation
- Department of Power

32. Ministry of Labour

33-34. Ministry of Law of Justice
- Department of Legal Affairs
- Department of Legislative Affairs

35. Ministry of Parliamentary Affairs

36-38. Ministry of Personnel, Training, Administrative Reforms, Public Grievances, Pension and Pensioners' Welfare

Department of and Training
Department of Administrative Reform and Public Grievances
Department of Pension and Pensioners' Welfare

39. Ministry of Petroleum

40-41. Ministry of Planning
Department of Statistics

42. Ministry of Railways

43-45. Ministry of Steel, Mines and Coal
Department of Steel
Department of Mines
Department of Coal

46. Ministry of Shipping and Transport

47-48. Ministry of Tourism and Civil Aviation
Department of Tourism

49. Ministry of Women and Social Welfare

50. Ministry of Works and Housing

51. Ministry of Youth Affairs and Sports

**Department**

52. Department of Atomic Energy
53. Department of Culture
54. Department of Electronics
55. Department of Environment
56. Department of Ocean Development
57. Department of Space
58. Cabinet Secretariat
59. President's Secretariat
60. Prime Minister's Office

It is now proposed to discuss the following Ministries in the present chapter:

1. The Ministry of Home Affairs
2. The Ministry of Finance

3. The Ministry of Defence

4. The Ministry of External Affairs.

**The Ministry of Home Affairs**

The Ministry of Home Affairs has always been considered to be of key importance in the Central Government, indeed in the entire governmental system of the country. This is despite the fact that a few functions which remained with this ministry since the inception were taken away from its purview under the prime ministership of Indira Gandhi. In June 1977, the Department of Personnel and Administrative Reforms was transferred to this Ministry.

This arrangement continued till January 1985 when the department of Personnel and Administrative Reforms was separated from it and placed directly under the Prime Minister.

The principal functions of the Ministry of Home Affairs are maintenance of internal security and management of public services. Its most important function, of course, is the maintenance of law and order in the country; and to this end, it has even set up para-military forces like the Central Reserve Police Force, Border Security Force, Central Industrial Security Force, etc. Besides, the Ministry of Home Affairs administers the programmes for the welfare of scheduled castes, scheduled tribes and backward classes. Matters relating to emergency provisions of the Constitution (except those relating to financial emergency) are the direct responsibility of this Ministry. It is also to be remembered that it is the Ministry of Home Affairs which administers the union territories numbering 9 at present.

The Ministry of Home Affairs is responsible for the following subjects:

1. Establishment and formation of new States.

2. Issues of notification of election of the President and the Vice-President.

3. Grant of pardons, reprieves, suspension, or commutation of a sentence of death.

4. Issue of notifications of appointment and resignation of the Prime Minister and other ministers and parliamentary secretaries in the Central Government.
5. Model Rules of Business for State Governments.
6. Issue of notifications of appointment, resignation and removal of Governors.
7. Administration of Union Territories.
8. Border Security Force.
9. Scheduled Castes, scheduled Tribes and other backward classes.
10. Matters relating to the emergency provisions of the Constitution.
11. Matters relating to the Rulers of former Indian States.
12. Intelligence Bureau.
13. Preventive detention.
14. Citizenship.
15. Immigration from foreign and Commonwealth countries.
16. Matters relating to code of conduct for legislators.
17. Code of conduct for ministers.
18. Census of population.
19. Matters relating to the Indian Police Service.
20. Matters relating to Central Industrial Security Force.
21. Central Reserve Police.
22. Civil Defence
23. Emoluments, allowances, privileges and rights in respect of leave of absence of the President and

Governors; salaries and allowances of ministers; deputy ministers and parliamentary secretaries of the Union.

24. Matters relating to national integration.

25. Criminal law and procedure.

26. Matters relating to the State of Nagaland.

**The Ministry of Finance**

The Ministry of Finance is an important ministry in the Central Government. Its political chief is invariably a minister of cabinet rank and politically powerful. The Ministry of Finance consists of the following three Departments.

1. Department of Economic Affairs.

2. Department of Expenditure.

3. Department of Revenue.

Till 1977, the Ministry of Finance had a fourth department also—the Department of Banking—which looked after all the banks (including foreign banks), matters relating to the Reserve Bank of India, cooperative banking, and other long-term financial institutions (excluding the Life Insurance Corporation and the Unit Trust of India). As already mentioned, the Department of Banking was abolished in May 1977.

The Ministry of Finance is among the key ministries in the Central Government. It prepares the budget of the Central Government and also sees its execution. It is responsible for taxation administration. It deals with currency and coinage, and regulates and controls both foreign investment in the country and foreign exchange. It negotiates bilateral and international aid and other matters for the economic development of the country. In short, this Ministry is responsible not only for financial management in the Government but also for fiscal management. Wide ranging, thus, are the responsibilities of the Ministry of Finance.

The Department of Economic Affairs deals with the following:

1. Administration of the Foreign Exchange Act.
2. Foreign Exchange Budget.
3. Control of the foreign exchange resources.
4. Foreign investment.
5. Import and export of gold and silver.
6. Technical and economic aid for economic development.
7. Currency and coinage.
8. Budget.
9. Preparatioin of the Central budget including supplementary budget.
10. Accounting and audit procedures.
11. Finance Commission.
12. Stock Exchanges.
13. Stock issues.

The Department of Expenditure deals with the following:

1. Financial rules and regulations and delegation of financial powers.
2. Financial sanctions relating to all ministries and offices of the Government of India.
3. Review of the staffing of Central Government establishments with a view to securing economy.
4. Indian Audit and Accounts Department.
5. Defence Accounts Department.
6. Statutory grants to states provided for in the Constitution.

7. Local taxation.
8. State Finance.
9. Capital Budget.
10. Planning and Development Finance.
11. Bureau of Public Enterprises, including Industrial Management Pool.
12. Grants to the Indian Institute of Public Administration.

The Department of Revenue of Insurance looks after the following:

1. The Central Board of Revenue.
2. Stamp duty.
3. Questions relating to income-tax, corporation tax, capital gains tax.
4. Excess profits tax.
5. Wealth tax, expenditure tax and gift tax.
6. Medical and toilet preparations.
7. Opium.
8. Administration of excise in the Union territories.
9. Central excise.
10. Life Insurance Corporation and matters relating to life insurance.
11. Preventive detention for reasons connected with the conservation of foreign exchange or prevention of smuggling.

**The Ministry of Defence**

The Ministry of Defence has under it two departments:

1. Department of Defence.

2. Department of Defence Production, and
3. Department of Research and Development.

While certain functions have been neatly distributed between these Departments, others continue to remain with the main Ministry. In this sense, therefore, the Ministry of Defence has really 4 units among which the functions relating to defence have been allocated.

The main Ministry looks after the following:

1. The Defence of India.
2. The armed forces, namely—army, navy and air force.
3. The reserves of the army, navy and air force.
4. The territorial army and the auxiliary air force.
5. The National Cadet Corps, the Auxiliary Cadet Corps and the Lok Sahayak Sena.
6. Works relating to the army, navy, air force and ordnance factories.
7. Remounts, veterinary and farms organisation.
8. Canteen Stores Department.
9. Civilian services paid from defence estimates.
10. Hydrographic surveys and preparation of navigational charts.
11. Formation of cantonments, delimitation/excision of cantonment areas, local self-go in such areas, the constitution and powers within such areas of cantonment boards and authorities and regulation of house accommodation (including the control of rents) in such areas.
12. Acquisition, requisitioning, custody and relinquishment of land and property for defence purposes. Eviction

of unauthorised occupants from defence land and property.

13. Matters relating to ex-servicemen including pensioners.

The Department of Defence Production deals with matters relating to defence production and organisations engaged in this work. The Defence Production and Inspection Organisations; Hindustan Aeronautics Ltd.; Bharat Electronics Ltd.; Mazagon Docks Ltd., Bombay; Garden Reach Workshops Ltd., Calcutta; Praga Tools Corporation Ltd., Hyderabad; Bharat Earth Movers Ltd.; Defence Research and Development Organisation; Matters connected with aeronautics, etc., have been placed under the Department of Defence Production.

The Department of Defence Research and Development deals with the following:

1. Planning for substitution of imports; requirements for defence purposes, particularly in the fields of electronics, instrumentation, vehicles and ship-building, and the preparation of detailed schemes in this regard.
2. Implementation of such schemes through the utilisation of the industrial capacity in the country for research and development work and for manufacture.
3. Coordination of scientific and technological research and development work in the country with the work of the Defence Research and Development Organisation.

**The Ministry of External Affairs**

The Ministry of External Affairs is one whose importance in an independent country cannot be overlooked or under-estimated. As its name suggests, this Ministry deals with matters relating to India's relationship with foreign countries. It is responsible for the following:

1. External Affairs.
2. Relations with foreign states and Commonwealth countries.

3. All matters affecting foreign, diplomatic and consular officers and United Nations officers and its specialised agencies in India.

4. Passports and visas.

5. Extradition of criminals and accused persons from India to foreign and Commonwealth countries and *vice versa*.

6. Preventive detention in India for reasons of state connected with external and Commonwealth affairs.

7. Repatriation of the nationals of foreign and Commonwealth states from India and deportation and repatriation of Indian nationals of foreign and Commonwealth countries to India.

8. All emigration under the Indian Emigration Act 1992, from India to overseas countries and the return of emigrants.

9. All consular functions.

10. Liaison work connected with Education Ministry's cultural scholarships, schemes and nomination of private students of Indian origin domiciled abroad to reserve seats in medical and engineering colleges in India.

11. Ceremonial matters relating to foreign and Commonwealth visitors and diplomatic and consular representatives.

12. Himalayan expeditions.

13. Coordination and development measures in border areas.

14. United Nations specialised agencies and other international conferences.

15. Indian Foreign Service.

16. Indian Foreign Service Branch 'B'.
17. External Publicity.
18. Political treaties.
19. Notification regarding commencement or cessation of a state of war.
20. Foreign Jurisdiction.
21. Piracies and crimes committed on the high seas or in the air; offenses against the law of nations committed on land or the high seas or in the air.
22. Demarcation of the land frontier of India.
23. Economic and technical assistance given by India to the Government of Nepal under the Colombo Plan for co-operative Economic Development.

8

# Central Civil Services

Unlike the all-India services, the Central Civil Services are under the exclusive control of the Central Government, and, secondly, the members of which man the positions only in the Central Government. The Civil Services of the Central Government comprise established services known as central civil services as well as civil posts created outside the established services, which constitute the general central service. Both the established central civil services and the civil posts are classified in the descending order of importance into Class I, Class II, Class III, and Class IV. There are, today, the following 33 Central Civil Services Class I, and 25 Central Civil Services Class II:

**Central Civil Services—Class I**

1. Archaeological Service 2. Botanical Survey of India 3. Central Engineering Service 4. Central Electrical Engineering Service 5. Central Health Service 6. Central Revenues Chemical Service 7. Central Secretariat Service (a) Selection grade (b) Grade I. 8. General Central Service 9. Geological Survey of India 10. Indian Audit and Accounts Service 11. Indian Defence Accounts Service 12. Indian Foreign Service 13. Indian Meteorological Service 14. Indian Postal Service 15. Indian Posts and Telegraphs Traffic Service 16. Indian Revenue Service.

(a) Customs Branch (Indian Customs Service) (b) Central Excise Branch (Central Excise Service) (c) Income-Tax Branch (Income-Tax Service).

17. Indian Salt Service 18. Mercantile Marine Training Ship Service 19. Mines Department 20. Overseas Communication

Service 21. Survey of India. 22. Telegraph Engineering Service 23. Zoological Survey of India 24. Central Legal Service (grade I, II, III and IV) 25. Railway Inspectorate Service 26. Indian Foreign Service Branch (B) (a) General Cadre, Grade I (b) General Cadre, Grade II 27. Indian Inspection Service 28. Indian Supply Service 29. Central Information Service (a) Senior Administrative Grade (b) Junior Administrative Grade (c) Grade I (d) Grade II 30. Indian Statistical Service 31. Indian Economic Service 32. Telegraph Traffic Service 33. Railway Personnel Service.

**Central Civil Services—Class II**

1. Central Secretariat Service, Section Officers' Grade 2. Central Secretariat Service Grade IV 3. Central Secretariat Stenographer's Service, Grade I 4. Central secretariat Stenographers' Service (Combined) 5. Labour Officers' Service 6. Central Health Service 7. Indian Meteorological Service. 8. Postal Superintendents' Service 9. Post Master's Service 10. Telegraph Engineering and Wireless Service 11. Telegraph Traffic Service 12. Central Excise Service 13. Customs Appraisers Service-Principal Appraisers and Head Appraisers 14. Customs Appraisers Service, Class II Appraisers 15. Customs Preventive Service, Class II Chief Inspectors 16. Customs Preventive Service, Class II Inspectors 17. Income Tax Service 18. Geological Survey of India 19. Botanical Survey of India 20. Survey of India 21. Zoological Survey of India 22. Central Electrical Engineering Service 23. Central Engineering Service 24. Indian Salt Service 25. General Central Service.

The day-to-day administration of these services rests with the individual Ministry under which the posts exist. Also, involved in the management of these services are the Department of Personnel which determines the conditions of service (of administrative nature) and the Ministry of Finance which is concerned with the pay-scales and other financial aspects of conditions of service like fixation of pay, grant of increments, pension and gratuity, contribution to provident fund, etc. It is now proposed to describe one central civil service, viz., the Central Secretariat Service.

**Central Secretariat Service**

The Imperial Secretariat Service was renamed, in 1948, as the Central Secretariat Service under the Central Secretariat Service

(Reorganisation and Reinforcement) Scheme, 1948. The cadre of Assistant Secretary was abolished, and the existing personnel of this cadre were included in the grade of Under Secretary. Originally, the service had the following (iv) grades.

| | | |
|---|---|---|
| Grade I | Under Secretary | Class I |
| Grade II | Section Officer | Class I |
| Grade III | Section Officer | Class II non-gazetted |
| Grade IV | Assistant | Class II non-gazetted |

Grade III was created primarily as a kind of training post for direct recruits. "The idea originally was that there would be an equal number of posts in the two grades of Section Officer—those in the lower grade would be in charge of smaller and less important sections. Further, for direct recruits the new grade was to be a raining grade." But the scheme did not operate in the intended manner, and there was free interchange of positions among the Section Officers of the two grades. "In the circumstances, and also, in the interest of improved recruitment," wrote the Second Pay Commission, "we recommend the amalgamation of the two grades." The Government accepted this recommendation, and merged the two grades into a continuous Class II grade. There is, also, the addition of a new grade called the selection grade comprising Deputy Secretariaties and above, 45 posts of Deputy Secretaries in the Secretariat were reserved for the Central Secretariat Service personnel. More recently, the Central Secretariat Service has even made indent on the level of Directors and Joint Secretary. 32 Deputy Secretariats in the Central Secretariat Service has been put in the select list for Director's grade (Rs. 1800-2000) while other 13 deputy Secretariats have been included in the select list for the posts of Joint Secretariats (Rs. 2250). Above the level of Joint Secretariaties the personnel of the Central Secretariat Service have not yet made their impact felt.

The present organisation of the Central Secretariat Service is as follows:

| | | | |
|---|---|---|---|
| 1. | Selection Grade | Jt. Secretary | Rs. 2,500 |
| | | Director | Rs. 1800-2000 |
| | | Dy. Secretary | Rs. 1100-1800 |

| | | |
|---|---|---|
| 2. | Grade I (Under Secretary or equivalent) | Rs. 900-1250 |
| 3. | Section Officers' Grade | Rs. 350-900 |
| 4. | Assistant's Grade | Rs. 210-530 |

Appointments to the Selection Grade is made by promotion of permanent officers of grade I, having five years' service in that grade, on the basis of merit. For the purpose of promotion a select list of officers of grade I is prepared. Similarly, appointments to grade I are made by promotion of permanent officers of the section officers' grade having at least ten years' service in that grade, on the basis of merit. For promotion to grade I, a select list of section officers is prepared.

Appointment to section officers' grade is made partly by direct recruitment and partly by promotion. One-third of the vacancies are normally filled up through direct recruitment, the remaining by promoting assistants with eight years' minimum service, and by holding, annually the limited department competitive examination. Assistants are appointed through direct recruitment and partly through promotion—the (respective quota being three-fourths and one-fourth) ratio being 3:1.

A significant development since 1962 has been the decentralisation of the Central Secretariat Service "in the interest of better personnel management and better utilisation of the training received in each Ministry." The Department of Personnel is the controlling authority in the case of Selection Grade and Grade I of the Central Secretariat Service. But the control over personnel up to and including the Section Officers' level has passed into the hands of the administrative Ministries. The decentralisation has, however, raised the following problems:

1. This has led to the atomisation of the Central Secretariat Service, preventing the personnel from acquiring a wide experience of the various activities of the Government. This will breed too narrow—and confining—specialism.

2. Consequent on decentralisation, no single agency is, as a matter of course, responsible for collecting,

keeping and processing vital service statistics in regard to various decentralised services. "The (Estimate) Committee feels that without a regular and systematic study of these statistics, it would hardly be possible to keep a centralised watch over the growth of individual cadres or to take effective steps to correct imbalances in promotion prospects of the decentralised categories of staff in different cadres."

3. Some Ministries are more expansion-oriented than others. The inevitable result is that the promotion prospects in different Ministries are bound to be uneven.

4. Allocation of staff to the decentralised cadres is being disturbed because of the frequent reorganisation of Ministries departments.

# Field Administration

New Delhi is supposed to be the hub of administration—a centre, from where the whole country is governed and administered. In practice, however, there is a plurality of administrative centres spread throughout the length and breadth of the country; and from the point of view of the citizens, these centres are decidedly more important. There is no ministry/department of the Central or Sate Government which does not have numerous field offices all over the land. Take a central department like the Posts and Telegraphs which has about one lakh Post Offices scattered all over the country, all arranged in a hierarchy—circle, postal, district division, sub-post-office area, and village post-office. Similar is the case with the Ministry of Railways, which has the following hierarchy of organisation.

| | | |
|---|---|---|
| "Headquarters" | | —Railway Board |
| "Field" | Zone | —Zonal Manager |
| | Division | —Divisional Superintendent. |

The picture is no different in the case of the administration at the State level. Take the Police and Revenue administration as an example. The hierarchy of organisation in these cases is as follows:

| | *Police* | *Revenue* |
|---|---|---|
| State Headquarters | Inspector-General of Police | State Headquarters—Board of Revenue: Division—Divisional Commissioner |

| | | |
|---|---|---|
| Range | Deputy Inspector General of Police | District—Collector/ Deputy Commissioner |
| District | District Superintendent of Police | Subdivision—Sub divisional Officer; Tahsil—Tahsildar |
| Circle | Circle Inspector | Revenue Circle— |
| Police Station | Sub-Inspector | Revenue Inspector |
| Village | Chowkidar or Patel, or the Headman | Village-Lekhpal or Patwari |

By the term 'headquarters', we mean the central or supervising office, usually in the capital, in contrast to regional or fieldoffice. .Concretely put, the "headquarters organisation of the Government of India comprises a number of Ministries and Departments," to quote from the Report of the Second Pay Commission. In contrast to headquarters, the offices which usually should get the approval before taking administrative actions from the headquarters and are under the control and direction of the latter, are called 'field-offices'. In Indian administrative jargon, headquarters is synonymous with the secretariat, and the term 'field' refers to attached and subordinate offices.

## Importance of Field

Just as proof of the pudding lies in its eating, the impact of legislation or any administrative action depends upon its 'administering'. Best intentions get thwarted by inefficient or soulless implementation. Since 'administering' is the responsibility of the field, the latter, in fact, makes the difference between good government and bad government. Importance of the field emerges from other factors as well, some of which are the following:

1. There are many times more public officials working in the field than at the national capital. Only one out of every 160 or so Central Government employees is in the headquarters at Delhi—the rest work in the field. This is true of other countries as well. In the U.S.A. for instance, "nine employees are stationed in the field for every employee stationed in Washington," according to James W. Fesler. This is the trend all over the world.

2. Expansion of services now being provided by government committed to the ideals of the Welfare State.

3. Increase in the regulatory activities of government.

4. Technological advances—particularly in the field of transportation and communication—have played an important role in the expansion of field organisation.

5. Democracy, too, has necessitated the creation of field organisations. Citizens now want services at their door. Also, there is a demand for greater citizen participation in both, policy-formation and execution.

6. Some field organisations are inevitable under any situation. A country, for instance, must maintain its diplomatic missions abroad.

**Field: A Neutral Concept**

A word need be said about an erroneous belief that 'field' necessarily connotes decentralisation and 'grass-roots' administration. Historically, the field organisation has been a tool employed for both the centralisation and decentralisation of government. Centralist emphasis, for instance, dominated field organisation under Mughal and British administrations.

**Criteria Governing Formation of Field Areas**

An important organisational question is: Should each department have its own field area suited to its own convenience? Or, should all the departments agree to have one common area? We may pose the same question differently, viz., should field areas be single purpose (special) or multi-purpose?

Each method of organising the field area has its merits as well as demerits. There is no virtue in either method. It may, however, be advised that the same area should be created for as many departments as possible. This results in—(i) citizen convenience, (ii) easy and direct communication between field officers of different departments operating in the same area in related problems, and (iii) pooling together of house-keeping activities with resultant economy and greater efficiency. District in India is the multi-purpose field area, common to most of the departments. Yet single-purpose area may look necessary in view of the peculiar or different requirements of a department. Thus, railways and posts and telegraphs have their own field areas suited to their own requirements.

The criteria governing formation of field area may be listed as follows:

1. Administrative economy including availability of funds with a department, and manpower;
2. Political pressures and need for citizen convenience and participation;
3. Nature of work to be performed by the department;
4. Historical consideration; and
5. Topography.

**Co-ordination between Field Level Agencies**

The activities of field functionaries of different departments must needs be effectively coordinated, as all these are engaged in the performance of activities which are interrelated, even interdependent, and which, when taken together, culminate in realisation or planned targets. All the departments are thus, partners in the joint enterprise of a modern welfare state. Agricultural development, to give an illustration, requires supplies, in proper sequence, and, what is more, in a timely way, of fertilizer, seed, water and credit, and arrangement for storing and marketing. Involved in these various tasks are the departments of agriculture irrigation, husbandry, co-operation, electricity, etc. Failure on the part of even one is liable to retard the achievement of targets, and, as a result, there could emerge a situation, which a block development officer describes in this manner:

"Although the state irrigation department provides overseers on almost all the blocks, there is, however, no coordination between the overseers and the block. He seldom comes to the block, and hardly consults the extension officers or listens to the problems or grievances of the villagers. As a result, the grievances of the villagers regarding channels etc., are not solved in time and effectively. These are dealt with through routine correspondence and are, thus, delayed."

Success in agricultural development programme depends upon how various developmental functionaries gear their efforts. Co-ordination of these various activities may be facilitated if all these departments adopt identical boundaries for their areas, and also locate their offices in the same town in close proximity to one another. In addition, institutionalised efforts are also called for, and in this respect, a brief reference may be made to the following three models: (i) in India the District Collector/Deputy Commissioner has been the traditional coordinator in the district committed to his charge, (ii) the Prefect performs this function in Fance, and (iii) some countries appoint a general area officer who provides common staff services to all other and also functions as the convener and coordinator for conferences of officials in that area.

Whatever be the method for effecting field-level coordination among various technical functionaries, one thing must be strongly emphasised. And, this is the paramount need for free, frank and frequent communication between field offices of various departments. For, their tasks are interrelated to a much greater extent than is generally realised or visualised at the headquarters. This is the 'procedural' supplement to the institutional models described in the earlier paragraph.

**Issues in Field-Headquarters Relationship**

Major issues involved in the relationship between the headquarters and field are two: (1) territorial—functional dichotomy; (2) communications and control.

***Territorial—Functional Dichotomy***

The organisation of the establishments from the standpoint of overhead direction and control may take either of the two forms—territorial or functional. Willoughby calls them unitary or multiple.

In the unitary or territorial form the central authority creates regional or area agencies which have overall charge of all the activities of the area. The officer in charge of the area is its head and the heads of all other specialised units at that level are his subordinates. All communications from the field station to the head office and back are routed through him, and he has responsibility for the acts of all other departmental heads. The position is very different in a multiple or functional form of organisation where the different divisions or branches of the head-quarters office have their corresponding field establishments at different area levels and maintain direct contact with them. There is no coordinating or integrating authority at the area level; each service or agency is treated as an independent entity unrelated to other services or agencies and the line of authority runs direct from it to its headquarters office. A good example of the territorial unitary type of field organisation is the Prefect in France. He is not only the head of the department (the largest unit of local administration), but also acts as the agent of the Central Government. He exercises general control and supervision over a number of public services in his department, e.g., education, public health, poor-relief, hospitals, and the preservation of order. The powers and functions of the Prefect have been lucidity expressed the Barthelemy as follows:

"This political agent, appointed and dismissed for political reasons, dependent upon the ministerial department most vitally concerned with questions of policy, represents not only the Ministry of the Interior, but all other ministries as well. Within the limits of his department, he personifies administrative authority, and possesses the power of deciding matters and appointing executives. The Prefect does not confine himself to directing, surveying and managing penitentiary and charitable institutions, which are under the Ministry of the Interior, . . . . he does not confine himself to acting the part of political watchdog upon officials of all kinds, magistrates, schoolmasters, officers, and drawing up a more or less secret and exact report on everyone of them, nor even to keeping an eye on the general police and the maintenance of public order. In addition, he takes decisions upon numerous technical matters and appoints a large number of technical agents."

The Indian counterpart of the Prefect is the Collector or the Deputy Commissioner in India, who, till 1947, was in a way the real executive chief and administrator of the tract of country committed to his charge, namely, the District. His relationship with other specialised agencies at the district level was described by the Montagu-Chelmsford Report of 1918, as: "Several other specialised services exist with staffs of their own. . . . but in varying degrees the District Officer influences the policy in all these matters, and he is always their in the background to lend his support, or, if need be, to mediate between a specialzied service and the people." The position of the Collector, however, has changed since, and today the District functions as a subcapital where the district offices of the various technical departments are located. The heads of these departments are technical persons who are directly responsible to their departmental chiefs at the state headquarters, and who are independent of the Collector's authority. There has come about a similar diminution in the authority of the French Prefect as there is apparent a growing tendency for the French Minister at Paris to handle economic and social problems in the various departments through their field officials.

The mechanism of the central control over field-offices has been graphically portrayed by Luther Gulick, who discerns three patterns of the organisation, namely—(i) "All Fingers"; "Short Arms, Long Fingers"; and (iii) "Long Arms, Short Fingers". In the "All Fingers" pattern, there are no geographical subdivisions and the field agencies are controlled by the headquarters office directly. In the "Short Arms, Long Fingers" pattern there are found centralised subdivisions, that is to say, these divisions are located in the central office itself, each with an extensive staff, and they communicate with and control field offices in their respective areas. Thus, the Ministry of External Affairs has a number of geographical sections, like Africa—I Section, Africa—II Section, America Section, Burma-Ceylon Section, South-East Asia Section, Indo-China Section, Pakistan—I Section, Pakistan—II Section, etc. These sections are located within the Ministry itself and not in the areas with which they deal. Under the "Long Arms, Short Fingers" pattern geographical subdivisions are decentralised. In other words, regional sub-offices are established in the field, far removed from the headquarters. A good example of this pattern is the district office in our country.

The headquarters office of any organisation is subdivided into specialised units, each of which is concerned with a particular programme of a segment of the total operation. Thus, the railway management in India, has a number of functional departments, like, Civil Engineering, Mechanical Engineering, Electrical Engineering, Operating, Commercial, Signal and Tele-communication, Accounts, Personnel, Stores, Medical and Security. All these departments necessarily have an impact on the efficient working of the railways. Each one of these departments has a field office at the zonal and divisional levels. Side by side with these functional offices the railways have introduced area officers, namely, the General Manager, who is in overall charge of the Zone, and the Divisional Superintendent who is in overall charge of the Division. The relationships between the functional officials at different levels and the area administrators at these levels as well as their relationships *inter se* at the same level constitute the crux of the headquarters-field relationships. An examination of the railway administration at the ministerial, zonal and divisional levels will throw some light on this complex and difficult situation.

The Ministry of Railways at the secretariat level is organised as a Railway Board which is functional in character. The Railway Board consists of five members—the Chairman, who at present happens to be in charge of staff, the Financial Commissioner, in charge of Finance, and three other members, each in charge of Civil (including Electrical) Engineering, Mechanical Engineering and Transport respectively. The Chairman is responsible for intra-Board coordination and is the administrative head of the organisation. He has the status of a Principal Secretary to the Government and has authority to overrule the other members except the Financial Commissioner. The Board Members deal with all aspects of technical subjects of which they are in charge. These Members are assisted in their work by five Additional Members respectively in charge of Works, Mechanical, Transport, Staff and Fiancee. In order to give relief to the Members of the Board from the enormous amount of work involved in controlling Railways and to enable them to give some time for touring and studying the wider problems of Railway policy, the Board is assisted by a number of technical officers, designated as Directors, each placed incharge of a Directorate. There are 16 such Directorates, namely—Civil Engineering, Establishment, Efficiency Bureau, Finance, Health, Mechanical Engineering, Railway Planning, Railway Stores, Railway Co-ordination. Security, Signals and Telecommunications, Traffic, Transport, Statistics and Economics, Wagon Production and Vigilance.

The level next below the Board in the field is the Zone, like the Central Zone, Northern Zone, Western Zone, etc., at the head of which is the General Manager. He is a top level official in the railway hierarchy and is in overall charge of the zonal railway system, and is the Chief Executive at that level. He is assisted by a number of official heads of various departments or branches, viz., Chief Engineer, Chief Operating Superintendent, Chief Commercial Superintendent, Chief Personnel Officer, Chief Signals and Telecommunications Engineer, Chief Electrical Engineer, Chief Mechanical Engineer, Chief Medical Officer, Chief Security Officer, and Chief Accounts Officer. All these technical officers are subordinate to the General Manager and are directly responsible to him for their work. The General Manager writes their 'confidential report'. He is responsible for bringing about coordination at the zonal level between all departments. All communications from to New Delhi to any departmental officer are routed through the General Manager except in purely technical and routine matters where the departmental officers are free to correspond directly with the technical officers, that is, Directors at the New Delhi headquarters.

Zones are divided into Divisions which are in overall charge of the Divisional Superintendent. He is a prototype of the General Manager in the Division and is assisted by as many technical officers whoa relationship "Deputies" to the "Chief" at the zonal level.

The above organisation may be presented in the form of a chart given ahead. (p. 155).

### *Communication and Control*

One of the real areas of difficulty in headquarters-field relationship is the establishment of a system of good communications between various levels. In our opinion, the chief reason for non-implementation or partial implementation of policies and programmes in our country is the absence on the part of field officials of a proper understanding of the purposes and objectives of programmes. These officials are seldom taken into confidence in determining policies and preparation of programmes; nor do they have any appreciation of the overall plan or objective. They are not even sure of the methods and techniques they use for executing these programmes. The only channels of communication open to them are 'noting on files' and Manuals. Communication is usually one way, i.e., from the top to the bottom in the form of orders, directives, notifications, circulars and memoranda. Above all, there are the 'sacred' Manuals laying down in categorical terms the role of officials, at various levels. Feedback from below to upwards is not encouraged, if not frowned upon. As regards Manuals, the complaint of the field officials is that the procedures and rules prescribed therein do not always fit the situation and often do not take into account operating realities. Dimock and Dimock call this phenomenon "Manualties" which is defined as "an occupational disease, generally found in Government. . . . that causes people to assume that everything in administration can be reduced to rule and embalmed in a procedure manual for the guidance of all employees in the organisation."

Another aspect of this relationship is the exercise of control by the headquarters over field agencies. There are a number of commonly accepted techniques and devices by which administration at one particular level of an organisation may control the performance of subordinate field agencies. Such techniques may be in the nature of control before action is taken, for example, prior approval of individual projects before initiation by an operating unit; the promulgation of service standards; budgetary limitation upon the magnitude of operations; approval of key subordinate personnel. Field agencies in the States find themselves particularly handicapped by the imposition of detailed financial control by the

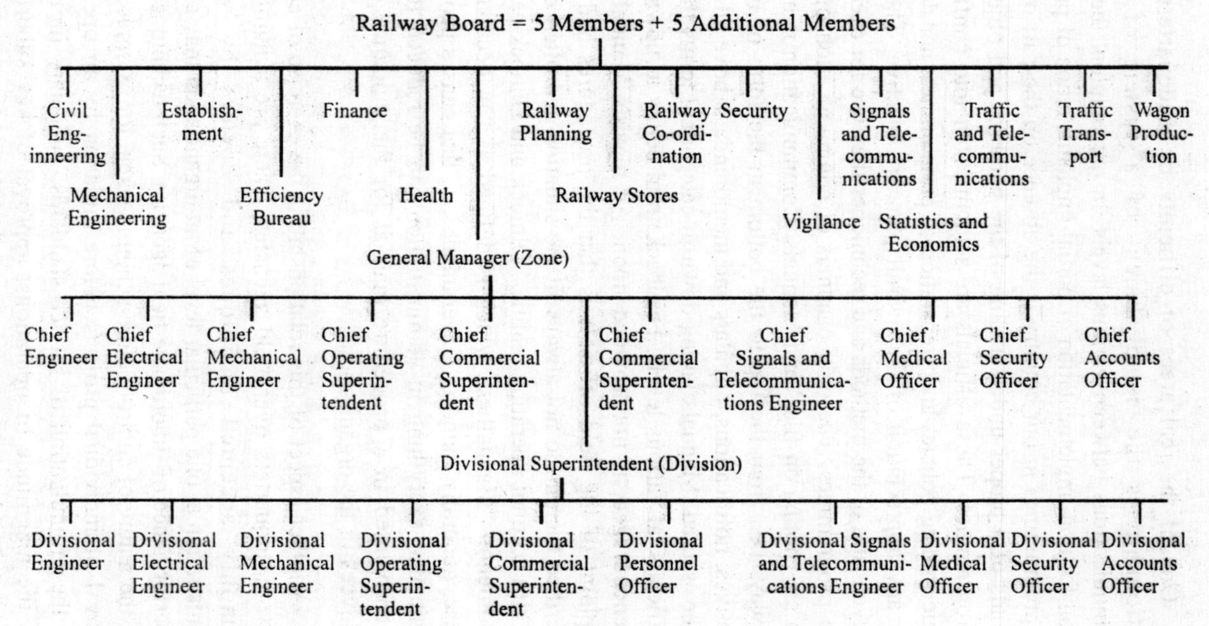
Railway Board = 5 Members + 5 Additional Members
Civil Eng-inneering
Mechanical Engineering
Establish-ment
Efficiency Bureau
Finance
Health
Railway Planning
Railway Stores
Railway Co-ordi-nation
Security
Vigilance
Signals and Tele-commu-nications
Statistics and Economics
Traffic and Tele-commu-nications
Traffic Trans-port
Wagon Produc-tion
General Manager (Zone)
Chief Engineer
Chief Electrical Engineer
Chief Mechanical Engineer
Chief Operating Superin-tendent
Chief Commercial Superinten-dent
Chief Commercial Superinten-dent
Chief Signals and Telecommunica-tions Engineer
Chief Medical Officer
Chief Security Officer
Chief Accounts Officer
Divisional Superintendent (Division)
Divisional Engineer
Divisional Electrical Engineer
Divisional Mechanical Engineer
Divisional Operating Superin-tendent
Divisional Commercial Superinten-dent
Divisional Personnel Officer
Divisional Signals and Telecommuni-cations Engineer
Divisional Medical Officer
Divisional Security Officer
Divisional Accounts Officer

Finance Department as also by the insistence on prior approval of the departmental headquarters office before any programme can be executed.

Control after action takes the form of reporting, audit, inspection and investigation. One of the traditional methods of exercising control over subordinate offices is for the headquarters to insist on receiving information from the field agencies in the form of returns, reports and statistics relating to the progress of field operations. The trouble with this method is that the returns and reports tend to multiply, thus entailing untold burden on the offices concerned. Audit may be defined as an independent examination of every financial transaction. The main purpose of audit is to prevent embezzlement, fraud, carelessness, errors, unauthorised expenditure, expenditure of excess allotment, and non-compliance with rules and laws. Two things to be noted about audit are: first, audit is a *post facto* function and is in the nature of a post-mortem scrutiny; and second, it has the limited function of examining compliance with rules and regulations in financial transactions. Inspection, literally speaking, means looking carefully at or over; viewing closely and critically. Inspection is designed primarily to ensure that the existing rules, regulations, procedures and practices are observed. It ensures compliance with instructions. In this respect, it resembles the audit function. What audit is to financial transactions, inspection is to administrative transactions. Such as limited view of inspection, however, is out of date in the present context of administration. Inspection, to be useful and effective, must develop a positive and affirmative character, and its scope should be widened to include some sort of audit of performance. It is not enough in a planned economy like ours, which calls for action-mindedness, that rules laid down in the Manuals are complied with the inspection authority must also evaluate the performance of the inspected agency as to whether it has fulfilled the purposes for which it had been set. Again inspections have to develop an O and M angle, that is to say, they should not stop at criticising the lapses but go further and suggest improvement organisation systems, methods and procedures with a view to increasing efficiency. Lastly, inspection is not a mere fault-finding process, and one of its essential elements should be instructing and guiding the person working in the inspected agency, and actually demonstrating on the spot as to how defects have to be rectified and discrepancies reconciled. In an ideal system of inspection, the inspectors have to regard themselves as a part of the administrative process and assume responsibility for the successful working of the office or project in the same sense as other officials engaged in the work. The effectiveness of an inspection system should be judged in the light of the above ingredients. Investigation is an inquiry into some alleged or suspected malpractice or abuse of authority. Its main purpose is to discover the guilty person and to prosecute him. Investigation is often personal and particular in character, and is usually on an *ad hoc* basis.

**Successful Administration of Field Offices**

"It has been said that there is both a headquarters and a field-way of life, the groups often viewing each other with smugness and suspicion. Field-workers insist that headquarters does not understand their problems.... Headquarters is characterised by an intellectual or research approach to problems in contrast to the field's practical approach." This statement has universal application. A general feeling is that a posting at the headquarters means a comfortable life, more amenities, special pay allowance, higher status, better 'contacts' and more powers. This feeling is obviously detrimental to the efficient administration of field offices.

Among the essential prerequisites to successful administration of field offices, the following may be enumerated:

1. Efforts should be made to create at the headquarters as well as in the field a full appreciation of the particular field situation so that they get induced to arrive at a decision appropriate to the situation. Orders should be, in the words of Mary Parker Follett, 'the composite decision of those who give and those who receive them' and this will maximize the chance of their acceptance Follett calls this process as the 'law of the situation'.

2. Field offices must be staffed by trained and competent personnel in adequate number, who can take sound decisions on matters falling within the sphere of their responsibility.

3. The responsibility of the fieldofficer must be clearly defined, and their limitations, too, should be made clear to them.

4. There should be free, frank and frequent communication between field-officers of different departments in the same area on related problems.

5. The powers given to field-officers must relieve the headquarters of unnecessary work. Because powers have been handed down, it does not follow that they will be used.

6. Special facilities including financial incentives should be provided in 'hardship' areas to attract competent staff.

7. Periodic transfers from field to headquarters and *vice versa* and between fields are useful in inculcating a balanced outlook on local requirements and national policies. The existing 'tenure system' needs to be strengthened.

8. Formal inspections, submissions of periodic returns and reports should be supplemented by informal visits by headquarters officers. These help build up rapport between the headquarters and field.

9. Training courses and conferences between field-officers and headquarters officers make them more competent, and keep them aware of each other's problems. This also result in the building-up of community of interests.

10. Field and headquarters officers must possess adequate knowledge of local needs and opinions, and, within the

framework following the governmental policy and procedures, strive to meet these.

11. Before a person is posted in the field he should be given briefing by the headquarters on his own assignment and the problems and issues involved in it. This helps him in understanding his new job quickly and more completely. Likewise, there should be de-briefing when he completes his field-assignment. De-briefing may take the form of a few terminal interviews with the headquarters personnel wherein he communicates the operational problems and difficulties he encountered in his work. This would provide the much needed feed-back to the headquarters.

# 10

# Guiding Principles on Civil Service Reform*

The paper is divided into six sections. The second section briefly outlines the purpose of the principles. The third three provide an overview of the general issues that need to be addressed or taken into account by donors when designing individual aid projects in support of CSR. The fourth section provides an overview of CSR design issues and the fifth covers implementation and monitoring issues. The last section identifies key issues for aid management.

## Background and Introduction

Civil Service Reform (CSR) programmes are increasingly being adopted in a range of African countries and in many cases they are closely linked to structural adjustment efforts. The results have been mixed and the effectiveness of the aid provided in support of these programmes has sometimes been limited. It is important to review CSR experience and to draw lessons that will enable Special Programme of Assistance to Africa (SPA) donors to improve the impact of their aid in this area and to inform the policy dialogue with recipient governments. CSR is also considered necessary to complement donor programmes at the sector level.

---

*Prepared by the Working Group on Civil Service Reform of the Special Programme of Assistance for Africa (SPA). The Guiding Principles were adopted by the SPA at its meeting in Paris in November 1995. Extracted from Ladipo Adamolekum, Guy development Luisgnam and Armand Atomate (Eds.), *Civil service* Reform in *Francophone Afria: Proceedings of a Workshop,* Abidjan, January 23-26, 1996 Washington DC, World Bank, 1997, pp. 49-56.

The following principles have been developed by the Working Group by drawing on a wide range of published material, the experiences of the donors in question and six case studies of major CSR programmes. In Uganda, Tanzania, Ghana, the Central African Republic, Benin and Burkina Faso, the case studies were specially commissioned by the Working Group to provide a more in-depth assessment of current CSR programmes from a cross-section of African countries.

## The Purpose of the Guiding Principles

The principles outlined in this paper are intended to provide general principles of guidance and pointers to donors wishing to assess the viability CSR programmes developed by African governments. As such, they provide guidance on the overall requirements for effective CSR and on the critical issues that need to be considered in appraising CSR programmes for possible donor support. This will help to promote a more consistent approach to the policy dialogue and donor support in this area.

The second aim is to provide guidance to assist aid donors contemplating involvement in CSR to design more effective aid interventions in line with current best practice. The third objective is to identify areas of weakness in existing CSR programmes and to purpose corrective action that can be taken by donors and recipients.

## Overall Approach

### *Purpose and Scope of CSR*

The purpose of CSR is to improve the effectiveness and performance of the civil service. The ultimate goal is to raise the quality of services delivered to the population, support economic and social development and to enhance the capacity to carry out core government functions.

CSR programmes therefore need to improve both core functions (e.g. revenue generation, financial management, personnel management, policy formulation, etc.) as well as sector-specific policy, management and organisation. Both aspects need to be covered in a coordinated manner.

In many African countries, the effectiveness of the civil service is constrained by poor governance, structural factors such as excessive staff and inadequate incentives as well as by a lack of administrative capacity. If performance is to improve, all these aspects need to be simultaneously addressed in a comprehensive reform programme.

### *Economic Reform and Adjustment*

Adjustment programme often emphasise the need to redefine the role government and to concentrate public sector activities on functions such as economic policy making, revenue collection, infrastructure provision and the delivery of social services. In such cases, CSR should be designed to assist recipient governments to review the role and function of the civil service and to identify how services can be provided most efficiently and effectively. This may result in changes to the balance between public and private sector provision including corporatisation and privatisation.

In some countries, CSR can contribute directly to macroeconomic stabilisation through supporting downsizing programmes which reduce the size and cost of the civil service to an affordable and sustainable level. This can assist governments in restoring budgetary stability. In such cases, downsising could be key component of CSR and a high priority for donor support along with other measures such as strengthening revenue collection. Support for capacity building should also be given a high priority for donor support in the early stages of CSR.

In developing CSR programmes and aid projects, recipients and donors need to ensure there is consistency with overall public expenditure plans, especially the target ceilings for the recurrent budget and the composition of expenditure. There will also affect the pace of some reforms and their longer-term financial sustainability. Planned improvements in civil service terms and conditions are particularly dependent on the availability of recurrent finance.

### *Leadership and Commitment*

High-level political commitment and support is an essential prerequisite for successful CSR but is not sufficient in itself.

Ownership of reform programmes needs to be more broadly based in dialogue with recipients donors should underline the need for policy statements on CSR to be endorsed ast the highest level of government as a foundation for the development of detailed programmes. Windows of opportunity such as change of governments should be used to initiate such dialogue and to build commitment.

The development of political commitment takes time and donors need to participate actively in the process through policy dialogue and acting as advocates of reform. Although the process of developing a reform policy and strategy must be led by domestic stakeholders, donors can sometimes facilitate debate and help to build involve consultation and communication and representatives from civil society.

Developing and sustaining political commitment often requires careful attention by recipient and donors to the timing of commencement and implementation of CSR projects and to the clear communication of reform objectives.

Donors should avoid taking the lead in diagnosing problems and devising reform strategies. This is likely to undermine ownership and commitment. Recipients need to develop their own reform strategies and to devise CSR programmes which they own and are prepared to implement. Where recipients lack technical capacity, donors should provide technical assistance to facilitate this process.

*Taking Account of Governance*

Good governance including accountability, transparency and the rule of law is conducive to effective CSR. This requires commitment to a more professional civil service with a greater emphasis on performance.

In developing CSR programmes, donor need to review the position in the country concerned and if appropriate, develop specific governance projects which complement efforts to reform the civil service. There is likely to be a need for this where there is a high degree of patrimonialism and endemic corruption.

Donor support for governance projects will typically go beyond the confines of the executive branch of government to include activities such as support for development of legislation governing the civil service, legal sector reform (including the relevant sections to the judiciary) and anti-corruption measures. CSR can itself promote improved governance and donors should aim to support activities which can help achieve this such as improving ethical standards or enhancing accountability.

## Programme Design

### *Diagnosis and Preparation*

Prior to the detailed design of CSR programmes, there is a need for an open and objective analysis of the constraints faced and a stocktaking of the current situation. It is important that this draws on the knowledge and experience of local decision-makers and officials in a participative way to diagnose the problems faced. It may also require donor funded consultancy studies on particular issues or aspects of the civil service.

Close attention needs to be paid to the process involved in carrying out such a diagnostic. Donors should seek to support a structured and participative approach involving all stakeholders in an attempt to reach a consensus on the problems and the required corrective action. Following this, it should be possible to develop a strategy and reform action plan to which local stakeholders are committed.

### *Vision and Strategy*

Donors should encourage recipients to develop a clearly articulated view about the scope and nature of the civil service they are trying to develop. Overall programme objectives should be driven by the intended outcomes. This vision should be noted in the expectations of the public. It will provide a framework for objective setting and minimise the risk of programmes (or individual components) being seen as ends in themselves which can sometimes lead to a build-up of resistance to reform.

Donors should aim to provide support for CSR in a programmatic framework. This requires a comprehensive reform strategy which addresses all the main constraints in an integrated way and sets specific objectives with targets/benchmarks against which progress can be judged. These should be linked to desired final outcomes such as improved services delivery or the size, structure and cost of the civil services.

*Sequencing and Timeframe*

Donors need to assess whether the proposed content, sequencing and pace of any CSR programme for which aid is requested is realistic. In part this depends on the specific situation and initial conditions of the recipient country. In practice, the precise sequencing adopted is often influenced by the availability of finance, the ease of carrying out a programme component and the degree of support for it amongst stakeholders.

The implementation phase of many African CSR programmes has typically included most of the following components: rationalisation and restructuring of ministries and departments; reducing the size of the civil service through downsising and rightsising; improving pay levels and incentives. Donors should encourage recipients to identify the linkages between these programme components and to implement them in a sequence which takes into account any interdependenceies.

In general, downsising and rightsising programmes should take place after Ministerial reviews because these will identify redundant posts and personnel to be retrenched. However, in some cases where there is a "ghost worker" problem and gross overstaffing, it may take place before this. Downsising programmes generally need to be preceded by efforts to establish a robust personnel information and establishment control system to prevent re-employment of retrenched personnel. Where pay reform is to be wholly or partially financed by downsising, this will have to await the implementation of the latter.

*Process Approach*

Donor assistance for CSR needs to give higher priority to process issues. More participative methods should be used to develop and design CSR programme components and aid projects.

Greater use should be made of stakeholder analysis and other participatory techniques such as workshops and team-based project preparation methodologies. Donors should also consider providing advisers and consultants with change management expertise and who adopt a more facilitative and supportive approach.

All the CSR components need to be developed in a participative way. However, the implementation of some components will require a more directive approach (setting global targets) led by higher-level authorities. Other (e.g. ministerial restructuring) will be implemented through further consultation.

Process approaches also require donors to adopt a flexible approach to project design so that programmes can be adopted and changed in response to evolving circumstances.

***Strengthening of Core Functions***

In developing CSR projects donors should aim to strengthen the core functions of government, thereby improving resource mobilisation and allocation, policy-making capacity and the effectiveness and independence of the judiciary. This can involve action by the recipient and specific donor support to increase the autonomy and accountability of revenue collection institutions; strengthen financial planning and budgeting systems; and strengthen policy-making through training and technical assistance.

Strengthening of core functions needs to take place across the civil service and take into account sector-specific management needs. The Public Expenditure Working.

***Ministerial Restructuring and Decentralisation***

Functional reviews and restructuring of ministries are crucial to improving the effectiveness of service delivery. Donors should encourage recipients to use process to help define sector objectives and to consider the appropriate division of responsibilities between government and NGO or private sector service providers.

The scope of ministerial reviews should be wide ranging and include an assessment of structures, establishment and staffing levels, and management systems. This must respect specific organisational and cultural factors. Management systems need to be introduced to encourage a strong focus on objective setting and to improve resource management. These will need to be consistent with civil service-wide systems managed by central ministries.

Where decentralisation is envisaged or underway, donors should emphasise the need for the ministerial reviews to be coordinated or integrated with these programmes. Once an agreed division of responsibilities between the central and local government exists, this can form the basis for ministerial restructuring.

*Downsizing*

Some donors are increasingly willing to provide aid financing for downsising and rightsising programmes, and it is important for them to ensure that recipients have well-designed and cost-effective programmes. This will involve assessing the total cost of retrenchment options including both additional pension payments as well as the costs of the severance package and ensuring that these are in line with international experience.

It is also important to ensure that the present value of the cost savings that will accrue to government overtime from the retrenchment programme outweigh the present value of the initial cost of retrenchment and any additional pension payments to those retrenched. In general, such programmes, should have a quick payback period and generate net budget saving for the government budget within a few years.

Retrenchment programmes can be difficult to design and there are usually several options to be considered. Donors should be prepared to provide technical assistance for this purpose and to help redesign and strengthen personnel management and control systems to prevent reemployment.

Particular attention needs to be given to the social consequences of retrenchment. Criteria for selection need to be open and transparent to prevent any discrimination on ethnic or gender grounds. Tracer studies of retrenched staff are also required to identify any adverse social consequences, to ensure the adequacy of severance packages and to consider the need for other measures.

### *Pay and Incentives*

Inadequate terms and conditions for civil servants remain a major impediment to improving performance in the civil service. Successful CSR requires a commitment by recipients to move basic pay towards a Minimum Living Wage (MLW) over time and to reform pay and benefits structures by restoring differentials, introducing performance-related aspects and monetising all benefits in kind. The performance-related element should be introduced as quickly as possible and should focus on measures such as attendance, achievement of agreed objectives.

Donors should encourage recipients to adopt pay reform as a key component of CSR and provide technical assistance to support the design and implementation of the programme. Support for comparative surveys of pay and benefits in the private sector and the design of performance pay and now pay scales is often needed Donors should also consider providing selective support to improve civil service offices and equipment.

### *Capacity Building*

Donors should assist recipients to design and implement in-country training programmes that would help to develop skills and build capacity in areas related to CSR. Such training should cover both technical as well as process aspects.

## Implementation, Monitoring and Evaluation

### *Management of Reform*

Donors should assist recipients to establish adequate capacity to manage and implement CSR. Recipients need to establish a CSR management with sufficient status and authority and for this to be overseen at the political level. This set-up requires adequate management technical capacity to cope with CSR and the design of the programme should be matched to the level of capacity available.

Donors should be prepared to assist the CSR management team by financing technical assistance which is capable of providing technical advice and support in a facilitative and supportive way whilst retaining local ownership. Such support can also build local capacity through developing staff motivation and skills, suitable administrative participative working methods. Specialised training for change management could be offered in support of this.

Reform of service delivery also requires the leadership and active participation of officials from ministries. This is likely to require the creation of ministerial teams and the development of capacity through team-building workshops and training.

The coordination and management of donor activities is an essential requirement for successful implementation of CSR. Donors should encourage recipients to lead the process and donor-funded experts or advisers should support the CSR management team to develop suitable coordination mechanisms. Joint donor and government project reviews should be held on a regular basis and the CRS management team should also develop a format progress reports and supply these routinely to donors.

***Baseline Surveys and Service Delivery Surveys***

Donors should provide support for recipients to assess the impact of CSR, including the provision of technical assistance to help build local capacity in this area. There is a need for a baseline study to be developed at the design phase of the project and for regular surveys to be repeated thereafter. This should focus on service delivery standards and the level of involvement, utilisation and access to public services by the poor and women. The initial survey should be used both to improve the design of CSR of well as to monitor the impact on service delivery. Repeat surveys should then be able to identify the need to take early corrective action to mitigate any adverse consequences.

Recipients and donors need to review the progress of the main programme components against qualitative and quantitative indicators and targets established for the CSR programmes. Monitoring systems and progress reporting should be designed to cover this aspect. Occasionally, specific studies of reviews of individual programme components are also likely to be required.

Tracer studies of personnel retrenched from the civil service would fall into this category. Donors should be pepared to assist with those studies if requried.

***Conditionality***

Carefully designed and selective conditionality is an important mechanism for stimulating initial action by recipients and as a means of allowing donors some influence over the pace and direction of reform. However, the conditions need to be realistic, developed jointly and negotiated with the recipient so that they are perceived as a government commitment to an agreed programme rather than being externally imposed. Conditions on CSR in Structural Adjustment Programmes can be an important catalyst for the development of programmes by recipients.

***Policy Dialogue***

Donors should pursue the policy dialogue on CSR in a coordinated fashion using the Consultative Group and Round Table process. This requires close consultation at the working level between bilateral donors and the multilateral agencies.

***Aid Mechanisms***

Where possible, donors should consider the provision of financial aid as well as technical assistance. Some donors may be able to consider providing recurrent financial support to the recipient budget over a limited time period and on a tapering basis. This mechanism could be used to support the introduction of pay reforms.

Donors should be prepared to consider a variety of options for the provision of technical assistance often over an extended period. The flexibility to recruit national consultants and experts can be particularly useful where local knowledge and contacts are required. While use of short-term periodic technical assistance should in general be encouraged, in certain circumstances the use of long-term advisers may be appropriate.

The quality of the technical assistance provided is crucial to the success of CSR. The terms of reference for consultants and experts should emphasize the importance of working in a facilitator and supportive manner with national personnel and the need for early skills transfer and capacity building. Donors should aim to provide consultants and experts with process and change management skills as well as expertise in the design and delivery of specific programme components.

***Local Compensation for CSR Management Team***

The successful delivery of CSR programmes often requires that monetary incentives be offered to personnel in the CSR implementation organisation. Donors need to ensure that such arrangements are open and transparent and consistent with any government regulations covering local salary supplementation and secondment of civil servants. Where civil servants are involved, they should either be employed by government on short-term performance related contracts or be seconded from the civil service for the period of the project.

Where the management team includes national consultants, they should be recruited in an open and competitive manner and their fees should reflect local market rates for their skills.

There is a need to manage the tension between the CSR team receiving incentives and other personnel who are responsible for implementing reform and are not included. Expectations need to be actively managed to prevent dissatisfaction and demotivation.

# Civil Service Reform in Developing Countries

In my presentation today I will look briefly at the types of problems faced by civil administrations in developing countries and then outline the elements of a reform programme.

I would like to welcome you to the World Bank's Conference on Civil Service Reform in Latin America and the Caribbean. At the Bank, we are beginning to realise that without effective government administration, structural adjustment programmes and other economic reform initiatives are seriously handicapped. I chose to link economic and administrative reforms not because I work in an institution concerned with economic development, but because I believe that development is not indivisible whole. A country's income is not likely to increase, for example, while poor institutional conditions continue to exist. Even if that were to happen, it would not represent real development but transient wealth without sustainable roots.

## Problems Faced by Developing Country Civil Services

You all know the most serious symptoms of administrative dysfunction: surplus employment, cost overruns, and poor performance. Some of these are the result of external factors, some of internal factors, but most are the result of a combination of both.

I am referring to three principal external factors. First increasing number of young people joining the labour force. Second is the poor economic growth rate, which means that the formal labour market cannot provide these young people with jobs. And third is the political expectation of many people that the state will always act as an employer of last resort. Together, these three factors have led to surplus employment in the civil service. It is important to note that they cannot be resolved rapidly, yet any reform programme that does not take these external factors into account is doomed to be overtaken by these same factors in the future.

Among the internal factors, most come under the heading of personnel management. For instance, many countries have adopted inappropriate policies for recruitment, such as the automatic hiring of graduates. Career development policies often are rather elementary and link promotion prospects to seniority rather than to performance criteria. Rigid policies on wages and compensation have constituted a fiscal drain on the state because governments have been unable to adjust wages. Perhaps as damaging has been the secondary result-contribution to the failure of the civil service to attract and retain the most qualified and committed people for the job. Less easy to discern and define among the internal problems is the general philosophy of the civil service, in other words, the image the institution has of itself. Public administration in many developing countries have failed to develop a professional ethic of political neutrality and a service minded approach to their relations with the public. It is these internal factors that have contributed most to the low quality and inefficient performance of public administrations.

## An Approach to Civil Service Reform

The principal elements of a comprehensive process of reform are, first, the elaboration of a clear vision of the role of the civil service and, based on this optimal role, the development of a comprehensive reform plan; second, the rationalisation of rules and regulations for the civil service; third, the design of modern management systems; and fourth, the implementation of the programme.

First, we need to define a comprehensive strategy. This begins with a rethinking of the role of the state generally.

Development theory at present firmly supports removing the state from the day-to-day running of the economy and allowing market forces to take over many of the old responsibilities of the state. Although this is a rather vague notion, it can be refined. For the civil service, it means retrenching the state from the provision of certain services, now best left to the private sector, and it means streamlining the ministries and regulatory agencies, particularly those responsible for the oversight of the economy. (For the state enterprise sector, it means less active participation of the state in the economy by limiting state enterprises to the provision of utilities and certain sectors of national interest.) Once the role of the leaner state has been defined, the mechanics of the new government need to be worked out, along with a plan to achieve this goal. This is what I mean by a comprehensive reform framework: a plan that outlines the specific reform measures needed, illustrates the linkages between them, and explicitly relates the relevance of short-term measures to long-term goals.

It is important that the reform effort have the full commitment of the political leadership. Bank experience has shown that effective implementation depends initially on the active participation of the most senior members of government. It is also important for the civil service management and rank and file to be involved in the process, to establish domestic ownership of the programme.

The second step is a legislative effort, it involves rationalisation of existing policies and rules and implementation of new legislation, to the extent necessary for the introduction of the reform programme. For instance, the administrative laws that regulate the internal workings of the civil service, such as personnel regulations, might need to be amended to allow for the downsising effort and to install flexible personnel management practices that are geared toward the recruitment of high-quality employees and that will, in terms of compensation and promotion, reward efficient performance. The other set of rules and policies that will need to be overhauled are those the civil service is charged with implementing. These range from foreign investment laws to the issue of building permits.

The third element of a reform process is the design of systems and programmes these systems have been based on private sector management approaches and have benefited from the flexibility gained and from the more up-to-date systems in use.

These include:

- A *modern data collection system*, which ensures accuracy and includes rules governing the confidentiality of information.
- A *financial system for budgeting and expenditure,* which includes budget planning and preparation, the control of expenditures, and a tender and contracting system.
- An *accounting and auditing system*, which ensures sound financial auditing.
- Modern *central personnel management systems*. These would include a *strategic planning system* at the ministry or agency level to forecast future staffing requirements over a period of, say, five years—and the consequent job reclassifications and specification of inputs—and to avoid a build-up of surplus staff, and a *personnel recruitment and management system* to recruit and promote qualified staff, particularly to high-level positions. This system may differ as to the degree of centralisation of the personnel function. It appears that systems with some degree of centralisation are more appropriate for developing countries generally. Another system would be a *human resources management system*, which ensures that the required skills will be made available and will be developed continuously through training programmes designed to broaden experience and improve efficient performance, and through relocation programmes. Finally, a *control and oversight system* would monitor staff performance and provide rewards and sanctions based on the efficiency of performance.

The main objective of these management systems is to ensure sustained and efficient staff performance and the achievement of the civil service's goals, as defined in the general strategy.

The fourth and final element of comprehensive reform is the implementation of the reform plan. This should begin with a determination of the numbers of employees and kinds of skills needed in each ministry and agency. This should then be followed by a survey of the work force (age, grade, position, and the like), including a determination of the skills available. The next step is to implement the elements of the reform programme, including installation of the modern management systems that, by now, have been modified to fit local needs and are ready for use. Such reform measures would have three objectives: to halt the increase in the size of the work force, to reduce its financial burden on the state, and to revamp the work force so that available skills and staffing levels meet the service's needs, all within the scheme of a new service-oriented, professional, developmental bureaucracy.

I can suggest a number of measures to control the size of the work force. These include a freeze on new hiring and salary increases, the elimination of automatic hiring programmes (for example, of graduates), the enforcement of retirement age, and the elimination of ghost workers. Voluntary exit programmes may be introduced at this stage. These need to be carefully designed to minimise the danger of adverse selection, that is, the most efficient workers leading first because the most readily find alternative employment in the private sector. One way to avoid this would be for the employer to retain a veto right. Another design issue for voluntary exit is the size of the compensation to be paid to existing workers. Of course, the principal aim is to minimise the fiscal burden on the state. As a final measure, involuntary retrenchment measures might be implemented. In view of the enormous human and political costs frequently associated with these programmes, great care must be taken in their design.

The second goal of a reform programme is cost-cutting, that is, the reduction of the financial burden on the state. This will be partly achieved by the decrease in the size of the work force. It can be further effected by introducing the modern personnel management and auditing systems prepared in an earlier phase of the reform process. For instance, the restructuring of existing wage and compensation policies might help both to reduce the wage bill and to improve the performance of the work force.

The third and final goal is the most important, and the most difficult to achieve. It is the elusive goal of changing sometimes monolithic institutions into lean and responsive administrations committed to developmental and social goals. In some countries this will require a radical transformation in the values and traditions of the institution, in others merely a revival of dormant professional ethics. Specific measures that can help are personnel management systems modelled on those prevalent in the private sector, which encourage efficient performance and reward accordingly. Other measures aimed at raising the prestige of the institution might also help attract better qualified candidates for management positions. Performance-based criteria should be introduced not only into wage and compensation determination, but also into promotion and career development. In some environments, it might be more appropriate that these criteria be group-determined rather than individually based.

*—Ibrahim F.I. Shihata*

# Managing the Civil Service—Reform Lessons from Advanced Industrialised Countries*

## Conclusions

This paper has reviewed established practice and emerging innovations in civil service management in advance industrialised countries in order to glean lessons for developing and transitional countries. In some instances, discussion about alternative approaches revealed ongoing debates, leaving uncertain the optimal reform strategy. The position assumed here, though, is that even with imperfect information reforming countries must choose some reform path to improve the management of their civil services. Rather than definitive conclusions, the guidance offered here constitutes at most hypotheses and at least "hunches" about what is likely to work under reforming country conditions. Focusing on three principal areas of CSM,—system organisation and management, quality of human inputs, and staff incentives and performance—the paper's main findings are summarised below:

- As a general reform principle, traditional, mainly centralised civil service management models provide the best starting point for many of the reforming country administrations. Agency approaches requiring

---

*Extracted from World Book Discussion Barbara Nunberg, *Managing the Civil Service:* Reform Lesson from Advanced Industrialised Countries, Wshington DC, World Bank, 1995, pp. 41-43.

technological and human resource skills beyond the present capacity of many reforming countries, may, however, provide models toward which some countries—especially the better endowed—can strive. Certain selected elements of agency reform might even now be successfully emulated by some reforming administrations. But any countries contemplating comprehensive agency-type reforms need to assess seriously the degree to which the requisite human and technical requirements can be met and to think strategically about the necessary steps to acquire them.

- Strong centralised institutions are usually be necessary to support fledgling civil service management functions in reforming countries. Shared power and good coordination among a limited number of organs at the centre ensures necessary checks and balances. To the degree that capacity can be developed in line entities, some de-concentration is desirable however, for responsive, flexible personnel management.
- Certain CSM functions should be given higher priority than others. This wisdom is even more powerful in reforming countries, where resources are scarce and starker choices about allocation need to be made. Two functions emerged as central: recruitment and establishment control.
- Establishment control provides the foundation for all other CSM functions. In reforming countries where this function has historically been poorly managed, centralised models are advisable. Advanced industrialised country experience with strategic, forward manpower planning could be enormously instructive to many reforming countries.
- Programmes to improve the rigour of recruitment standards should receive high priority in reforming countries. Despite serious pitfalls, some aspects of

"Mandarin" systems offer many advantages to reforming countries building a professionalised civil service. They compensate for other system failings. Governments should take measures to moderate the elitist characteristics of the mandarin approach and, as appropriate, judiciously introduce market flexibilities to recruit scarce skills.

- Senior Executive Services, or similar programmes to develop professional elite cadres, have proved difficult to design and implement in advanced industrialised countries, but many flaws can be corrected in adapting them to reforming country contexts where there is often an urgent need to group higher-level civil servants. Such services may complement recruitment rigour. These programmes must be carefully designed to include career mobility and training as well as remuneration features, and exclusion of political appointments is essential to their credibility.

- Assuming necessary minimal levels of establishment and budgetary control, unified pay and classification in reforming countries could arguably be relaxed, following the lead of increasing numbers of advanced countries. The common tendency toward circumvention of existing unified norms in many reforming civil services, along with the need to target scarce skills more directly with appropriate remuneration packages, reinforces this view.

- The benefits of performance *pay* remain to be demonstrated in industrialised country public sectors, and the management requirements and costs of installing such systems can be considerable. Resistance may subvert efforts to effect performance pay arrangements. Given these difficulties and the urgency of other CSM tasks for reforming country administrations, lower priority should be given to this reform at present. Performance-related *promotion* systems, on the other hand, even if imperfectly implemented, can help move civil service values toward standards of competence and merit.

**Suggestions for Further Work**

These conclusions represent best guesses for reforming country policy directions based on an initial, broad review of administrative experience in some advanced industrialised countries. The intention was not to carry out rigorous research but to begin to elevate the quality of Bank operational advice on civil service management by flagging topical issues in worldwide administrative reform. Naturally, this work has raised a series of questions that require systematic investigation in order to move beyond the realm of speculation. The following are a few suggestions for further inquiry.

- Rigorous comparisons of civil service performance across countries do not exist due to the absence of suitable methods for measuring civil service performance, the lack of comparable cross-national data on most questions, and the inherent difficulties in controlling for a range of intervening variables such as politics and culture. Research to develop a methodology for measuring civil service performance would be a valuable contribution in trying to determine which systems and approaches work best under which conditions. Initial comparative work might begin by developing performance measures for single, relatively simple function carried out by most central governments.

- Research on the relationship between pay and performance in the public sector is not well advanced, and often policies are adopted on shaky empirical bases. Further work on this issue, particularly in reforming country contexts, would be useful.

- The effect of private-public pay differentials on civil service management functions could not be determined in this project and would require significant data generation and collection. Comparative research might be worthwhile in this area.

- The relative effectiveness and efficiency of agency reform systems versus traditional civil services need to be studied rigorously before credible policy prescription can be extracted for reforming countries. Given the recent origin of many of the reforms, such research might be appropriately undertaken after a suitable period elapses.

- Given the urgent need in many developing and transitional countries to build governmental capacity, a more active form of applied research on civil service management topics might be an appropriate parallel approach to those suggested above. Pilot experiments could be carried out in reforming country administrative "laboratories" to examine the relative merits of, say, different recruitment, pay and classification, or performance appraisal systems on a comparative basis. While the actual "experiments" in one or another civil service management improvement in a particular country could be financed as a lending operation, the exercise could simultaneously be set up as comparative, cross-national research by undertaking baseline study.

# 13

# Structure of Organisation—Boards and Commissions

The Commission form of organisation has been extensively employed in the administration of public affairs, though, generally speaking, unitary control of administrative services is now increasingly favoured. The history of this form of organisation dates back to Middle Ages when many European Governments created boards and commissions for conducting public affairs. The commission form of local government in the U.S.A., is largely modelled on this basis. In international administration, the boards and commissions have been in vogue since the nineteenth century with a view to giving representation to all independent states. In Europe, the commission form has today fallen into disfavour. In the U.S.A., on the contrary, there has been a constant increase in the number and variety of boards. This increase is partly due to the looseness of the American administrative system, and partly to a desire to escape the pervasive influence of party politics in administration. In India, too, boards and commissions have been extensively made use of. The commissions in India may be classified into three broad categories from the point of view of their source of origin.

The Constitution of India mentions a few of such organisations; for example, the Election Commission, the Union Public Service Commission, etc. These organisations are, thus, backed by constitutional sanctity. Secondly, boards and commissions may be set up by Acts of Parliament. The University Grants Commission, the Railway Board, the Central Board of Revenue, the Oil and Natural Gas Commission, the Atomic Energy

Commission, the Flood Control Board, etc., have been set up under statutes passed by the Indian Parliament. Thirdly, the commissions may be brought into being by an executive resolution of the Government. The Central Social Welfare Board, the Handicrafts Board, the Handloom Board, the Central Water and Power Commission, etc., may be cited as examples of boards and commissions created by the resolutions of the Government.

Of these three categories, the commissions mentioned in the Constitution enjoy the greatest amount of autonomy: they are appointed directly by the President of India, and do not come under the general administrative control of any particular Ministry in their day-to-day functioning. The statutory boards are put under the general administrative control of the Ministry concerned, but are free from the regular departmental procedures. The third category of bodies like the Handloom Board, the Handicrafts Board, etc., are created for a specified period of time, and their existence depends upon the will of the Ministries concerned. They are attached to the Ministry and are known as Attached Boards.

The Constitution of India enumerates the following bodies to be set up on the commission model: the Finance Commission, the Union Public Service Commission, the Election Commission, the Backward Classes Commission and the Official Language Commission.

**The Finance Commission**

The Finance Commission is constituted at the expiration of every fifth year or at such earlier times as the President considers necessary. It consists of a chairman and four other members to be appointed by the President. The Finance Commission recommends on the following:

*(i)* The distribution between the Union and the States of the net proceeds of taxes which are to be or may be, divided between them, and the allocation between the States of respective shares of such proceeds;

*(ii)* The principles which should govern the grants-in-aid of the revenues of the States out of the Consolidated Fund of India; and

*(iii)* Any other matter referred to the Commission by the President in the interest of sound finance.

The recommendations of the Commission are laid before each House of Parliament.

**The Union Public Service Commission**

The Union Public Service Commission conducts examinations for appointments to the services of the Union. It shall be consulted:

*(i)* On all matters relating to methods of recruitment to civil services and for civil posts;

*(ii)* On the principles to be followed in making appointments to civil services and posts, and in making promotions and transfers from one service to another, and on the suitability of candidates for such appointments, promotions, or transfers;

*(iii)* On all disciplinary matters affecting the Central Government employees;

*(iv)* On any claim by or in respect of Central Government employee in a civil capacity, that any costs incurred by him in defending legal proceedings against him in respect of acts done in the execution of his duty should be paid out of the Consolidated Fund of India; and

*(v)* On any claim for the award of a pension in respect of injuries sustained by a Central Government employee.

The members of the Union Public Service Commission are appointed by the President for a period of 6 years or till the age of sixty-five, whichever may be earlier. The authorised strength of the Commission is nine.

**The Election Commission**

The superintendence and control of all elections to Parliament and to the Legislatures of the States and of the President and the Vice-President of the Union, are vested in the Election Commission consisting of a Chief Election Commissioner and such other Commissioners as may be appointed by the President. Originally, it was proposed to set up one Commission to deal with elections to Parliament and separate Election Commissions for each State to be appointed by the Governors of the States. But now there is only one centralised Commission. "The centralised election machinery has, thus, stemmed from the national urge to curb and thwart any intention of the State Governments to project regionalism into the preparation of the electoral list."

## The Backward Classes Commission

The Backward Classes Commission investigates the conditions of socially and educationally backward classes within the territory of India and the difficulties under which they labour, and to make recommendations as to the steps that should be taken by the Union or any State Government to remove such difficulties, and to improve their condition and as to the grants that should be made for the purpose by the Union or any State Government. The report of the Commission is laid before each House of Parliament. This is not a standing commission.

## The Official Language Commission

The Official Language Commission set up at the expiration of five years from the commencement of the Constitution and thereafter at the expiration of the ten years from such commencement, recommends to the President as to:

*(i)* the progressive use of the Hindi language for the official purposes of the Union;

*(ii)* restrictions on the use of the English language for all or any of the official purposes of the Union;

*(iii)* the language to be used for all or any of the purposes in the Supreme and the High Courts, etc.;

*(iv)* The form of numerals to be used for any one or more specified purposes of the Union; and

*(v)* Any other matter referred to the Commission by the President as regards the official language of the Union and language for communication between the Union and a State, or between the State and another and their use.

The Commission consists of a chairman and such other members representing the different languages as the President may appoint.

The Commissions envisaged in the Constitution itself manifest some common traits. The members are appointed by the President, and Commissions do not come under the general administrative, control of any Ministry. Their reports are placed on the table of each House of Parliament. Further, the members cannot be removed from office except by a special procedure, ensuring thereby independence of members.

A study of all the three categories of boards/commissions reveals that their composition varies from one another. They may be composed of government officials who are full-time members, or the members may be non-officials including members of Parliament or State Legislatures, giving only a part of their time to the work of the Commission. Finally, the Commissions may consist of members holding offices under the Government and by virtue of such offices being *ex officio* members.

The relative merits of the Commission form of organisation have been debated in all countries. W.F. Willoughby argues that the Commission is better fitted than the Bureau:

*(i)* where duties involve the exercise of discretion on an important scale in the formulation of policies and rules affecting private rights and the adjudication of claims;

*(ii)* where the functions involve general control of character;

*(iii)* where it is desirable to have a number of different interests represented; and

*(iv)* where it is necessary to eliminate party politics and influence of pressure groups.

The board or commission type of headship is generally recommended if the public policy has not been fully finalised, and, therefore, joint discussion and deliberation should precede its formulation. Secondly, this form is appropriate in those areas where several interests are to be represented, adjudged, or reconciled. Labour disputes, involving the interests of capital and labour, are usually entrusted to boards for settlement; for, a plural body, it is generally believed, commands greater confidence of concerned parties than a single individual. Thirdly, plural headship is appropriate where wide discretionary or controlling powers are exercised. The examples are the Public Service Commission, the Central Board of Revenue, etc. Fourthly, this form of organisation may be preferred in the interest of administrative integrity against external pressure. For, a single individual may more easily succumb to external pressures than a plural body.

The plural executive, however, suffers from a number of drawbacks which, in effect, severely restrict its large-scale adoption. It results in lack of unity of purpose, lack of energy in execution, absence of well-defined responsibility, and not unoften, lapses of co-ordination. "While Commissions, at times, operate smoothly and energetically, they often develop friction and conflict among their members. Differences spread inevitably into the subordinative staff, forming factions, one of the worst type of administrative plague." That the plural headship is a guarantee to sound decisions is also a doubtful proposition. The single executive, on the other hand, displays energy, vigour and courage in execution and is, therefore, to be preferred where the major policy has been settled, and work is of a routine character. Even where Commission type of organisation exists, the implementation of the decisions is very often entrusted to the charge of a single executive officer. "Substantially universal experience demonstrates the fatal weakness of the direction of day-to-day operations by a plural body. To 'administer' in this sense of the term is the job of one, not of many." The merits of the single executive are, thus outlined by Alexander Hamilton.

"A single man, in each department of the administration, would be greatly preferable. It would give us a chance of more knowledge, more activity, more responsibility, and, of course, more zeal and attention. Boards partake of a part of the inconvenience of larger assemblies. Their decisions are slower, their energy less, their responsibility more diffused. They will not have the same ability and knowledge as in administration by a single man. Men of the first pretentions will not so readily engage in them; because they will be less conspicuous, of less importance, and have less opportunity of distinguishing themselves. The members of Boards will take less pains to inform themselves and arrive to eminence, because they have fewer motives to do it."

The above discussion does not establish a conclusive case for either of the two types of headship. Choice of one as against the other, should be determined by the administrative circumstances of each case. It may, nevertheless, be pointed out that plural executive lacks ingredients of effective management. Boards are expensive, cause delay, result in diffusion of responsibility, and precipitate occasional deadlocks. The board form renders difficult co-operation and co-ordination between different agencies. As L.D. White observes, "in general, the burden of proof is one the advocates of a board in preference to a single executive." John A. Fairlie observes, "For the conduct of administrative services, there should be a responsible single executive. There will remain, however, a place for boards in conducting inquiries and in planning new undertakings, as well as in the management of emergency or temporary tasks. Furthermore, they will find a function as advisory agencies and as regulators of general policy even in cases where a responsible single executive will carry out the actual administrative work. This division of function has already developed to a considerable extent in the control and management of educational affairs; it promises the possibility of deriving from the use of boards the greatest possible benefit with the least possible disadvantages. There will, of course, exist danger of conflict between the supervising boards and the administrative official."

It is appropriate to point out here that the Indian Commissions are not like the Independent Regulatory Commissions of the United States. The former are not independent in the sense in which it is understood in the U.S.A. In that country, the Commissions are virtually free from the Presidential control. The Commissions in

India do not enjoy such a degree of independence. The U.S. Congress labours under perennial distrust of the Executive *i.e.*, the President. Consequently the Congress has preferred to create special bodies to regulate and control, when regulation and control become necessary with the economic advancement and industrialisation of the country. Of course, a feeling that quasi-judicial, quasi-legislative work should be entrusted to separate bodies independent of the executive has also been behind the creation of such bodies. Nevertheless, the paramount factor behind the emergence of the Independent Regulatory Commissions has been the Congressional distrust of the President. It is, therefore, necessary to point out that India, with its parliamentary system of government, is not likely to have the Independent Regulatory Commissions of the U.S.A. model.

**Independent Regulatory Commissions**

The Independent Regulatory Commissions are characteristically American device to undertake public regulation of private economic activities. The need for such regulation and control became apparent with the growing industrialisation of the country during the nineteenth century. Appearing first at the state level, the first Independent Regulatory Commission set up by the Federal Government, was the Inter-State Commerce Commission, established in 1887. At present there are the following nine regulatory Commissions in the Federal Government of the U.S.A.:

1. Inter-State Commerce Commission.
2. Civil Aeronautics Board.
3. Federal Power Commission.
4. Federal Communications Commission.
5. Federal Trade Commission.
6. National Labour Relations Board.
7. Securities and Exchange Commission.
8. Board of Governors of the Federal Reserve System of Banks, popularly called the Federal Reserve Board.
9. Tariff Commission.

Broadly speaking, the Regulatory Commissions perform two sets of functions. First, they set up standards and rules to govern the behaviour of a particular industry in future. Secondly, they also enforce these standards and rules, and prosecute the defaulters. The Commissions are, thus, engaged in administrative legislation (or, rule-making) and administrative adjudication. These bodies are marked by the following three features:

1. These Commissions are manned by experts and are relatively small.
2. They are collegial, consisting of a group of men discussing and arriving at decisions by majority vote.
3. They are relatively independent of the Chief Executive, *i.e.*, the President.

A Commission is set up under a statute passed by Congress laying down its constitution and functions. Though the members are appointed by the President with the approval of the Senate, they are not responsible to him. The overlapping of terms of the members also strengthens their independence of the President in the functioning of the Commission. The President cannot remove the personnel of the Commission except on grounds specified in the statute creating the Commission. The members of the Commission are not to be treated like the civil servants who can be removed by the President at his will. This position was established in the famous Humphrey case. It may, nevertheless, be stressed that the independence of the Regulatory Commissions is relative, not absolute. Their actions are subject to judicial review, which means judicial control in three principal aspects—(i) "in assuring the use of correct procedures in administrative action; (ii) in preventing action in excess of powers conferred by the legislature; and (iii) where administrative action depends on a factual record in making sure that the evidence in the record is sufficient." Further, the Commissions are subject to Congressional control. They receive annual appropriations from the Congress, which may order an investigation into the operations of the Commission, amend its constitution, and, even abolish it; although this last step, in the words of the Hoover Commission Task Force, is a "blunt instrument and not likely to be resorted to except under the extreme circumstances." Moreover, in personnel administration, the Regulatory Commissions are controlled by the Civil Service Commission. Lastly, their budgets are subject to review by the Bureau of the Budget.

Regulation of private business activities is a difficult task. The organisation entrusted with this function must manifest impartiality to all concerned. At the same time, it must not be hampered by provisions which interfere with the discharge of the vital function of regulation of private business activities. "The industries affected by regulation are often powerful and politically influential, and regulation controls their profits, their services, and their finances. The combination of a wide administrative direction, on the one hand, and great private influence, on the other, plus high stakes in the relationships between them, involves serious risks of corruption and unfairness. In this situation, the independent Regulatory Commission seems most nearly to meet the need." Elucidating the merits of this type of administrative organisation, the Hoover Commission Task Force commented: "The number of members and their security of tenure are intended to assure freedom from partisan control or favouritism. The group is able to resist outside influence more effectively than an individual, and each member is free from a threat of removal as a source of pressure. Moreover, since the activities of the Commission may be more subject to public scrutiny than would be a single bureau in a large department, there is greater opportunity for exposure of pressures or improper actions. Finally, while provisions for hearings and similar safeguards against arbitrary actions are not peculiar to Commissions, they may be more effective when combined with group action."

Despite these advantages, independent Regulatory Commissions have been subjected to varied criticism. Indeed, there are fundamental differences of opinion regarding the suitable administrative organisation for the performance of regulatory functions in the economic field. The main indictments are summarised below:

In the first place, the system of independent Regulatory Commissions has created a 'headless fourth branch' in the U.S. Government, violating the accepted tripartite separation of powers. They are 'headless' as they are not subordinate to the President. They lie outside the administrative system headed by the President, and may be called 'islands of autonomy' within the United States administrative organisation. Consequently, the latter has become 'disintegrated', resulting in the diminution of the President's effectiveness as the Chief Executive. In the words of the Brownlow Committee (1937), "They (Independent Regulatory Commissions) are in reality independent governments set up to deal with the railroad problem, the banking problem, or the radio problem. They constitute a headless fourth branch of the Government, a haphazard deposit of irresponsible agencies and un-coordinated powers. They do violation to the basic theory of the American Constitution that there should be three branches of the Government, and only three. The Congress has found no effective way of supervising them, they cannot be controlled by the President, and they are answerable to the courts only in respect to the legality of the activities." This Committee further declared that "though the Commissions enjoy power without responsibility, they also leave the President with responsibility without power."

Secondly, the combination of the functions of law-making, prosecution, and decision has been inherently unfair and is likely to lead to arbitrariness, endangering thereby the rights of individuals. In this connection, Robert E. Cushman writes : "The Commissions are being asked to perform judicial tasks interwoven with determination of policy which at times are the subjects of acute partisan controversy or economic class antagonisms. This is not the atmosphere in which the rights of individuals ought to be judged. It is a vital and inherent weakness of the Independent Commission system..."

Thirdly, it is argued that the Commission device has not been an effective one, either in protecting the public interest, or in assuring the long-run progress of the industry. This is because the Commissions act through case-by-case procedure, and they are separated from one another. This defect impressed the Hoover

Commission (1949), which pointed out : "The chief criticism that can be made of the Regulatory Commissions is that they become too engrossed in case-by-case activities and, thus, fail to plan their roles and to promote the enterprises entrusted to their care. Typical of this is the attitude by which the Civil Aeronautics Board and the Inter-State Commerce Commission have approached the problem of building a route structure for the nation.

Fourthly, the Regulatory Commissions are subject to the charge that they have been unduly lax. This slackness is engendered partly because the Commissions, being relatively free from executive supervision, are liable to drift into a condition of dependence upon the interest with which they deal, partly because "in practice, the Commissions are not responsible to the legislative body in any orderly way holding out the possibility of various forms of interference, and partly because of the Commissions' fear of being reversed by the courts." In the opinion of Arthur M. Macmahon, all these three factors may make the commissioners timid.

Fifthly, the Regulatory Commissions have been criticised on the score that the Commission type of organisation is inherently weak. This criticism can, however, be made pointless by developing the administrative role of the chairman. Indeed, the Hoover Commission has recommended the strengthening of the chairman's role. As a result, the chairman's administrative role has been strengthened to some extent.

Sixthly, the system of independent Regulatory Commissions has resulted in lack of co-ordination. This is because they adopt the case-by-case procedure, are outside the administrative system headed by the President, and are even separated from one another.

**Attempts at Reforms**

The independent Regulatory Commissions have been the subject of study and investigation by individuals as well as commissions. The President's Committee on Administrative Management (popularly called the Brownlow Committee) severely criticised them declaring that "though the commissions enjoy power without responsibility, they also leave the President with responsibility without power." The Committee was of the opinion that the work of the Commissions should be assigned to appropriate departments, the former to remain as autonomous adjudicatory boards within the departments for the handling of cases involving administrative adjudication. Such activities as planning, investigation, initiation of prosecution should be looked after by the bureau of the department. The Congress, however, rejected this recommendation. The Brownlow Committee's plea that the regulatory work should be sought under the departmental auspices, and the Regulatory Commissions should survive as the adjudicatory boards, was criticised by the Attorney General's Committee on Administrative Procedure, reporting in 1941. The Committee observed : "A separation of functions would seriously militate against what this Committee has already noted as being numerically and otherwise the life-blood of the administrative process—negotiations and informal settlements. Clearly, amicable disposition of cases is far less likely where negotiations are with officials devoted solely to prosecution and where the prosecuting officials cannot turn to the deciding branch to discover the law and the applicable procedures." This Committee, thus, defended the Commission system.

The second Hoover Commission called the Regulatory Commission 'an outstanding development' in the American federal government, though, at the same time, it drew attention to the haphazard, un-coordinated nature of their growth in response to the immediate needs of the government. The Commission said, "...it is found that a large part of the work of the Commission is not closely related to that of the rest of the Government and requires no active co-ordination to avoid conflicts." It pleaded for enhancing the powers of the chairman, and better salaries for the commissioners.

The independent Regulatory Commissions confront any scheme of federal administrative reorganisation with a challenging problem. In the words of Robert E. Cushman, they are 'areas of unaccountability' outside the sphere of Presidential direction and responsibility. How can they be made to fit into the broad pattern of the United States Government? There are the following four alternatives:

1. Integration of the Regulatory Commissions into the executive branch of the government making them subordinate to the President;

2. Strengthening of the congressional control of the Commissions;

3. Strengthening of the judicial review of the Commissions' activities; or

4. Segregation of the legislative, administrative and judicial work of the Commissions, each phase of work to be appropriately performed.

It appears that, despite their shortcomings, the independent Regulatory Commissions seem impregnable. James W. Fesler stresses the need for the recognition of certain fundamental factors in the functioning of the Commissions. He writes, "first, the quality of men and women appointed to the Commissions is more important than the details of organisation. Second, judicial work should be carried on in an impartial manner, free from the bias characteristic of the prosecution function. Third, co-ordination of policy formulation and administrative management among government agencies is essential, especially during periods when government plays a positive role in the economy. The chief executive appears to be the only responsible and effective focus for such co-ordination. And fourth, independent Commissions should be subject to the same control by the legislative and judicial branches that applies to all other regulatory and service agencies of Government".

# 14

# Civil Service in India

## Introduction

"The function of the Civil Service in the modern State is not merely the improvement of government; without it, indeed, government itself would be impossible.... Its numbers are a measure of the activities of the State and an indication of its measure."

"Of no country can it be said more truly than of India that 'government is administration'," wrote the Indian Statutory Commission, commonly known as the Simon Commission, after the name of its Chairman, in its Report on the Indian Constitutional Reforms, in 1930. Commenting on the character and importance of Civil Service in India, the Commission stated : "In a country of small cultivators, with no accumulated resources and little experience in organisation ...private enterprise cannot undertake new and costly experiments. The task of bringing within reach of such a society the benefits of the administrative experience and the applied science of the West was possible for one agency only—the Government; no other had the necessary knowledge or machinery. Thus, the Civil Service of India, which in origin was little more than revenue collecting agency, gradually took upon itself a very wide range of duties. As the work became specialised, new services had to be created....India looks to Government to do many things which in the West are done by private enterprise." The brilliant statement serves to explain the origin, nature and purpose of the Indian Civil Service.

The expansion of governmental activities has been going on at a fast rate since the above lines were written, and more so since

Independence in 1947. With the adoption of the concepts of Welfare State and "socialistic pattern of society", the sphere of Government has expanded enormously resulting in an immense increase in the magnitude of administrative services, and an additional big increase in future might well be anticipated. Comparing the strength of the Indian Civil Service with that of the Civil Service in the United States, Appleby writes: "The Government of the United States, apart from its armed services but including state, country and municipal governments, had 6.13 millions of employees in 1951. Excluding persons employed in governmentally financed schools and universities, the total number of employees was 4.44 millions. India has altogether 2.15 millions in comparable employment. Since the population of India is 2¼ times as large as that of the U.S. and since India is undertaking through government a good many activities which in the U.S. are carried on privately, it is safe to say that the number of employees in governments at all levels here will increase enormously in years to come."

**All-India Services**

Like other federal polities, the Union (Centre) and the constituent States, under the Indian Constitution, have their separate public services to administer their respective affairs. Thus, there are Central or Union Services to administer Union subjects, like defence, income-tax, customs, posts and telegraphs, railways, etc. The officers of these Services are exclusively in the employ of the Union Government. Similarly, the States have their own separate and independent Services to administer State subjects like land-revenue, agriculture, forests, education, health, etc. The officers and employees constituting the State Services are exclusively in the employ of the different State Governments. A unique feature of the Indian Administrative system, however, is the creation of certain Services common to both the Union and the States, namely, the All-India Services which, as a form of personnel organisation, are perhaps unparalleled except in Pakistan. These Services are composed of officers who are in the exclusive employ of neither the Centre nor the States, and may at any time be at the disposal of either. These Services are recruited on an all-India basis with common qualifications and uniform scales of pay, and, notwithstanding their division among the States, each of these Services forms a single Service with a common status and a common standard of rights and remuneration.

**Why All-India-Services?**

Commenting on the need for the setting up of such Services, in a speech before the Constituent Assembly, B.R. Ambedkar, the Chairman of the Constitution-Drafting Committee, said : "...It is recognised that in every country there are certain posts in its administrative set-up which might be called strategic from the point of view of maintaining the standard of administration...There can be no doubt that the standard of administration depends upon the calibre of the civil servants who are appointed to these posts....The Constitution provides that, there shall be an All-India Service, the members of which alone could be appointed to these strategic posts throughout the Union." Ambedkar, thus, emphasised the contribution such a Service could make in brining about greater efficiency in the administration of the Union as well as the States. Secondly, there are others who emphasised the cohesive aspect of such Services, which, it is claimed, will ensure the uniformity of the administrative system throughout the country. Apropos of this, the Simon Commission wrote: "A proper circulation (of Services) between the provinces and the Centre is essential if contact is to be maintained over so vast an area." In the third place, in the words of A.D. Gorwala, "...it would make a valuable contribution to the cause of national unity. Each province would, then, in its administration, present a replica of many of the elements that contribute to the varied richness of this ancient land. A great dramatist imagines a world government in which the local administration of each country is conducted by inhabitants of other countries, thus ensuring impartial administration and at the same time impressing upon the inhabitants of all lands the essential unity of the planet. We, in India, are fortunate enough to be able to carry out, if we will, that experiment in large measure, thus providing an effective check to fissiparous tendencies and obtaining an essential uniformity." Fourthly, the high remuneration, authority, prestige, status and tradition attaching to this Service, secure for it recruits of a class for which other Services may have no attractions. It is a tempting prize and the best products of the universities compete for it. In the fifth place, since the responsibility for the administration of a State, in the event of the breakdown of the normal constitutional machinery, is vested in the President, the existence in the State of a certain number of officers of All-India Services occupying key-posts in the administration will certainly be helpful to him. He can count more on the co-operation of officers, who, in the last analysis, are Union Government's employees, than on the officers of the State Government proper. Lastly, it should always be kept in mind that the new All-India Services are but a continuation of the old arrangement.

## History of All-India Services

For the sake of convenience the development of these Services may by divided into three periods (1) pre-1947; (2) 1947-1950; and (3) present position after 1950.

*Pre-1947*. Ever since the creation of Indian Civil Service in the days of the East India Company there has always existed in India an all-India cadre of service. Gradually, the all-India cadres were introduced almost in all departments of the Central Government. The number of all-India cadres and the strength of each one of them, as reported by the Lee Commission in 1924, was as follows:

| *S.No.* | *Name of Service* | *Strength* |
|---|---|---|
| 1 | I·.dian Civil Service (I.C.S.) | 1,350 |
| 2 | India Police Service (I.P.S.) | 732 |
| 3 | Indian Forest Service (I.F.S.) | 417 |
| 4 | Indian Service of Engineers (I.S.E.) | 728 |
| 5 | Indian Educational Service (I.E.S) | 421 |
| 6 | Indian Agricultural Service (I.A.S.) | 157 |
| 7 | Indian Veterinary Service (I.V.S.) | 53 |
| 8 | Indian Medical Service (I.M.S.) | 420 |
| | Total | 4,278 |

These Services formed the highest rung of the bureaucratic ladder in India. The British Government in India, depending as it did for its strength primarily on its civil servants, loaded them with all kinds of favours, concessions and privileges. These Services, thus, were not even under the control of the Governor-General ; they were directly under the Secretary of State for India and his Council. No All-India service officer could be dismissed from his service by any other authority than the Secretary of State-in-Council. He had a right of appeal to that body if he was adversely dealt with in important disciplinary matters. The Governor of a province was required to examine the complaint of any such officer who thought himself wronged by an official superior, and to redress the grievance if he thought it equitable to do so. No order affecting his emoluments adversely, and no order of censure on him could be passed without the personal concurrence of the Governor, and orders for his posting to appointments also required the personal concurrence of the Governor. His salary, pension etc., were not subject to the vote of any Indian legislature.

These Services, entrenched in their privileged positions and irresponsible to public opinion, found it difficult to adjust themselves to the reform-era introducing very limited responsible government under the Government of India Act of 1919. Criticism of individual members of the Services by questions in the Provincial and the Central Legislatures, the 'ignominy' of working under Indian Ministers in the provinces, the Non-cooperation Movement of 1920-1922 putting the officers and their families in personal discomfort, the insufficiency of the salaries due to the high level of prices prevailing in the wake of the First World War—all these embarrassed and discouraged European members of these Services and many of them expressed a desire to retire. The Secretary of State-in-Council, therefore, adopted a scheme under which all-India officers, selected for appointments before January 1, 1920 and not permanently employed under the Government of India, were allowed to retire before they had completed the normal full service on a pension proportionate to their length of service actually rendered. Under this scheme by 1922, two hundred all-India officers had retired and by 1924 the number had risen to 345.

Meanwhile, the pressure of Indians to enter these services in increased numbers could not be ignored for long. It was under these circumstances that the Royal Commission on the Superior Civil, Services in India, of which Lord Lee was the Chairman, was appointed. The Commission submitted its Report in 1924.

The Commission recommended the abolition of certain all-India services, particularly those dealing with departments that had been 'transferred' to Indian hands, namely, Indian Educational Service, Indian Agricultural Service, Indian Veterinary Service, and the Roads and Building Branch of the Indian Service of Engineers. It, however, recommended the retention of the Indian Civil Service, Indian Police Service, Indian Forest Service, Indian Medical Service and the Irrigation Branch of the Indian Service of Engineers. It also recommended the increasing Indianisation of these Services. The commission further recommended that any British officer should be free to retire on a proportionate pension if at any time the department in which they were employed should be transferred to the control of responsible ministers. Effect was given to these recommendations.

Further changes were made in the position of these Services by the Government of India Act of 1935. Indian public opinion had always been demanding the abolition of the Secretary of State's Services. It was argued before the Joint Select Committee of the British Parliament considering the draft of the Act of 1935, and emphasised by the 'British India' delegation in their Joint Memorandum that further recruitment by the Secretary of State of officers serving under the Provincial Governments which were to be handed over to the popular control was incompatible, and that Services in future be recruited and controlled by the authorities in India. The Joint Committee, however, only partly accepted such demands, and recommended the continuance of I.C.S., I.P.S. and I.M.S. (Civil). This recommendation was embodied in Section 224 of the Act of 1935. Thus, at the time of transfer of power in 1947, recruitment was open only to two all-India services, namely, the I.C.S. and the I.P.S., the recruitment to the I.M.S. has been suspended. Besides, there were the surviving incumbents of the defunct all-India services. The most important and the highest ranking of all such services was the famous Indian Civil Service commonly known as I.C.S. which owing to its very high remuneration and enormous authority and prestige, was nicknamed as the 'Heaven-born Service', and constituted the 'steel frame' of the British Government in India.

The British Government, depending as it did for its strength on its civil servants, loaded them with all kinds of favours, privileges and concessions to the effect that public service grew to become a 'special interest' and demanded safeguards for the protection of its privileged position. As shown earlier, many British officers chose to retire prematurely rather than serve under the Indian ministers after the introduction of the 1919 reforms. The Government of India Act of 1935, therefore, included the protection of the interest of the Public Services in the list of the Special Responsibilities of the Governor-General and the Governors (Sec. 247-9). Thus, if any officer of the Secretary of State's Services was affected adversely by an order relating to his conditions of service, he had a right of complaint to the Governor (as the case may be), and the latter was to deal with the matter "exercising individual judgement," that is, acting without consulting his Minister. As a matter of fact, the introduction of limited responsible government in 1920 and its extension in 1937 had been marked by frequent clashes between the Indian ministers and the British officers. Even a strong man of the stature of the late Sardar Patel, the then Minister for Home Affairs in the Interim Administration of 1946-47, was unable to take any action against a British officer for a serious misconduct. Revealing his helplessness before the Constituent Assembly, he said: "I tried to get the District Magistrate of Gurgaon (a district in the Punjab) transferred. I could not succeed...I tried hard. I wrote to the then Governor of the Punjab; I pleaded with the Viceroy, but I found it difficult to remove him." All this happened just a few months before the transfer of power.

The solicitude of the British Government for its civil service was carried during negotiations for transfer of power, and it insisted that before the transference of power, arrangements must be completed about the conditions of service of the officers of the Secretary of State's Services to the satisfaction of the British

Parliament, and that transfer of power could take place only when such guarantees had been given. Adequate guarantees were, thus, embodied in the Indian Independence Act of July 1947 (Sec. 10-2). Moreover, Indian leaders gave public assurances to the Services not to make any change in the conditions of the services to their disadvantage. Although some members of the Constituent Assembly protested against the continuance of the privileges of officers even in a free India, the Government was averse to repudiating its promises, and the Constitution of 1950 (Art. 314) provides for protection of the rights of the existing officers of the Secretary of State's Services. The prematurely retiring British officers were given general proportionate pensions.

*1947-1950.* While guaranteeing the rights of the old Services, the new Indian Government had foreseen the need for replacing them with Services controlled and manned by Indians. In fact, as early as October 1946, Sardar Patel, the then Home Member in the Governor-General's Executive Council, had secured the agreement of the Provincial Governments to the formation of the two new all-India services, namely, the Indian Administrative Service (I.A.S.) and the Indian Police Service (I.P.S.), which were to replace the old I.C.S. and the I.P.S. The emergence of a free India on August 15, 1947 found the country facing a personnel crisis. Not only had the volume of work greatly expanded, but the new government had increased its functions also considerably. But while India's requirements of trained personnel had, thus, increased greatly, the administrative Services had seriously weakened. On the eve of Independence, most of the British officers had retired from service, and due to the partition the majority of the Muslim officers had opted for Pakistan. Thus, nearly 600 members of the Indian Civil Service left India, leaving only about 400 officers in that Service. The Indian Police Service, too, suffered a similar depletion in ranks. The acute shortage of trained personnel can be judged from the fact that while the External Affairs Ministry needed some 300 officers to man its diplomatic posts, not more than 50 were available for the purpose.

The new government promptly and courageously set about the task of filling the gaps in the Services. The first step in this direction was to invite applications to fill about 200 to 300 posts in the newly created Foreign Service. The applications were invited from persons from all walks of life, and the age-limit was specially raised to 45 years. The idea was to attract the best available talent to the Foreign Service from wherever it could be got. About 16,000 applications were received, and of these about 2,000 were called for interview by the Civil Service Commission. To suit the convenience of candidates, the Commission was split into groups to interview candidates at different centres in the country. The Commission was aided in its work by a high official of the External Affairs Ministry who sat at the interviews. The commission, after a long and arduous series of interviews submitted its list of eligible candidates. Strangely enough, this list was never made public, and not many persons from it were appointed. The Ministry perhaps did not feel satisfied with the recommendations of the Commission, and made its own appointments. Thus was born the idea of setting up a Special Recruitment Board for filling the newly created posts in I.A.S. and I.P.S. This decision led to a controversy between the Federal Public Service Commission, which was the only legally constituted body under the Act of 1935 (still in force) to recommend candidates for appointment, and the Home Ministry which sponsored the idea of establishing a new Board to make emergency recruitment. The controversy was ultimately resolved by making the existing Commission the nucleus of the Board and adding a few more members to it including one or two public men. The new Recruitment Board was set up in 1948. Its task was to survey the available administrative manpower in the country both inside and outside the ranks of the permanent services, and to select men of the requisite standard in order to make good the deficiency in services. As in the case of the Foreign Service jobs, applications were invited from the open market, and about 350 to 400 appointments were made. Besides this recruitment from the open market, the recruitment was also made out of the Provincial Civil Services. Each Provincial Government recommended certain officers of its own Executive Service for promotion to the ranks of the I.A.S. and the I.P.S. Such persons were interviewed by the Special Recruitment Board and on a favourable recommendation by it were appointed. By this two-fold process, the critical gap in higher ranks of administrative service was met on an emergency basis. This was, however, merely a stopgap arrangement, and the Special Recruitment Board came to an end with the inauguration of the new Constitution on January 26, 1950.

*1950 and After*. The Constitution also provides for the all-India cadre. It adopts specifically the I.A.S. and the I.P.S. cadres which had already been created earlier (Art. 312-2). Besides, it empowers the Union Parliament to create more of such all-India services whenever it is deemed necessary or expedient in the national interest, provided the Council of States (the Upper House) passes a resolution to the effect supported by not less than two-thirds of the members present and voting (Art. 312-1). Since the Council of States is composed of the representatives of different States, its support will ensure the consent of the States to the creation of new Services. The Constitution also authorizes the Parliament to regulate by law the recruitment and the conditions of services of persons appointed to these Services. Accordingly, the All-India Service Act was passed by the Parliament in October 1951. Since the inauguration of the Constitution, the following new all-India services were planned but only one, namely, the Indian Forest Service, has been set up:

*(i)* Indian Service of Engineers (Irrigation, Power, Buildings and Roads);

*(ii)* Indian Forest Service; and

*(iii)* Indian Medical and Health Service.

Two more all-India services—Indian Educational Service and Indian Agriculture Service—are on the anvil.

It should be noted that not all all-India services have the same pay-scales and status. Even the I.P.S. which is an original all-India service, differs from its compeer—the I.A.S —in two ways: (i) most of the officers in this Service work only in the States since there are only a few police posts at the Centre; and (ii) its pay-scale and status are lower than those of the I.A.S. From the point of view of remuneration, status and prestige and topmost all-India service is the Indian Administrative Service. Thus, the only typical all-India service is the I.A.S. and it is this Service which we shall now consider at some length. By the end of 1964, there were 2,145 officers in I.A.S., and 1,196 in I.P.S.

**The Indian Administrative Service**

*Character*. The Indian Administrative Service, commonly and conveniently called the I.A.S. is the direct descendant of the old Indian Civil Service. It was on the initiative of the late Sardar Patel, the Home Minister in the Central Government, that a conference of the Chief Ministers of the various Provinces was called to meet in Delhi to discuss the question of creating the all-India cadre of service. The conference endorsed Patel's proposal to create an Indian Administrative Service in place of the defunct I.C.S. The very manner of its origin, therefore, determined the dual character of the Service, namely, a Service common to the Centre as well as the States. The control and management of such a Service is necessarily a joint co-operative affair. As an all-India service, it is under the ultimate control of the Union Government, but is divided into State cadres, each under the immediate control of a State Government. The salary and the pension of these officers are met by the States. But the disciplinary control and imposition of penalties rest with the Central Government which is guided, in this respect, by the advice of the Union Public service Commission. The State Government can only administer a reprimand at the most. On appointment, the officers are posted to different State cadres, and they carry this nomenclature with them throughout their service. Thus, there are Bombay civilians (officers), Bengal civilians, Madras civilians, etc. The strength of each State cadre, however, is so fixed as to include a reserve of officers who can be deputed for service under the Union Government for one or more 'tenures' of there, four or five years before they return to the State cadre. This ensures that the Union Government has at its disposal the services of officers with first-hand knowledge and experience of conditions in the States, while the State Governments have the advantage of their officers being familiar with the policies and programmes of the Union Government. Such an arrangement works for the mutual benefit of both governments. The majority of individual officers have an opportunity of serving at least one spell of duty under the Union Government; many have more than one such spell. The need for reverting I.A.S. officers from the Centre to the States after the required period is clear, and has been emphasised by the Chief Ministers' Conference, held in August 1961. This Conference recommended: "The rule of rotation of officers in the existing all-India services between the Centre and the States should be more rigorously followed." The practice of rotating senior officers in and out of the Secretariat positions—known in official parlance as the tenure system—continues to be mater of controversy. It is not, however, true that "senior officials occupying Secretariat positions of responsibilities are rarely rotated now." It was recently stated in reply to a question in Parliament that on December 1, 1960, there were 333 officers serving at the Centre, from the Indian Administrative Service, including members of the Indian Civil Service, as against a Central deputation quota of 399 provided in the various State cadres of the Service. During the period since 1949, two hundred forty-five officers went back to their respective States after the expiry of their tenure of deputation. According to information laid before Parliament earlier on February 2, 1959, there were only 26 officers on that date who had remained beyond their normal tenure of deputation at the Centre; of these 12 were of the rank of Secretaries. In respect of Secretaries, it had long been a matter of dispute whether they should be subject to strict rules of the tenure system. If the posts of Secretaries are excluded, there were in 1959 only 14 officers who had stayed beyond their tenure. Though in theory the tenure system is still in operation, many officers are seen to overstay at the centre.

Another distinctive feature of this Service is its multi-purpose character. It is composed of 'generalist administrators' who are expected, from time to time, to hold posts involving a wide variety of duties and functions; for example, maintenance of law and order, collection of revenue, regulation of trade, commerce and industry, welfare activities, development and extension work, etc. In brief, the I.A.S. is intended to serve all the purposes formerly served by the I.C.S. except providing officers for the judiciary. Thus, this Service is a kind of omnibus service, and its officers are liable for posting in almost any branch of administration. It may be interesting to note that in one of the States, an officer of the I.A.S. held the appointment of the Director of Health for over two years.

*Strength of Cadre.* So far no fixed quota has been determined for this Service, which is being continuously expanded to meet the growing administrative needs of the country. To start with, the Service was introduced only in Part 'A' States (the former Governors' Provinces), but as the former princely States became integrated into the Union and were constituted as Part 'B' States, the cadre was extended to them as well. Thus, about 400 to 450 emergency appointments to this cadre were made in 1948-49. Special recruitment was again made in the years 1955-1958. In addition, regular appointments are made every year on the basis of a competitive examination, the number varying according to requirements.

Another mode of recruitment to the I.A.S. is from amongst the members of the State Administrative Services (old P.C.S.). Until May 1977, the quota of the State Administrative Service personnel was 25 per cent of the total annual intake into the I.A.S. This quota has been raised to 30 per cent in 1977.

The authorised strength of the I.A.S. 4,705 in January 1982, but the actual number of officers being in position was 4,125. The cadre has been registering a steady expansion as revealed by the following figures:

| *Year* | *Authorised Strength* |
|---|---|
| 1952 | 1,201 |
| 1956 | 1,542 |
| 1957 | 1,672 |
| 1958 | 1,676 |
| 1959 | 1,785 |
| 1960 | 1,862 |
| 1961 | 2,010 |
| 1962 | 2,147 |

| *Year* | *Authorised Strength* |
|---|---|
| 1963 | 2,278 |
| 1964 | 2,470 |
| 1965 | 2,567 |
| 1966 | 2,855 |
| 1967 | 2,882 |
| 1968 | 3,035 |
| 1969 | 3,234 |
| 1970 | 3,199 |
| 1971 | 3,225 |
| 1974 | 3,794 |
| 1975 | 3,884 |
| 1976 | 4,195 |
| 1977 | 4,267 |
| 1981 | 4,599 |
| 1982 | 4,705 |
| 1983 | 4,859 |

Such a rapid expansion of the I.A.S. cadre is a consequence of more and more posts getting reserved for members of this service. The I.A.S. is a formidable institution in India and its members control virtually all levers of administrative power and patronage. All services reach a pleateau after some interval, and the total membership stabilises around a certain figure. The present degree of expansion of the I.A.S. is not a very healthy feature, for it is bound to introduce deep distortions within the civil service.

A word may now be said about the distinct role of the all-India services, especially the Indian Administrative Service. The Indian arrangement creating a common pool of officers, who are in the exclusive employ of neither level of government and fill the top posts in both Union and State administrations, comes nearest to the ideal federal administrative system. The essence of federalism is as much joint action, co-operation and co-ordination, between the two levels of government as the distribution of power between them. One single integrated federal service common to both the Centre and the States will be a negation of State autonomy. On the other hand, if the federal government is denied its own services, one of the two results may follow—either the State services will be reduced to the status of being mere agents of the Central Government, or the Central Government may find itself helpless in the face of the non-cooperative attitude, nothing to say of disobedience on the part of the State services. Responsibility divorced from power is the worst principle of administration. The Indian experiment avoids both pitfalls by providing separate and independent Union and State services and yet facilitates co-ordination and co-operation, and, if necessary, joint action between the two levels of government by creating a common cadre of officers at the top level. It also avoids the possibility of the best brains preferring Federal service to State service, leaving the latter to be manned by the second or the third best. As it is, the all-India services, being recruited by the Union Government on an all-India basis, attract the best persons who are then posted to different States. Such service cadres, thus, are a means for carrying a wider stock of talent to States. No better way of strengthening the State services can possibly be suggested. Again, constant transfers of such officers from the States to the Centre and back makes them aware of, and conversant with the administrative problems at both levels of Government. Such officers, therefore, can be the best agents for carrying out administrative co-ordination between the federal and State administrations.

Secondly, one of the great weaknesses inherent in a dual polity is the possibility of a conflict of loyalty and responsibility on the part of the public servants as between the Central and State Governments. Unseemly quarrels and wrangles over federal versus State interests are not uncommon. The State services, not unoften, develop a parochial attitude, and tend to look upon the Central services as foreign and even their suggestions as interference. On the other hand, the federal services often betray a lack of appreciation of the state point of view and tend to regard themselves as superior. The Indian system aims to obviate both these defects inasmuch as the all-India services without ignoring

State interests, develop an all-India outlook whose importance in a country with heterogeneous elements and fissiparous tendencies cannot be too much emphasised. Their loyalty and responsibility to both levels of government make them truly federal services. Moreover, by vesting the ultimate control of these services in the hands of the Union Government, it is hoped that in the event of a clash between the Centre and a state the top officers in the State will choose the higher loyalty to the Union as against the lesser loyalty to the State. Such an arrangement is in keeping with the spirit underlying Indian federalism which provides for the turning of the federal structure into a unitary one in times of emergency. These services, therefore, may well prove to be a force in fostering national unity in India—and India needs nothing so much as this.

Lastly, whatever may be said about the efficiency of the services at the lower level, there can be no doubt about the efficiency of all-India services. The old Indian Civil Service was, indeed, famous for its high efficiency throughout the world. Even such an inveterate critic of administration as Gorwala has to admit, "Though it must not be forgotten that in many instances the few senior officials in charge have been able, at any rate during periods of stress and emergency, to get excellent work out of their inexperienced, newly promoted juniors, and indeed, in many provinces, the quality of specific portions of work has, on occasion, been as good as, if not better than in the past. That these officers could earn the unstinted praise of no less a person than the late Sardar Patel, the then Home Minister and Deputy Prime Minister, is the best testimony to their efficiency. Defending the guarantees given to the members of all-India services and safeguarding their rights and privileges before the Indian Constituent Assembly, Patel said: "I wish to assure you that I have worked with them during this difficult period. I am speaking with a sense of heavy responsibility and I must confess that in point of patriotism, in point of loyalty, in point of sincerity and in point of ability, you cannot have a substitute. They are as good as ourselves...I wish to place it on record in this House that if, during the last two or three years, most of the members of Services had not behaved patriotically and with loyalty, the Union would have collapsed." It must however be admitted that there has been a certain decline in the efficiency as well as integrity of the members of these Services since the seventies.

Nevertheless, it must also be stated that, at least during the early days of Independence, some of these officers had entertained somewhat strange views about their own position in the emergent administrative set-up, and found it rather difficult to act in complete harmony and co-operation with the newly-introduced political element in the government, *viz.*, Ministers. Sri Prakash, the former Indian High Commissioner in Pakistan, recalls the difficulties he had encountered in getting his instructions implemented by an I.C.S. officer who was his deputy in the embassy. He, finding consolation in a similar discomfiture experienced by even Jawaharlal Nehru, writes: "It would be interesting to recall that even the Prime Minister had his own sad experience. He told me, when comparing notes about the time that high-ranking I.C.S. officers thought that government should be run according to their own directions, and that he himself had difficult times keeping them in check and getting his policies implemented. When he had to encounter such opposition, the position of small folks like myself can well be appreciated."

# Civil Service Reforms

This paper illustrates the degree to which new areas of consensus are emerging in the implementation of reform. It reflects the findings of the Roundtables and proposes a framework for sharing experiences of successful civil service reforms.

At their 1991 meeting in Harare, Commonwealth Heads of Government reaffirmed their commitment to the Commonwealth principles for democratic development and identified sound and accountable administration as a key priority for the Commonwealth. Subsequently, the Secretariat's Management and Training Service Division organised a series of Roundtables and consultations with Governments. The aim of these was to learn from successful experiences and explore ways and means of strengthening Commonwealth cooperation in the area of administration and managerial reforms.

The dialogue highlighted both the diversity and the commonality of reforms programmes, and the key distinctions between domestic and external pressure for change. Discussions also revealed a movement from "macro" concerns relating to the role of government in socio-economic development, towards a more "micro" concern with the development of specific strategies for improvement in public sector management. In summary, the debate had moved from the problems to the solutions.

## Pressure for Reforms

Since the mid-1970s, governments have been increasingly concerned with adapting and developing structures and values of civil service which will achieve greater efficiency, and more responsive and flexible services. This movement has been motivated by unprecedented economic crises which led to reduced financial resources for governments and by rapid changes in political and public opinion.

A combination of economic pressure acted as forces for change. These included problems related to balance of payments faced by most countries in the Commonwealth which eroded their exchange rates and the purchasing government's power. The terms of trade were such that developing countries could not cover their needs for imports of manufactured products—many of which were needed by government agencies.

Also, the high levels of government expenditure as a proportion of Gross Domestic Product (GDP) were increasing every year, while the sources of government revenue could not keep pace. Thus, the cost of government was becoming unsustainable. Hence, there was a need for urgent reductions in government expenditure.

This concern with economic growth has led to reforms directed towards national goals affecting society generally, rather than those limited to improving administrative efficiency within government. Reforms have also attempted to improve the context for private sector development. In some settings, this has led to changes resting on the premise that government is intrinsically an obstacle to development which must be removed, rather than a potential solution which must be appropriately targeted.

Against this general background, managerial pragmatism and political conviction have both played their part in motivating reform programmes. Whether explicitly stated as a goal or not, economic growth has been of paramount concern, particularly at a time of widespread recession.

**The Changing Role of Government**

The role assigned to government in the planning and management of national economic and social activities has undergone fundamental reassessment in both the industrial and developing economies within the Commonwealth. At the same time, major political reorientations in the level of state intervention in social and economic spheres have taken place.

A crucial development has been the change in strategy being pursued by most countries for achieving economic growth and broader development objectives. In the late 1980s, the question of "perestroika" posed fundamental challenges far beyond the boundaries of the Soviet Union. This occurred at both a practical and an intellectual level and to both policy-makers and managers alike. The issue of moving from an economy in which activity has been planned mainly in terms of physical quantities, to one in which consumers indicate their preferences by means of the monetary valuations they put on at least some goods and services, is one of the key managerial and intellectual challenges of our time.

These developments, combined with political and social changes around the world, have had an impact on various economies. As well as reawakening a spirit of economic liberalism, they have also impacted on the functions of governments. However, despite consensus on the need for change, there continues to be controversy on what the appropriate role of the state should be.

In most industrial Commonwealth countries in the 1980s, market-oriented, private sector techniques emerged as the sole path to holding down public sector budgets while allowing some opportunity to meet increasing public expectations. As some of the ideological rigour underpinning this approach softened, a more dispassionate view of the advances made has been possible. Sound management supported by pragmatism, enterprise and a clear sense of mission, have emerged ahead of ideological conviction.

Many countries are now seeking modes of administration which avoid the errors of both Soviet-style planning and the grandiose corporate planning approaches popular in the 1960s. The need to change the role of the state has found acceptance as a route towards improved economic efficiency in many countries. The restructuring which followed has been shaped differently by the ideological, political, structural and cultural contexts in the perceived role of government from acting the principal vehicle for socio-economic development to guiding and facilitating that development.

Many of the difficulties faced by developing countries are due not only to defective and ineffective policy instruments but also to complex institutional mechanisms which make it difficult to implement various policies effectively. In this context, attention needs to be given to management structures and institutional mechanisms within the government for creating the capacity and capability for effective policy management involving identification of strategic choices, policy analysis for outlining implementable programmes of action and monitoring of policy implementation.

Although policy formulation remains one of the main functions of government, the role of the government in implementing policy decisions is changing. The strong movement towards liberalisation of economies has been accompanied by a desire to appraise what government does best. As a result, issues related to economic liberalisation, transfer of state-owned enterprises to the private sector, reductions in the size of the state bureaucracies, and contracting out work, have been placed higher on the strategic agenda.

The situation, however, is far from straightforward. Underneath the general current towards "leaner and meaner" administrative structures, there are many eddies in the opposite direction. Economic liberalisation brings with it an increased requirement for regulatory activity, as does the increasing concern for the environment. Equally, the strong pressure towards consumer-oriented services can lead to requirements for more rather than less government, with an emphasis on "transparency" rather than size.

Within this climate of change, there are underlying concerns to achieve efficiency, cost-consciousness, responsiveness and accountability. The motivation for such reform are emphasised by increasing public expectations concerning the quality of government services.

This very striking managerial shift has been strongest in industrial and newly-industrialised countries, but the reform themes relate closely to the changing mood within other settings. Such managerial focus on systems and structures embodies a powerful set of ideals, and has recently been described as "the emergence of entrepreneurial government".

In different settings, different paths are being followed towards a similar set of goals. In UK and New Zealand, systemic and radical reform measure have been adopted, utilising the new managerialism to the full to reorient the civil service and to decentralise its functions. In other settings, such as Singapore and Malaysia, the new approaches have added to the existing administrative tool kit available to government. These new tools have facilitated incremental reform of a more traditional and centralised position towards enhanced managerialism, within a border focus on the "well-performing government organisation".

**Common Themes**

The Roundtable highlighted several common themes to the introduction of reform programmes. These individual components indicate that a substantial reform programme, with roots deep in a changing conceptualisation of government, is under way.

Examination of these themes emphasised the complexity of the challenges, the potential which such reform programmes might realise, and the remarkable similarity about the concerns and changes taking place in very different settings. These themes are as follows.

**Redrawing the Political/Administrative Boundary**

The research for enhanced clarity of role and tighter lines of accountability extends to a desire to refine the relationship between political policy-making, and administrative policy implementation. As a policy goal, its roots lie in the concern that the civil service requires a clearer political lead, and the belief that in distinguishing the role of senior administrators from that the politicians, strategic objectives will be more easily distinguished from operational processes.

**Selecting Appropriate Options**

In order to maintain an effective capacity for strategic intervention in all areas of socio-economic activities, governments must select the most effective structured reform option from an increasingly broad portfolio, from corporation through to contracting-out. The difficulty is that this occurs within a climate of accelerating change and globalisation. Selecting the appropriate option requires a willingness to dispassionately evaluate models for their effectiveness, regardless of whether those models are traditionally associated with the public or private sectors. Also, it implies a managerial style which facilitates a rapid response and which is capable of driving through change.

**Emphasising Accountability**

This identification of responsibilities, where policy formulation is separated from implementation, is a necessary precursor to strengthening accountability. Enhanced accountability fits with a broader concern to adopt a more managerial approach. Such an approach suggests that accountability is enhanced by tighter definition of tasks, measurement of performance, devolution of resource control, strengthening monitoring, and clarifying incentives.

**Achieving A "Synergy" Between the Public and Private Sector**

Recognition that the public sector is dependent on the services of the private sector, as well as being ultimately responsible for the climate in which that sector thrives or otherwise, requires a clear conceptualisation of the boundary between the two. This entails clarity in the mechanisms for the exchange of goods and services across that boundary. In turn, this requires a clear model for government purchasing of externally-produced services and an ability to specify the government's intended outcome in strengthening the capacity of the private sector. Within the more pragmatic management culture increasingly adopted by governments, a broader range of choices is available for the intervention in, and withdrawal from, areas of social and economic activity. The public/private "synergy" is maintained by a flexible and frequently tactical choice of strategies and actions.

**A Concern for Efficiency**

The reform programmes reflected the two broad aims of increased efficiency and effectiveness. The concern for heightened efficiency is both an organisational value implying amoral dimension to any apparent waste in government, and an instrumental concern resting on the premise that inefficiency within government represents a drag on national productivity.

The concern to ensure efficiency in state-owned enterprises is mirrored in the concern to achieve a civil service more oriented towards achievements and outputs than consistency of procedures—the model which has traditionally underpinned civil service activities. This refocusing of the civil service is made possible when clear lines of accountability and sharp definition of purpose are introduced into government.

**Reducing Corruption**

In varying degrees, corruption is a fact of life in all areas of government. While perceptions of its nature and extent vary, it provides a strong impetus for reform on two levels. First, concern exists in some countries that independence left a residue of endemic corruption. Fundamental reform was seen as necessary to change the value base and the procedures which sustained this state of affairs. Second, and contrast, other countries have more recent concerns regarding the growing number of public sector scandals, which could related to the fast pace of change.

**A Dual Focus on Staff and Structures**

Discussions indicated clearly that successful reforms are built on a foundation of attention to both the organisational and attitudinal dimensions of public sector reform. In some settings, the comprehensive revision of traditional personnel policies within the civil service, supported by tight monitoring to total staff numbers and costs, have clearly assisted in developing a new culture in which quality and accountability to the public are being emphasised through a conscious process of reorientations.

Such a deliberate process of changing attitudes, in step with reforming structures, highlights the central role of staff commitment to change. The process of reform must capture the imagination of existing staff if they are to lead to sustainable service improvements.

## Changing Values and Attitudes

The question of attitudes underpins all concrete issues concerning possible civil service reforms. Increasing concern with the quality of service provided to "customers" has acted as a particular catalyst in developing an organisational culture where concern for the finished product is a major preoccupation. Attitudes concerning commitment to the job, belief in quality, and flexibility, have been associated with many recent developments. Such reforms within the public sector have represented a major challenge to the traditions and assumed values of the civil service.

In some settings, a concern for quality and identification with the public served are important aspects of the new culture. This gives rise to the possibility that a new public sector value system is emerging. If this is the case, it might represent the ethical dimension of the revised boundary between the public and private sectors referred to earlier. Such developments raise fundamental questions about the very notion that the public sector is distinct and separate from the private sector and should operate on different principles.

## Technological Opportunities

The growing power of information technology has opened up possibilities which have not existed previously. The rapid processing and dissemination of information is allowing the development of a broader range of organisational structures and systems. Flatter structures allowing for tighter monitoring of service outputs and delivery of better services to the customers and improved information interface with the public at large are some of the development in this area.

## Key Strategies of Civil Service Reforms

Along with the common themes, a set of key strategies of civil service reform programmes within the Cõmmonwealth governments emerged. Details of these strategies are summarised below.

## Securing Leadership for Change

The importance of securing the highest level of political authority, namely the commitment of ministers and senior officials, to an administrative reform programme, was identified. Equally important is the institutionalisation within the government machinery of the skills necessary for the continuation and development of good management in government. Thus, reviewing and defining the relationship between ministers and the most senior officials was particularly highlighted.

As well as high-level political support, encompassing both the Prime Minister and President and Cabinet, such reforms also require the support of the Chief Executives at the organisation level.

Most successful reforms are politically driven at the highest levels as was the case in UK, Malaysia, Singapore and New Zealand. By contrast, Canada's Public Service 2000 was seen to have suffered from a deficiency of political will and intent.

Such support was evident in Jamaica when the Hon. Prime Minister stated that he did not envisage that the new role of government as minimalist or resulting in its eventual disappearance. Rather, he said that it suggested that government of a somewhat different nature and better kind. It certainly implied movement towards catalytic government: one that concentrates on facilitation, regulating, and monitoring; one that focuses more on "steering than rowing".

In Uganda, a public service review and reorganisation commission was appointed in 1989 with the major objective of redefining the role of government in meeting the development needs of Uganda and raising the efficiency and effectiveness of the public sector.

In Zimbabwe, civil service reforms involved the setting up of institutional machineries to implement and monitor the reform programme. In this regard, a number of units had been created. These include a monitoring and implementation unit in the office of the President and cabinet, a human resources and management service directorate and efficiency unit in the Public Service Commission and the training directorate in the Ministry of the Public Service. A Public Service Commission was appointed in 1987 by the President to undertake an in-depth study of civil service in Zimbabwe.

The Government of Malta appointed a Public Service Reform Commission when it initiated a radical reform of its civil service in 1987. The role of the Commission was to "examine the organisation of the public service, and recommend means by which the Service can efficiently respond to the changing needs for effective government".

In Trinidad and Tobago, in 1991, a cabinet minister was appointed and given a mandate, for the first time, to implement public service reform.

**Policy Development and Strategic Planning**

Strategic planning deals with strengthening the core policy development, management and coordination capacity within the government. The lack of policy analysis skills has been identified as a key weakness within the civil service in many developing countries.

In some countries this has been addressed by strengthening offices of President/Prime Minister/Cabinet through development of policy units (Britain, Australia, New Zealand, Zambia). In other countries, inter-ministerial committees have been set up for special policy issues and national forums involving private and public sectors (Malaysia: Malaysia Inc. and Ghana: National Renewal Programme). Also, special committees of secretaries and task forces have been set up (Zambia, Malaysia). Some countries have also facilitated the setting-up of independent policy institutions.

Strategic planning also deals the civil service improvement programmes, and in particular, the development of priorities with responsibility through clear systems of delegation.

In Jamaica, one of the first priorities of the civil service reform was also to establish the necessary capability under the Prime Ministers personal authority to command and control the formation of strategy and the policies for development of resources money and people to implement it. The Prime Minister's Office (PMO) has to take over full responsibility of bringing together issues which bear on government strategy and presenting them to Ministers and to take a lead role in corporate planning for the government as a whole.

In UK, most policy proposals originate from Ministers and all those civil servants who are especially designated to produce policy advice. Political advisers play a part in this process and the PMO has its own advisers in the form of the Number 10 Policy Unit. This Unit is headed by an officer of Deputy Secretary level who is in charge of a team of eight people producing ideas on domestic, economic and foreign affairs for the Prime Minister.

**Making the Most of Staff: Human Resource Management**

Improved human resource management systems within the public service should aim to encourage and reward both team and individual performance. Increasing managerial autonomy over departmental and agency human resources management practices allows for innovations in producing, measuring and rewarding individual performance.

A number of governments have successfully experimented in this regard: developing flexibility in working conditions (Australia and New Zealand); moving collective bargaining from the entire public service to the work-place (Australia and UK); and the application of private sector law to the public sector (New Zealand).

Some of the most successful Asian economies recognize the importance of recruiting the most talented people available and improving their skills through constant training. Hong Kong and Singapore carry out aggressive recruitment at entry level, entice high-flyers for further training and generally pay attractive salaries compared with the private sector.

**Tailored Training**

Current reform programmes are adopting a highly pragmatic approach to maximising the effectiveness of all levels of staff. Training programmes to ensure competency are increasingly tailored to individual needs. Performance appraisal techniques which identify the strengths and weaknesses of individual contributions, and personal career planning to ensure the personal ambitions and aspirations are harnessed towards the overall service of government, are also being introduced.

Imaginative training initiatives have been initiated in a number of countries. In UK and Mauritius, training is being tailored to rank; and Singapore Ghana, Australia and Trinidad and Tobago have all instituted customised training for staff. The Malaysian government's focus on establishing key national institutions capable of providing highly targeted training to strategic personnel provides a useful example of current developments in this field. The Botswana government has set up a specialised training centre, Botswana Productivity Centre, for training in productivity and quality improvement programmes. The Ghana Institute of Management and Public Administration (GIMPA) has expanded its activities to meet the increased demands of training as a result of civil service reform in Ghana. Throughout the Public Service of Canada, staff training and development is given high priority. Close attention has been paid to the purposes, coordination and cost-effectiveness of training and development, so that overall effectiveness has increased.

**Rewarding Achievement**

Incentive packages, such as the Malaysian New Remuneration System, which ensure that skills and, in particular, personal achievements, are recognised and rewarded, are also becoming more widespread.

Open recruitment procedures, with wider recruitment for senior posts, helps to ensure that vacancies are filled on the basis of skills and competence. As a result, the assumption of a career-based civil service with semi-automatic promotion is weakening. At senior levels, low reward, high-security positions are being replaced with the exact opposite.

The Canadian government has made it a policy to inform employees of the results expected of them in the performance of their work; to make them aware of the standards against which their performance will be judged; to provide them with informal feedback on a continuing basis and periodic formal feedback; and to act upon the conclusions of employees' performance reports.

**Establishing A Fast Track**

As the emphasis continues to shift from high-security careers, shaped by length of service and seniority, towards shorter term employment contracts and achievement-oriented promotion, a new cadre of responsive managers is emerging in many settings.

This shift away from a career civil service has been emphasised by the establishment of Senior Executive Services in Australia and New Zealand, offering appointment contracts, performance measurement, and intra-service mobility. The expectation in that public sector managers, often recruited from the private sector, will have a high level of managerial skills and talent and will be flexible enough to manage effectively in any government agency.

Singapore has maintained a systematic focus on efficiency as the sole criterion for retaining or retiring senior civil servants. Seniority is no longer the basis for promotion and many of Singapore's Permanent Secretaries are comparatively young.

**Managing the Political/Administrative Boundary**

Reform programmes are increasingly seeking to demarcate the political/administrative boundary more clearly. Authority is explicitly delegated to senior officials in exchange for accountability for performance. Power is provided on the basis that its use and, very particularly, the result achieved with it will be monitored.

Such monitoring is often achieved through performance agreements and the specification of expectations within short-term contracts for staff at senior levels to provide the basis for ministerial review of achievements.

**Clarifying Public Service Accountability**

An emphasis on personal and institutional accountability runs through all the current reform programmes. Personal contracts and public reporting of the planning and delivery of services are the practical mechanisms by which accountability is highlighted. This enables public exposure of poor performance by senior officials, agencies, departments or other institutions, including that caused by corrupt practices.

If enhanced accountability is to act as a pressure for performance improvement, it must be matched by enhanced managerial authority. Devolving responsibility to senior managers allows them the financial and procedural latitude necessary to deliver the outputs for which they are held responsible.

Modernising the role of the Public Service Commission represents a particular aspect of this necessary devolution to managers or agency chief executives.

In Australia, state public service boards are being abolished in favour of smaller commissions, and their controlling role is changing to one of personnel service provider, training resource, and review body.

The nature of accountability is increasingly affected by the changing nature of relationships between the public sector and the community. A shift towards formalised and specified contractual relationships, capable of being monitored and where necessary enforced, is occurring. While this increased formality enhances accountability by offering rights of redress not previously available, some accountability is increasingly legalistic rather than cooperative.

**Anti-Corruption Measures**

Current reforms are translating the broad appeals for transparency and accountability in government into operational systems for specifying the expected performance of staff and institutions.

The experience of Singapore indicates how strong political leadership and rigorous anti-corruption measures, enforced by powerful and incorruptible idle agencies, can turn corruption from a low risk-high reward activity into high risk-low reward activity.

The increasingly business-like approach implicit within many reform programmes is allowing anti-corruption measures to be supported by tighter employment frameworks for senior officials. Contracts are for short terms, with more detailed specifications, to ensure that performance monitoring is more rigorous. Significantly, the development of large sticks is being matched by the growth of larger carrots. Salary levels are increasingly comparable with private sector positions to reduce the temptation of inducements to corruption.

The Mauritius Civil Service, like all big organisations, is not exempt from various forms of malpractice. Corruption is one problem which is perceived to have reached disquieting proportions in some areas. To remedy the situation, the following measures have been taken: an Ombudsman's Office has been created, an Anti-Corruption Tribunal has been set up, a code of ethics to promote "responsible behaviour" within the service is under preparation; and a Public Complaints Bureau will be set up to examine complaints from members of the public.

**Redundancy Management**

It was emphasised that the management of redundancies is a reform component of last resort. Ideal or otherwise, it is however a pressing issue within many Civil/Public Service bodies, Particularly following structural adjustment programmes.

Major programmes of redundancy management within the public sector must be linked to more systemic approaches to controlling workforce size, and procedural mechanisms to achieve this must be founded on a "culture of realism".

The Singapore experience of a zero growth strategy and financial capping, and the Malaysian experience of public sector salary cuts, introduced into these settings during periods of national economic difficulties, provide powerful examples of public sectors being tutored in this culture. The zero-based reviews of public sector structures and costs undertaken in Singapore every five years further emphasise this culture of realism by focusing on what is to be done rather than what has already been achieved.

It is essential to have clarity of purpose in driving through a contentious but unavoidable redundancy programme. Experience emphasises that a rational and purposeful approach is most politically and administratively feasible when popular support for the government is at its highest, and when there is internal political and managerial cohesion.

A major component of the Civil Service Reform programme in Zimbabwe is the reduction of the size of Zimbabwe's civil service. Since 1992, the Zimbabwean government, through the Public Service Commission, has adopted various strategies to reduce the size of the civil service. First, those posts that remain vacant in excess of twelve months were abolished. However, some professional technical posts which remained unfilled for a long period because of shortages of required skills were reinstated. Second, obligatory reductions were effected in the form of giving up a certain percentage of their positions in each of the Ministries. Third, downsising the service was done through voluntary retirement.

**Making Government More Efficient**

Another common component was the need to review and re-examine structures of government, including the potential for decentralisation and divestment, and to establish efficiency and market testing programmes.

**Structuring for Efficiency**

Traditionally, the primary structural choices facing government concern the height and breadth of departmental bureaucratic pyramids. Accountability is assumed to flow upwards, with the administrative dimension funnelled smoothly towards the Permanent or Chief Secretary and, in the political dimension, towards the Minister. By contrast, recent experience shows governments are choosing from a considerably broadened range of structural options. This development has reduced the previous consistency across the machinery of government. Unity remains a feature of the civil service, but uniformity is assuming less relevance.

The establishment of Statutory Boards in Singapore, Executive Agencies in the UK, and the experience of corporatisation in Australia has allowed a clear delineation between the functions of policy formulation and policy implementation. In this way, areas of relative freedom from bureaucratic constraint have been created in which a more business-like climate can be maintained. Establishing an operational unit around a clearly demarcated and coherent set of functions allows the development of operational goals, uniting staff with a clarified sense of mission.

As a result, commercialising of government departments (Malaysia, Ghana) and decentralising financial responsibilities through management contract (India, UK) has been made possible. In some countries, responsibilities are being devolved to provincial and local levels (South Africa, Sri Lanka, India, Nigeria).

The Statutory Boards in Singapore were created to achieve specific social development goals. They are designed to counter the traditional civil service emphasis on regulation and monitoring, and were structured specifically to encourage the return of talent previously lost to the private sector.

The establishments of Executive Agencies in the UK were intended to redress the historical preference for policy development over service delivery within the civil service.

Where successful, such developments have been supported by a strengthened managerial role for senior staff Traditional bureaucratic/administrative models have seen some separation between the financial, strategic, and personnel responsibilities of senior managers, particularly in the context of the historically strong roles given to Public Service Commissions and similar bodies. Within more autonomous functional units, these three responsibilities can be brought together, enhancing the managerial authority of the agency's chief executive.

The establishment of executive agencies or similar bodies has the consequence of fragmenting the traditionally uniform civil service, and is replacing the traditional procedural concerns of the public service with the pursuit of explicit objectives. In some settings, this re-orientation has served to emphasise the "vertical" relationships within government, increasing accountability to the political leadership, while simultaneously reducing "horizontal" linkages between ministries. As a result, this reduces the focus on the collective interest associated with more traditional models of public service.

In Trinidad and Tobago, the organisational structure of ministries/departments Minister, who determines the functional description of ministries based on the political mandate. Each ministry/department has been asked to develop strategic plans which will identify core purpose statements and clarify their major function and sub-functions.

The Canadian Government, in its White Paper of December 1990, include the establishment of special operating agencies as one of the key items for public service reforms.

**Establishing An Efficiency Programme**

Efficiency programmes comprise both cost reduction (without lower standards) and performance improvement (at no higher, and preferably lower cost). They question whether a task should be done at all, whether it should be done by government directly or by contractors paid by government, or done by the private sector.

Since government resources are always under pressure (demand exceeds supply and expectations exceed what can be afforded) there is an on-going requirement to review activities to ensure that resources are used to best effect and that government can demonstrate sound stewardship. Consequently, the point of entry for programmes to improve efficiency is commonly a requirement to reduce operating costs as part of budgetary restraint.

Based on the UK experience, typical steps in establishing an efficiency programme carried out with in-house skills include the establishment of a small unit (which may be directly accountable to the Prime Minister) which had the responsibility for vetting and approving proposals from various ministries for efficiency savings. Such a unit is responsible for reporting on savings and benefits, which are publicised in the public service to create a climate of achievement.

A more fundamental and sophisticated approach would be to progressively review, under the overall direction of an Efficiency Unit, the functions of all ministries with a view to ensuring that only essential activities are undertaken. Where there is not strategic reason why an activity should be conducted within the government, privatisation corporatisation or contracting-out should be considered.

**Introducing Market Testing**

As part of the hierarchy of reforms in public service management, the policy of market testing has been increasingly introduced. Market testing works by putting the activity in question out to competitive tender, with internal and external bids assessed against the same criteria. Such market testing determines whether contracting out will be the most efficient way of carrying out a civil/public service activities which clearly need to remain the ultimate responsibility of the public sector.

There are number of benefits from the market testing process. First, when considering whether to accept an in-house bid or give the work to an outside contractor, the evaluation will look at improvements in the quality of service available from innovative methods of service delivery.

Second, there may be cash savings. It is axiomatic that where an activity is market tested, and an external bid is successful, it will be because that bid offers greater overall long-term value for money than the current method of provision. Where an in-house bid succeeds, the process of opening up that public sector activity to competition in itself often creates opportunities for greater effectiveness. In the central government of one Commonwealth country, saving arising from market testing, in its initial stages, have averaged about 25 per cent of the original cost whether or not the activity has remained in-house.

Third experience suggests that market testing will lead to raised standards by making expectations explicit within contractual arrangements. Greater clarity about standards of service and better monitoring of performance against those standards, regardless of whether the work is retained in-house, is a vital feature of public sector reforms.

It is, however, important to note the dangers of rapid introduction of competitive tendering without preparation, and the weakness of the private sector in some settings. The process also opens up the possibility of cartel formation after abolition of in-house providers, and the problem of fixed wage costs even after staff transfers.

**Improving Quality of Services**

The introduction of quality management and customer-oriented programmes was also highlighted as a common component in reform.

**Introducing a Quality Management Approach**

Quality management is the creation of a culture of commitment to identifying and meeting customer requirements throughout the whole organisation, within available resources. The approach defines standards for each area of activity, from which performance standards are set for each member of staff and unit of management. Performance is then regularly assessed against customer expectations and satisfaction. Commitment to quality management is openly vowed and performance is made public. The term customer has a broad meaning: any citizen engaged with government, or any person acting as proxy for the public. New Zealand includes the Minister as a proxy customer for the policy advice outputs of the department.

The idea of quality management originated in the private sector, but has become increasingly relevant to government as rising expectations have highlighted areas of unacceptable low standards of service to the public, to officials and to politicians. There is growing experience in Commonwealth countries in applying quality management approaches as a firm base for sound government.

Quality management is closely linked with human resource management, particularly leadership and team-building, training and development including management and leadership training, performance management, especially specification of outputs, organisational change, frequently leading to flatter pyramids, and workforce reductions.

This change in work culture and systems has encouraged respect for excellence at all levels. Success within the public sector is recognised and rewarded. Practical and measurable quality standards are set, with participative mechanisms established to ensure that the need for quality has a broad "Ownership" at all levels of staff. The Malaysian Civil Service provides a clear example of successful strategy for recognising excellence, through the series of award it offers. Singapore was the first civil service to introduce Work Improvement Teams, developed from the Quality Control Circles employed in successful and innovative private sector companies to allow groups of staff from varying levels to discuss obstacles to quality openly and honestly, and to divide practical solutions for service improvement. India also has introduced some Work Improvement Teams. The Botswana Government introduced the productivity and quality improvement programme in 1993 by creating work improvement teams (WITS) within various institutions and departments.

**Developing a Customer Orientation**

Productivity improvement within government has encouraged acceptance within government that public service, like those produced in the private sector, are products to be tested against the needs of service users. This shifting emphasis has been encouraged by a conscious reshaping of the work culture to achieve a customer orientation. Courtesy campaigns, customer care training, and comprehensive complaints procedures ensure that service users are seen as active freely choosing customers rather than passive recipients of monopolistically provided state services.

The Malaysian Government has emphasised that its public administration is operating in an era where the customer's needs are paramount. The new public administration document emphasises that the focus of the new public management has shifted from tasks to processes involved in delivering the final product or service. In the UK, two government documents "The Citizens Charter" and "Competing for Quality" provide a comprehensive agenda for change towards consumer culture. The broad principles in the government's Citizens Charter include standards, information and openness, choices and consultation, courtesy and helpfulness, putting things right and value for money.

The main focus for the British Government reforms are to widen choice and competition and improve value for money. Countries such as New Zealand, Malaysia Namibia, Singapore and, Mauritius are seeking to emulate this innovation.

**Developing A Public Sector Ethos**

Creating a working culture based on quality, performance and openness and transparency necessarily involves employees and the public in the change process. The new civil service reforms are aimed at developing the organisational culture to manifest itself in strengthened employee involvement, consistency in the change process, rewards from team work and individual perfection and consultation with clients and users.

Trinidad and Tobago have recognised that the critical element for the successful implementation of civil service reform is focusing on the process that will ensure successful change. Consequently, the government has developed processes which identify "Change Sponsors" and "Change Agents" and emphasise that members of the public service organisations should feel a sense of involvement in the process, share the new vision and own the change. Malta has set up management committees in each ministry to aid internal consultative processes.

The formal development of codes of ethics within government marks a significant step in moves towards codifying public sector values at a time of rapid change within the culture and practice of the public sector. The Malaysian programme for inculcating positive attitudes provides a successful example of a practical approach to the establishment of appropriate values within an increasingly entrepreneurial public sector.

**Improving Partnership with Organisations Outside the Government**

The development of partnerships with non-governmental organisations (NGOs) and the private sector has emerged as a key element in implementing development policies and programmes.

State monopolies have been maintained by complex regulatory regimes designed to ensure safety or equity. At the same time, these have served to maintain areas of public service as the exclusive preserve of government organisations. Opening up areas of public service to private or NGO suppliers, while maintaining standards in areas where consumer choice will have insufficient impact, requires a complex readjustment of such restrictions. Extensive and successful experience is now available illustrating strategies for measured deregulation and regulation.

An example of a government which has successfully facilitated and managed such partnerships is illustrated by the establishment of the German Bank in Bangladesh which has effectively developed programmes and direct benefits for poor sectors of society.

India has also had successful experiences with the NGO role in implementing education, national planning and rural development programmes.

Partnerships have been built with the private sector in Britain, Australia, New Zealand through the contracting-out of work previously exclusive to the public domain. Contracting out has been well-tested within government. Although specialist services have always been purchased from the private and NGO sectors, it is the development of market-testing techniques which is providing a strategy for assessing the ability of the market to provide goods or services historically considered to lie at the core of government. Significantly, market-testing is showing considerable potential as a technique for stimulating change through the assessment of internal efficiency. In some limited situations where contracting-out is not feasible because of market weaknesses or political restrictions, the developments of internal markets is being explored with as yet uncertain results.

Efficiency within government has also been improved through some restructuring of central/local, or federal/state inter-governmental boundaries. Clarification of mutual roles and responsibilities and, in particular the rationalisation of mechanisms for financial transfer between levels of government, has heightened efficiency and enhanced fiscal transparency. Flexibility and a concern for service quality and sustainability, rather than preconceptions concerning the efficiency of the private sector, have been the key futures of successful initiatives.

## Making Management More Effective

The use of information technology and the development and use of internal and external advising skills were highlighted in improving management systems and skills.

## Information Technology

Major improvements have been achieved by the use of information technology (IT) for efficient revenue collection, financial management and accounting, and interdepartmental communication systems.

Significant automation programmes have been implemented in Australia, Singapore, Malaysia, Malta, Mauritius and UK. Information technology has also been used in providing better interface with customers by developing "one-stop/non-stop" service centres and public information systems in Malaysia.

Within the UK civil service, a body called CCTA, the Government Center for Information Systems (part of the Office of Public Service and Science, itself part of the Cabinet Office) is responsible for promoting business effectiveness and efficiency in government through the use of information systems.

In Singapore, the National Computer Board (NCB) was formed on August 15, 1981, to promote, implement, and guide the development of information systems in the Singapore Civil Service.

In Malaysia, IT planning takes place both at the macro and micro level, at the micro level, there is the National Committee on Data Processing (NCDP) which has been entrusted with the role to formulate national policies and that will promote the usage of IT for administrative modernisation and national development. The Malaysia Administration Modernisation and Planning Unit (MAMPU) is the Secretariat to NCDP.

In Malta, one of the key parameters of the strategic plan for civil service reform is based on maximising the information resource through the sharing of information within the confines of Malta's legislation to avoid duplication in information collection and maintenance.

**Internal Management Advisory Capacity**

Successful developments within government have recognised that the need for an increasingly responsive government machinery provides little organisational stability in a rapidly changing climate. Shifting consumer needs, and funding are revenue assumptions, call for rapid structural and policy changes, and the broadened range structural options available to government emphasise the need for a strong evaluative capacity.

The work of the Canadian Auditor-General's office illustrates the degree to which internal advisor capacities are increasing. Recent institution audits have focused on constraints to productive management, attributes of well-performing organisations, and values which drive managers to perform well.

**Participative Review Group**

Particular managerial review exercises can involve staff with direct experience of the areas requiring review. The UK scrutiny exercises, and the Singapore programme for staff reduction, both relied heavily on staff seconded from their substantive positions for limited periods to assist the reviews. Training and technical support from specialist units within government is crucial in maintaining the quality of the review team's work.

**External Policy Advice**

External management advisory capacity available to governments is being strengthened to respond to these challenges. Outside government, a market of contestable policy advice is available to government by purchase or through presentations as lobbying platforms. This allows the independent testing of strategic options and increases both the planning capacity and the policy development transparency of government.

In Malaysia, the practice of opening ministries doors to receive public views on policy formulation is highlighted under the

Malaysian incorporated policy. In the process of making a policy proposal, ministries solicit views from certain sections of the public. For example, the Ministry of International Trade and Industry through its annual trade industry dialogue with trade associations gets feedback on the effectiveness of government policies in trade and industry.

In Trinidad and Tobago, formal consultations with the public take place through tripartite committees, a standing committee, which is chaired by the Ministry of Labour and comprises representatives of government, private and public enterprises and labour.

In UK, there are suggestions that the provision of policy advice should be put on the same customer basis through contractual basis that now applies to service delivered mechanisms for other departments. The Treasury and Civil Service Committee of the House of Commons recently examined this topic and heard suggestions from some quarters that senior officials should be employed on fixed term contracts with a clear remit related to producing answers on policy issues.

In Botswana, government is in the process of setting up an independent institute of development policy analysis.

**Improving the Management of Finance**

Major structural and institutional reforms have taken place in the area of financial management, making it more performance or output-oriented. Other developments in this area include the provisions of efficiency dividends to the departments (UK, Australia), the introduction of developmental charges for the use of capital (New Zealand), payments by department for internal government services (Australia) and a shift from cash to accrual accounting (New Zealand). New Zealand's financial reporting is completely output-oriented and Malta and Australia carry out three-year forward plan estimates.

The financial management reforms in New Zealand have illustrated the significance of adopting appropriate accountancy approaches from other sectors. Accrual accounting supplements cash accounting systems to ensure that the financial information available to managers is current and provides a meaningful analysis of resource usage within the department. Capital charring ensures that the opportunity costs of typing up capital within departments are fully captured.

Capital charging underlines the significance of goods estate management. The developments in UK and other settings indicate the growing concern of governments to ensure that fixed aspects are fully utilised and regarded as investments requiring careful husbandry. The end point of these developments is ascertaining a market price while allowing other aspects of market discipline to be introduced, in a situation where government services are fully contestable. This encourages heightened efficiency and economy.

## Output-Oriented Procedures

The traditional financial concerns of government emphasise probity. Public money must be fully accounted for and procedures must emphasise upward reporting of financial decisions, and strict enforcement of tightly specified budget headings.

Some current reforms are underpinned by fundamental changes in the emphasis of financial management systems. The concern with probity is matched by a growing concern to enable managers within government to act as public sector entrepreneurs, fully utilising the value of capital, goods, and staff within government to deliver specified objectives.

In New Zealand, the output orientation is the main emphasis in financial accounting. This is coupled with capital charging, and the need for adequate information on capital investments and governments subsidies.

## Delegation

The move towards an output-orientation fixes attention on the range, quality and volume of service which government is seeking to provide within its financial allocations. Delegation of financial responsibility gives managers some leeway to consider alternative methods for ensuring that the agreed services are provided.

In New Zealand, this approach is developed to the point where Ministers are effectively purchasing the outputs (goods and services) from departments. The outputs required from departments are precisely detailed in the specification of the performance required of the fully accountable Chief Executives. This provides room for entrepreneurial flexibility in meeting targets by offering them greater control over the purchase, use and sale of departmental assets necessary to produce the required outputs.

The delegation of authority to levy user charges on corporate-customers for some academic institutions in India is providing an incentive to market services more activity.

**Introducing Capital Charging**

The New Zealand experience of accounting for the cost of capital through a policy of explicit capital charging is conducive to good financial management in government. Benefits can be obtained from explicit recognising and accounting for the cost of capital. Capital charging makes clear the full costs of goods and services produced by departments, so that Ministers can make more informed decisions about the costs and benefits of government policies. The specific objectives in doing this in a public sector entity are to provide information and the incentives needed for efficient management of the government's investment.

If departments do not bear the cost of capital, they may be seen as the preferred provider, even when more efficient producers exist. Therefore, ignoring this cost is likely to result in poorly-informed decision-making the misallocation of resources. The government is more likely to achieve value for money when capital is no longer treated as being free, because the bias in favour of capital-intensive production is addressed.

Many departments supply goods and services to third parties. If the piece charged does not recover the total costs, including the cost of capital, then the government is effectively providing subsidy. A government should be in position to decide explicitly whether to subsidize a particular activity, and the amount of the subsidy. If the total cost exceeds the price that the government wants consumers to pay, then transparency could be achieved by making a specific budget appropriation to cover the expected shortfall.

Capital charges are most effective when combined with a consistent financial management framework and accrual accounting. Together, these changes provide departmental Chief Executives with the opportunity, incentive and information to produce desired "outputs" at the lowest cost.

Incentives for efficient performance are also enhanced by delegating control over inputs (for example, cash, fixed assets and human resources) to Chief Executives, and then linking this increased authority with accountability for the production of agreed outputs.

Before implementation, reliable information on department's net assets need to be available. In New Zealand, this information is provided in audited accrual accounts (including a balance sheet) which all departments are required to produce.

**Improving Estate Management**

The land, buildings (and equipment and, perhaps, infrastructure) owned by the government (the estate) represents a massive occurred investment. This huge resource is commonly neglected and often not systematically recorded or valued. Management of this resource is now being recognised as a key area for reform and development and is illustrated here on the basis of New Zealand experience.

Increased awareness and understanding of the size, nature, value and condition of property coupled with increased management authority, responsibility and accountability for the estate, brings added value for money to the public sectors mainstream activities by allowing for better use of these assets and releasing cash and management time. By making it apparent that the estate is not available free of charge, by allocating management time to its active development, by making the estate finances visible and by demonstrating a committed will to change ingrained habits and behaviours, the estate can and should make a valid contribution to better value-for-money from government expenditure.

Since the estate is a part of mainstream activity, it should feature as strongly as other topics mainstream management training courses. The objective should be to train managers to take an active informed interest in the whole of their assets base. Managerial awareness will increase if manager's performance on their property assets is judged and valued with the same vigour as their people management or financial skills.

It must be recognised that the benefits are derived over a long time-scale. Major restructuring of large complex estates cannot be achieved quickly but with professional help, significant benefits will be forthcoming.

**Introducing Accrual Accounting**

The experience in this area is very strongly influenced by the innovations implemented within the New Zealand public sector.

Good practices in decision-making on the allocation of resources, and in the specification and subsequent assessment of financial performance, require financial information that is timely, relevant and reliable. In both the public and private sectors, accounting systems are a major source of this information.

Since cash accounting records money received at the time it is banked and money spent at the time it is paid out, it does not provide enough information to measure the full cost of producing goods and services in a given period. In addition, it provides only limited information on the value of assets and liabilities.

While cash-based accounts give an accurate view of an entity's cash flows, accrual-based accounts give a fuller picture of its operations and overall financial position, since it relates activities to the period in which costs are incurred or revenue in earned, regardless of when or whether money changes hands. It keeps track of assets and liabilities, and records change in their values.

Accrual reporting thus gives a clearer view when financial implications extended beyond a year and encourages a longer-term focus in decision-making. It also facilitates more meaningful assessment by Ministers and Legislators of the performance of government entities (including departments), and of the managers responsible for them.

Accrual accounting is a logical tool of accountability when viewed from purchases and ownership perspectives. In the case of departments, the government is in many cases the principal purchaser of their "output" (the goods and services produced) and at the same time is their owner.

The information yielded by accrual accounting is of use in specification and assessment of performance in respect of both output delivery and stewardship of assets entrusted. The purchase interest requires information on quantity, quality, time and place of delivery, and cost of outputs. The ownership interest requires financial information which distinguishes capital and current expenditure and revenue, and reflects a notion of capital maintenance. Accrual accounting provides information relevant to these interests and facilities comparisons between competing providers.

The period required to implement full accrual accounting is heavily dependent upon the level and availability of accounting skills.

In New Zealand, the move from cash to accrual accounting was scheduled to take two years. This involved departments in specifying their "outputs" as well as installing new computer software, and introducing new banking, costing, monitoring and reporting systems. The scale of the change to long established procedures was huge. Most departments employed consultants to assist with the transition, and many have retained staff with scare skills on contract.

**Public Reporting**

Developments in the style of public reporting by agencies and departments to expose the financial position and annual performance achieved to public scrutiny has further encouraged a climate of opened and public accountability. The annual audited financial summary statements in Canada and the consolidated balancesheets prepared for the Crown in New Zealand represent significant developments here. Strengthened roles for government auditors and the increasing use of value for money reviews are further steps in this direction.

**Conclusion**

Reducing the size of government while remaining effective and efficient has been the main objectives of civil service reforms aimed at developing a new public administration capable of meeting the emerging and complex challenges. However, individual governments have adopted a much more discriminating approach in seeking to enhance civil service performance while maintaining the overall objective of improved public administration and the delivery of high-quality public service to citizens.

While global concerns exist about the nature of civil service reforms, there is no unique solution or approach. There are as many lessons to be learned from the successful experience of the developing countries, as from the industrial countries. Each country needs to identify its priorities according to the local circumstances, drawing upon the mix of other experiences from both industrial and developing countries, and look at achievements and implications. In short, countries have to develop local solutions to global challenges.

Most successful reforms are politically driven at the highest level. There should be sufficient political will in developing countries to implement such reforms. Reform programmes should be holistic, have a clear vision and objectives and simple priorities.

Successful reform programmes require support to be mobilised from within the civil service. In this context, it is important that successful organisations are recognised and that individuals who understand and support change are involved in the reform process. Governments must empower those who are working for change.

Although, working in the civil service is about working with constraints, it is possible that amidst those real world constraints, civil servants to have choices available to them. Politicians and civil servants in developing countries should be prepared to make difficult choices. It is important to look for values which successful civil service reforms bring with them. Such reforms must emphasise accountability and transparency of government processes.

Finally, civil service must be a part of the international and national change process. For government to succeed, civil service should be at the forefront of the national change process-initiating, guiding and managing change.

—*Mohan Kaul*

# 16

# Position Classification

## Classification of Positions

The verb 'to classify' means 'to arrange, distribute or place persons, things or ideas into groups based upon similar or like qualities.' Classification is the act of classifying and is an everyday experience and a useful aid in comprehending and managing things. In a library, for example, books are grouped or classified by subjects, such as, public administration, political science, economics, sociology, etc.

Classification of governmental position is recognised as indispensable to a career service based on merit. It enables rational standards or norms to be set up of the selection of personnel, permits, uniformity in the method of describing different types of jobs and establishes an alike basis for giving equal status and equal pay for equal work. Since the administration of the civil service itself takes up a major slice of budgets of modern governments, classification of positions has become a primary concern for the legislator, the budget official as well as the tax-payer. The prevailing bases for classifications of positions are educational qualifications required in their incumbents, competence on the job, level of responsibility entailed in the job, rank and personal status of the employee, etc. The precise mix of them depends, of course, on a country's administrative value system and culture.

What is stressed in the above paragraph is that classification of posts is absolutely essential to a modern public personnel administration. But the basis on which posts are to be classified may not precisely be the same all over the world. Indeed, there are two well-known systems of classification used by the different countries: (i) Rank Classification, and (ii) 'Duties Classification'.

**Rank Classification**

This system is in vogue in India, Pakistan, Britain, France, Germany, Malaysia, Laos, etc. As the term explains, the basis of classification is the rank and personal status of the incumbent rather than the precise duties inhering in the post.

In India, the public personnel are classified into 'Classes' as well as 'Services'. There are, in descending order, 4 Classes— Class I, Class II, Class III, and Class IV, corresponding to differences in the responsibility of the work performed and the qualifications required.

Class I and Class II include personnel performing higher administrative and executive responsibilities in the Government. Class III includes clerical personnel. Class IV, which is the lowest in the hierarchy, includes peons, orderlies, watchmen, carpenters, drivers, cooks, khalasis, daftaris, sweepers, etc.,—all engaged in manual work.

Another way of classification is into 'Services'. Public Personnel in India are directly recruited to distinct services. Thus recruited, they continue to be the members of the particular service until they retire (or, resign), there being no inter-service mobility. Secondly, the civil servants hold their posts by virtue of their membership of a particular service.

The Central Government has two categories of higher civil services: (i) All-India Services, and (ii) Central Civil Services. Reference has already been made of the All-India Services. Suffice it to say that there are the following three All-India Services in existence at present: (i) Indian Administrative Service, (ii) Indian Police Service, and (iii) Indian Forest Service. The All-India Services are Class I Services. The Central Civil Services belong to Class I as well as Class II Services. The Central Civil Services (Class I) consist of the following 33 Services:

1. Archaeological Service (Class I).
2. Botanical Survey of India (Class I).
3. Central Engineering Service (Class I).
4. Central Electrical Engineering Service (Class I).
5. Central Health Service (Class I).
6. Central Revenues Chemical Service (Class I).
7. Central Secretariat Service:
   *(i)* Selection Grade.
   *(ii)* Grade I.
8. General Central Service (Class I).
9. Geological Survey of India (Class I).
10. Indian Audit and Accounts Service.
11. Indian Defence Accounts Service.
12. Indian Foreign Service (Class I).
13. Indian Meteorological Service (Class I).
14. Indian Postal Service (Class I).
15. Indian Posts and Telegraphs Traffic Service (Class I).
16. Indian Revenue Service:
    *(i)* Customs Branch (Indian Customs Service, Class I).
    *(ii)* Central Excise Branch (Central Excise Service, Class I).
    *(iii)* Income-Tax Branch (Income-Tax Services, Class I).
17. Indian Salt Service (Class I).
18. Mercantile Marine Training Ship Service (Class I).
19. Mines Department (Class I).
20. Overseas Communication Service (Class I).

21. Survey of India (Class I).
22. Telegraph Engineering Service (Class I).
23. Zoological Survey of India (Class I).
24. Indian Frontier Administrative Service:
    (i) Grade I.
    (ii) Grade II.
25. Central Legal Service (Grades I, II, III and IV).
26. Railway Inspectorate Service (Class I).
27. Indian Foreign Service—Branch (B):
    *(i)* General Cadre, Grade I.
    *(ii)* General Cadre, Grade II.
28. Indian Inspection Service (Class I).
29. Indian Supply Service (Class I).
30. Central Information Service:
    *(i)* Senior Administrative Grade.
    *(ii)* Junior Administrative Grade.
    *(iii)* Grade I.
    *(iv)* Grade II.
31. Indian Statistical Service.
32. Indian Economic Service.
33. Telegraph Traffic Service (Class I).

The Central Civil Services (Class II) include the following 26 Services:

1. Central Secretariat Service, Section Officers' Grade.
2. Central Secretariat Service, Grade IV.

3. Central Secretariat Stenographers' Service, Grade I.
4. Central Secretariat Stenographers' Service (combined).
5. Grades II and III.
6. Labour Officers' Service (Class II).
7. Central Health Service (Class II).
8. Indian Meteorological Service (Class II).
9. Postal Superintendents' Service (Class II).
10. Post Masters' Service (Class II).
11. Telegraph Engineering and Wireless Service (Class II).
12. Telegraph Traffic Service (Class II).
13. Central Excise Service (Class II).

    Superintendents, Class II (including Deputy Headquarters), Assistant to the Collector and District Opium Officers, Class II.
14. Customs Appraisers Service, Class II:

    Principal Appraisers and Head Appraisers.
15. Customs Appraisers Service, Class II Appraisers.
16. Customs Preventive Service, Class II Chief Inspectors.
17. Customs Preventive Service, Class II Inspectors.
18. Income-Tax Service, Class II.
19. Geological Survey of India, Class II.
20. Botanical Survey of India, Class II.
21. Survey of India, Class II.
22. Zoological Survey of India, Class II.
23. Central Electrical Engineering Service, Class II.
24. Central Engineering Service, Class II.
25. Indian Salt Service, Class II.
26. General Central Service, Class II.

Rank classification claims many advantages. Firstly, it is easy to understand and administer. Secondly, as the system is characterised by rank in man, the individual civil servant under it experiences greater security of job because he remains unaffected by possible changes in duties and responsibilities of a post. Thirdly, Rank classification lays emphasis on the career opportunities of individual civil servants by establishing an identity between his post and the one of his promotion. Flexibility in the operation of this system is its fourth advantage. Fifthly, it lays premium on generalist rather than specialist qualities in the civil servant—something which many in the society prize. Sixthly, it promotes mobility in the civil services by facilitating transfers within the services. Seventhly, it induces loyalty to the totality of the civil service rather than to a specific post in it. Finally, it is regarded as a better system from the point of attracting competent and promising personnel to the civil services.

The limitations of the Rank classification are many and serious. In the first place, it violates the principle of 'equal pay for equal work'. As pay and other privileges are determined according to the rank of the particular civil servant, identical posts are seen to carry differing emoluments, which is indefensible. This is not only manifestly unfair in itself but also causes low morale in the civil service. Secondly, it overlooks the claims of merit as the basis of holding a particular position, the system being amorphous and ascriptive. Besides, the Administrative Reforms Commission's Study Team on Promotion Policies, Conduct Rules, Discipline and Morale (Chairman: K.N. Nagarkatti) has pointed out the following other disadvantages of rank classification:

1. It does not define the contents of any job in detail. It does not describe what is expected of a post, and consequently, the performance of its incumbent may not be rationally measured.

2. It is not conducive to the formulation of scientific standards on which selection of personnel, training, posting, transfer, promotion, career development, etc., may be organised.

**'Duties' or 'Position Qualification'**

The other system of classification is 'Duties' or 'Position Classification' and is presently in vogue in the U.S.A., Canada, Philippines, Taiwan, etc., Historically, the object of position classification has been to provide a basis for fixing fair pay for work performed—for translating into action the principle of 'equal pay for equal work'.

The literature on this subject employ a variety of terms having technical connotations: job analysis, job description, job specification, occupational group or class specification, class series, etc. The purpose of the present chapter is to familiarize the reader with the broad concept of classification in public personnel administration, not to impart technical knowledge of the subject. Nor is latter immediately necessary for the Indian reader for the simple reason that it is not yet practised in Indian public administration.

In 'Duties' or 'Position Classification' the starting-point is the individual positions in the machinery of public administration. A position is a basic organisational unit. Each position represents certain well-defined duties and responsibilities, the latter two terms signifying the work assigned to a position and the matters for which an employee is held accountable. A position must remain differentiated from its occupant. From the point of classification, it is immaterial if the post is occupied or is lying vacant. To repeat, a position is a set of current duties and responsibilities, which are, as Glenn Stahl observes, "the bricks in the classification wall." Like positions are grouped together in a 'class'; a class, thus, is made of positions with duties that are similar in level and kind. To again quote Stahl, "If positions are the raw material of classification, the class is the operating unit." The different criteria for evaluation of jobs for purposes of determining their class are:

1. Nature of occupational field;
2. Complexity and difficulty in performing duties;
3. Scope of responsibility; and
4. Knowledge and skill needed.

Duties in a class should be sufficiently similar so that, (i) the same title may be applied to all the positions in a class, (ii) the same test can be used to fill all the positions in all classes; (iii) persons with the same minimum qualifications (education, training and experience) can do the work assigned to all positions in the same class; and (iv) the same salary, range may be applied to all positions in the same class. "the term 'class' means a group of positions established under these rules sufficiently similar in respect to the duties, responsibilities and authority thereof that the same descriptive title may be used with clarity to designate each position allocated to the class, that the same requirements as to education, experience, capacity, knowledge, proficiency, ability and other qualifications should be required of the incumbents, that the same test of fitness may be used to choose qualified employees, and that the same schedule of compensation can be made to apply with equity under the same or substantially the same employment conditions." In preparing the description, of a job, the duties responsibilities, degree of difficulty and required qualifications are clearly brought out. Each job is broken down into factors, such as, required experience, training, mental efforts, physical efforts, etc. The various jobs are then ranked in order of relative difficulty and grade levels are defined after each job has been ranked. After this, standards are developed for all levels of jobs. The requisite strength of personnel at various levels is determined on the basis of these standards.

There are 4 steps in the development of a position-classification: "(i) Analysing and recording the duties and other distinctive characteristics of the position to be classified (job analysis and description); (ii) grouping the positions into classes upon the bases of their similarities; (iii) writing such standards or specification for each class of positions as well indicate its character, define its boundaries and serve as a guide in allocating individual positions to the class and in recruitment and examinations; and (iv) installation by allocating individual positions to the classes thus described."

Position classification claims many benefits. Firstly, each person under this system gets a clearer understanding of his individual responsibilities and is at the same time given sufficient authority to carry them out. He also knows the objectives of this section or branch as well as the objectives of the department or organisation as a whole. Secondly, position classification induces competitiveness in the totality of the civil service: as such, and thus there is more emphasis on merit rather than seniority. Thirdly, it provides a definite target for recruiting personnel possessing specific qualifications to perform specific duties. Fourthly, it paves the way for an objective evaluation of the performance of personnel. Fifthly, it provides a basis for 'equal pay for equal work' and ensures that public personnel are paid according to the difficulty and responsibility of their work. Sixthly, the system is helpful to those who undertake organisational analysis, work distribution in the organisation, etc. Seventhly, it permits lateral entry into the civil service from outside the government. Eighthly, the placement practices (*i.e.*, postings and appointments) are shaped by the requirements of the job to be done rather than to provide a job to a person who has been assigned a certain status by virtue of membership of a particular service or cadre. The mobility of personnel is, thus, not haphazard but is objectively planned by rotation of the personnel among related jobs. Finally, position classification provides a uniform occupational terminology; by grouping similar positions into classes and allied classes into occupational groups, a common language is established with a uniform, significant and defined terminology for the naming of positions. Classification enables all concerned to speak about positions in commonly understood terms.

Nevertheless, position classification suffers from several limitations, which, too need to be pointed out. In the first place, its basic assumption—that duties and responsibilities of a post are capable of clear identification and must be measures—may be seriously questioned at least in the developing societies. A not fully "differentiated" society cannot have completely "differentiated" (or, structured) posts in its public bureaucracy. Can one precisely document and define all the duties and responsibilities of a district collector, a block development officer, or a village level worker? Duties of many functionaries, particularly those holding line positions, remain even at the best of times more undefined than defined. Secondly, since the pace of change in a developing society being inevitably rapid, the duties of civil servants necessarily undergo corresponding changes. This implies that the classification plan will have to be kept under continuous revision which would be quite onerous as well as costly. This apart, there will be constant pressures from sections of the bureaucracy to seek more favourable job descriptions for themselves. Need we give encouragement to them at this juncture in our history? Thirdly, position classification requires for its introduction and installation technical skills of a wide variety and sophisticated order. It is quite expensive and time-consuming to develop them and besides, many governments may not be able to afford such a paraphernalia.

Should position classification be adopted in public personnel administration in India? This has become a debating point in the country, advocated by the members of the specialist services and opposed by the generalist services like the I.A.S. It is to be noted that the Administrative Reforms Commission (1966-1970) has lent its support to this system of classification. It has observed: "The posts in the civil service should be grouped into categories, so that all those which call for similar qualifications and involve similar difficulties and responsibilities fall in the same category. The same pay scale should be applied to all posts in the same category. In carrying out such an evaluation, the following considerations should be borne in mind:

*(i)* In those services which have field as well as headquarters posts like the all-India services (technical as well as non-technical) and many of the central services (technical as well as non-technical), the liability for service all over the country will have to be reflected in the pay pattern and grading system that may be adopted.

*(ii)* For other services which work either only in the field or at the headquarters but not in both, the grades of pay scales would have to depend only on the duties and responsibilities attached to the posts.

*(iii)* The fact that the state services are required to work only within the confines of a state, and do not carry a liability for functioning all over India, should be reflected in their grades of pay.

*(iv)* Posts in which highly important research work has to be carried out may have to be graded high, even though they may carry little or no administrative responsibility.

*(v)* As far as practicable, the ratio which the increment in an entry scale bears to the difference between the maximum and minimum of that scale should be the same in all other entry scales.

The number of grades may have to be somewhere between 20 and 25. But we do not propose to make any recommendation regarding the number of grades. They can only be fixed by Government after making a detailed study of all the issues involved. The task of grading is onerous, but should not be an impossible one. A start can be made with the Class I posts under the centre and those to be manned by all-India services officers in the states. The number of these officers is small compared to the total strength of the civil service. All these posts could be evaluated and assigned, say, nine common pay scales, each representing a grade. These nine grades may be divided into three levels, namely junior, middle and the senior."

It is rather difficult to pronounce a verdict on this issue, particularly at the present moment. It is always difficult to uproot basic administrative arrangements which have struck roots in the soil. It is even more difficult to successfully graft foreign institutions and practices on an on-going administrative system. A fuller examination of the theory and practice of position classification is absolutely necessary before a firm decision in its favour is taken. The path of wisdom may perhaps lie in mending the existing rank classification. The prevalent 'service' concept in Indian personnel administration can be reinforced with the use of techniques of position classification, especially, at the lower levels of the country's civil service, for quantification of jobs is more practical at such levels.

# Civil Service Reform and The World Bank

Despite data constraints, the findings...suggest some lessons to guide present and future civil service reform. These can be summarised as follows:

- Most of the middle-range employment reduction mechanisms, such as voluntary departure schemes and early retirement programmes, may be useful and politically astute when applied in combination with more stringent retrenchment measures. But they have not yet proved effective in reducing employment in any significant manner. Thus, they do not provide a substitute for biting the bullet and making explicit dismissals.

- Technical analysis and support activities, such as functional reviews and competency testing, for example, have been useful in providing a rational basis for cost containment measures. Their major contribution, however, may be the symbolic assurance they provide that the reform process has been undertaken with fair and equitable intentions.

- Retraining, redeployment, credit, and public works programmes for redundant employees have certainly has a utility, but one that is more symbolic and political than economic. From a financial and technical perspective such programmes have had limited impact and have proved administratively difficult.

- Some reform programmes have promoted interim solutions to pay and employment problems through specialised incentive schemes for topping up executive-level salaries for key government posts, or, more broadly, by widely supplementing civil service salaries through donor-financed activities. Most observers familiar with the use of these mechanisms recognise their limitations and costs. The problem is that neither hard-pressed governments nor operational staff have alternative means at their disposal. Still, what must be recognised is that these salary supplement methods do not provide during answers to the fundamental problems of civil service incentives; indeed, they ultimately undermine the likelihood of devising a durable solution.

- The impact of programmes to contain the cost and size of civil services through emergency pay and employment reforms has so far been small. Effort in most countries to reduce the wage bill and to decrease the number of civil service employees have yielded only modest results. Attempts to correct distortions in the structure of pay and employment through the decompression of wages and the rationalisation of the remuneration system have also had limited success. This record suggests that reforms to date have been insufficiently ambitious in scope to bring about the degree of change that is needed. Meaningful change is going to require more forceful reforms.

- The question of whether more aggressive reforms are feasible is partly technical but mainly political. As discussed previously, the political economy of pay and employment reforms needs further conceptualisation and analytical work. Nonetheless, it is possible to hypothesise from the few examples of countries where programmes have been carried out that the political costs of implementing pay and employment reforms have been lower than most governments and donors

> anticipated. Organised opposition to reforms has not resulted in regime destabilisation, and social upheaval as a result dismissals has not occurred. In part, this way have been a function of the surprising capacity of private sector labour markets—especially in agricultural and informal sectors and particularly, but not exclusively, in Africa—to absorb surplus government workers. It may also have been a function of the unexpectedly agile handling of political factors, including the skill with which regimes generated supporting coalitions and managed contesting groups.

What this suggests is that perhaps regimes can (for political reasons) and should (for economic reasons) make deeper cuts. How far any given government can push these reforms is, of course, unknown. But the relatively mild consequences of the minimal reforms undertaken so far can, it is hoped, influence governments' perceptions of political risk and encourage them to take bolder actions in the future.

Most activities in civil service reform have concentrated, understandably, on short-term cost containment measures. Considerably more emphasis will have to be given to longer-term management issues if sustained improvement in government administrative capacity is to take place. More attention needs to be paid to devising a coherent, overhearing strategy for civil service reform, and detailing the set of tactics by which the strategic goals will be achieved.

In light of a mixed record on civil service reform efforts, the possibility that major donors will retreat from these activities as too difficult looms as a real and present danger. Such a retreat would, however, be tantamount to a denial of the crucial importance of government administrative capacity to implement economic and social programmes. A more responsible and realistic approach is to improve such programmes through a trial-and-error process. The review of experience presented here and in the case studies in the volume is intended to contribute to this process.

# Panchayati Raj in India

India is rightly regarded as the land of villages. In a country where eighty per cent of the population dwells in over five lakh seventy-five thousand villages, the importance of rural local government, popularly known as panchayati raj in India, looks self-evident and beyond any doubt or dispute. Indeed, thoughts on rural local government are but part of the larger concern for social and economic amelioration of the people, a task to which the country is irrevocably committed.

Panchayats have been amongst the oldest political institutions of India, and the very use of this term has a deeply nostalgic association tending to take the mind to the distant and dim past. But in the form in which it is constituted and made to function today is a modern innovation. One need not very much go into the past and may, instead, start with the inauguration, on 2nd October, 1952, in the country, of the Community Development Programme. This date was deliberately chosen to synchronise the Programme with the birth anniversary of the Father of the Nation, Mahatma Gandhi, to whom nothing was dearer than rural amelioration. One cannot overestimate the significance of Community Development which was designed to be an ever-widening programme eventually to cover the whole countrywide.

In 1957, the Team for the Study of Community Projects and National Extension Service, popularly known as the Balvantrai Mehta Committee after the name of its chairman, published its Report recommending a three-tiered system of rural local government, called panchayati raj in India. The principal thrust of the Balvantrai Report was towards decentralisation of democratic institutions in an effort to shift decision centres closer to the people to enable their participation, and to put the bureaucracy under local popular control. Though constitutionally 'local government' falls within the jurisdiction of the states, the latter were persuaded to accept the recommendations and decentralise adequate powers to popularly elected panchayati raj bodies, making them responsible for developmental activities within their jurisdiction. Rajasthan and Andhra Pradesh were the first to have adopted the panchayati raj form of rural local government, the year being 1959. They were joined by other states in course of time. Everywhere panchayati raj was introduced with great fanfare, and it easily constitutes the most conspicuous measure of reform in the system of governance in Independent India.

But panchayati raj has in India come to be associated with three broad images. It is viewed as an instrument for the realisation of the ends of Community Development. Equally, if not more importantly, it is perceived as an organ of the state government to execute the Community Development Programme and such other schemes as the latter may entrust to it. There is also the local government approach to panchayati raj, it is in the first place—and ultimate analysis—an extension and embodiment of democracy at the village level. In contrast to the first approach which looks at panchayati raj as but an instrumental value; the second belief makes panchayati raj as in itself a purpose, an end, a value. Panchayati raj is also a cardinal part of *Sarvodaya*; and especially Jayaprakash Narayan looked at it, not as a unit of the existing social system but basically as the harbinger of a new order of the society which is to be ushered into existence through this institution. Panchayati raj has, thus found itself subject to a variety of interpretations, perceptions, even pulls. To the state government as well as the bureaucracy, it has an agency role, and its relevance essentially lies in terms of the Community Development Programme. To the politician particularly of the grassroots level, it is, first and foremost, local self-government and thus consciously modelled after the western type democracy. Finally, to the *Sarvodaya*, it is a bulwark or a new social order to replace the present exploitative system.

The multiplicity of images did not pose a problem in the beginning. Rather, all shades of thought assured, even extended support to panchayati raj institutions. It was only after some interval that differing perceptions came in conflict with each other. Since mid-sixties, panchayati raj has been in particularly low profile. As a form of local government, it has fallen out of favour everywhere, even in Maharashtra and Gujarat, where it has been relatively more successful. Increasingly, its justification is sought purely in terms of an agency to augment agricultural production. The ascendancy of this view may be accounted for by four major factors. The new national and state level political leadership which emerged around 1966 had much thinner links with the ideals of Mahatma Gandhi and thus much weaker ideological commitment to panchayati raj. *Secondly,* the mounting food shortage of this period and the crop failures of 1966-67 led to a reshuffling of priorities in the Community Development Programme itself resulting in an overriding emphasis on agricultural production. In the process, a comprehensive concept of rural development got reduced to a mere project for agricultural production. *Thirdly*, the trend of Indian political system has been markedly centralised since the mid-sixties but the pace towards centralisation of power got considerably accelerated since 1971. Under the contemporary political leadership, the state governments were being made subservient to the central government. This exactly is not the climate under which panchayati raj can grow and flourish. *Fourthly*, the technology discovered at this time served only to reinforce the already powerful centralised pressures, in the process, relegating panchayati raj to a lower even unimportant status. New varieties of wheat had been discovered, making what has come to be called 'green revolution' possible in many parts of the country. From now on, a distinct technological orientation began to be given to agriculture, inducing the central government to make direct inroads into this sphere of activities to the detriment of both the state and local governments. Backed by the new technology, the central government began to develop its own independent administrative hierarchies to carry out the special programmes, and in the process the panchayati raj institutions were systematically by passed. Mention must here be made of special resource development programmes like the Intensive Agricultural

Development Programme (IADP), Command Area Development Project (CADP) and special economic programmes designed for 'target' groups like the Small and Marginal Farmers' Development Agency (SFDA), Drought Prone Area Programme (DPAP), Intensive Tribal Development Programme (ITDP), etc. All these programmes are financed and operated by the Central Government and they have no relationship, whatever, with the panchayati raj institutions. Even the Employment Guarantee Scheme (EGS) started by the Maharashtra Government is controlled by the district collector and the zila parishad is kept completely out of the picture. The present practice is to use the bureaucracy for the transfer of technology in rural development and to keep out popular institutions. Nor has the bureaucracy been kindly disposed towards panchayati raj which has provided for the primacy of the grassroots politician in the ordering of affairs and has thus come to be viewed as some kind of a thorn in the local-level administrative flesh.

As a cumulative result of all these forces, panchayati raj, today is but a dull echo of its former self. Indeed, it may not be very inappropriate to say that India is on the way to having a strong rural *administration* but not rural *government.*

It was in this overall context that the Central Government appointed, in December 1977, the Committee on Panchayati Raj Institutions under the chairmanship of Asoka Mehta to suggest measures to strengthen the panchayati raj institution. The Committee submitted its Report in August 1978, making nearly 100 recommendations. As this Report was subjected to extended discussion and debate throughout the country, a few observations on it are pertinent.

The Asoka Mehta Committee's principal thesis is the functional necessity for decentralisation of administration. Where millions of people are involved and where the lot of the poor is sought to be improved through a very large number of micro projects, decentralised administration is an unavoidable necessity. At the same time, in order to remain continually sensitive to popular will and aspirations, it requires democratic supervision. This is how the Committee has what it calls a 'new approach' towards panchayati raj. This is: "The formulation of structure, functions and the utilisation of financial administrative and human resources of panchayati raj institutions should, in our opinion, be determined on the emerging functional necessity or management or rural development." Such a philosophy or—'approach'—conceives of panchayati raj in somewhat narrow terms. It gives one a feeling that panchayati raj is a mere administrative contrivance whose justification lies only in terms of rural development. It may have been more secular if panchayati raj, or rural local government, is regarded, like its counterparts at the state and central levels, as a system of government having a measure of autonomy in the matter of its function and existing in its own right. The committee is a too closely focussed definition of rural local government and it needs to be liberalised and made more open ended.

The most significant recommendation of the Committee is for the creation of a two-tiered system of panchayati raj. It regards the revenue district as the first-point of decentralisation below the state level which assures the technical expertise of high order required for rural development. In short, the zila parishad should be the executive body—as in Maharashtra and Gujarat. Below the zila parishad is to be a mandal panchayat which is to be constituted by grouping a number of villages. The Committee wrote: "While our preference is for two tiers—a district-level zila parishad and mandal panchayat—we are conscious of the fact that two other tiers are already in existence and it may take time for the suggested institutional design to take shape and become fully operational. The block-level panchayat samitis, where they exist now would be converted into non-statutory executive committees of zila parishad and when the mandal panchayats become active, most of their functions would be taken by the mandal panchayats. As a transitional structure, the block can, therefore, continue as per the convenience of the states keeping in view their requirements and the stage of development. At the village level, the people would be involved in mandal panchayats through village committees which would look after the municipal functions and related welfare activities. Till the mandal panchayats are constituted, a federation of existing village panchayats may be desirable." The Committee's listing of functions to be performed by the decentralised structure is satisfactory, and if accepted, would be an exercise in genuine decentralisation. Of course, the position cannot remain static and has to be reviewed periodically to see whether some more functions may be devolved upon the panchayati raj bodies.

That zila parishad should be the level of democratic decentralisation which is to be entrusted with functions of an executive nature is a pattern already in operation in some parts of India. But the suggestion for the creation of mandal panchayats (which are to be the implementing bodies) covering a population of 15,000 to 20,000 is a new and novel one. The Asoka Mehta Committee adduced technological and administrative arguments in support of its recommendation for mandal panchayats. According to it, a mandal panchayat would alone be able to ensure a balance between technological requirements and possibilities of popular participation in decision-making. The size of the proposed lower tier would be such as to make projects and schemes economically viable. Besides, there are many programmes which need a larger unit than the present block to handle them. In short, mandal panchayat would ideally bring about symbiosis between technology and democracy. Thus runs the argument.

The Committee's recommendation favouring a two-tier form of panchayati raj needs to be discussed carefully and dispassionately. The Committee does not recognise a need for an elective participative organism at the level of the village: it is content with village committees. Such a view makes the village too conspicuous by its absence in the Mehta scheme of reorganisation. Political institutions do not operate in a vacuum, and by overlooking the village, which is an organic entity, the Asoka Mehta Committee runs the risk of suggesting precisely such a kind of remedy. It may perhaps do us good to decentralised structure upon it.

This apart, the Committee has to clear some other doubts as well. The present structure of panchayati raj was designed in the early sixties, and it necessarily takes time for it to grow roots and enter into the minds of the rural people. Rural people have their own psyche; they are rather slow in accepting innovations but having accepted, rather sceptical about proposals for their abandonment. It is only recently that the panchayati raj glossary has gained their understanding and even acceptance, words like 'block', 'panchayat samiti,' 'gram panchayat,' etc., have now become household expressions in rural India. One would like to be convinced more than the Committee had done in its report about the inadequacies of the present structure and about the distinct superiority of the proposed scheme. Perhaps, the weaknesses of the panchayati raj system are rather inaccurately ascribed to the structure alone. The fact is that it has not been given a really fair trial—and sympathetic analysis. It appears that the proposed two-tier system of panchayati raj and the exact location of the tiers are structural manifestations of an oversensitivity on the part of the Committee to technology and a studied under-reaction to democracy at the grassroots.

As regards taxation, the Asoka Mehta Committee wants the panchayati raj institutions to have 'compulsory powers of taxation' to mobilise the necessary resources on their own thereby reducing their dependence on devotion of funds from the state government. As we know from experience this is easier said than done: the centre, too, exhorts the state governments to display vigour in the matter of taxation but without visible effect on the latter. It is necessary that panchayati raj overcomes its shyness in levying taxes. The Committee has hinted at areas such as profession tax, entertainment tax, house tax and special taxes on lands and buildings. The problem here is that at certain levels of income these are the zones of the state governments while at a lower level, there is not enough income left for these local level bodies to levy taxes on.

A central feature of the local government in India is lack of its inherent power of taxation as the Constitution of India does not specify any taxes for its exclusive use. This, however, was not always the position. During the period 1921-37, the local government was endowed with a separate tax domain. The Government of India Act, 1919, which came into force in 1921, contained a local list comprising the following taxes:

1. Toll;
2. Tax on land and land values;
3. Tax on buildings;
4. Tax on vehicles and boats;
5. Tax on menials and domestic servants;
6. Tax on animals;
7. Octroi;
8. Terminal tax;
9. Tax on trade, professions and callings;
10. Tax on private markets;
11. Tax imposed in return for services rendered, such as (a) water rate, (b) lighting rate, (c) drainage rate, (d) fees for use of markets, and (e) other public conveniences.

The Government of India Act, 1935 did not include any local list of taxes, and so, with the inauguration of the Act in 1937, the local government was deprived of the special position in regard to taxation. Nor does the present Constitution enumerate, as it has done in the case of both the central and the state governments, taxes reserved for use of or by the local government only. This has occasioned a demand that local government in India be given a separate list of taxes, and that, in order to ensure definite and elastic sources of revenue, the Constitution needs to be suitably amended to include, on the lines of the union and the state lists, a list of local taxes also. The Asoka Mehta Committee examined the larger question of according a constitutional base to panchayati raj and wanted the central government 'to give careful consideration' to the proposal. One wishes that the Committee had lent a more positive support to the plea for making panchayati raj a part of the organic law of the land. A constitutional base is apt to impart both sanctity and stature to the grassroots government.

A remarkable feature of the Mehta Report is its recommendation favouring 'open participation' of political parties in panchayati raj affairs. This marks departure from the hitherto followed policy. It may, however, be mentioned that West Bengal and Jammu-Kashmir have held panchayat elections on party basis. In many states, where partyless polls are claimed, the political parties have been upto their necks in the fray. The fact is that the partyless polls acquire in practice the same competitive character, except, of course, for the labels. The recommendation that political parties be allowed to contest the panchayat elections is thus pragmatic. It is desirable too. Not only are the political parties the main channels of mass involvement in current issues including local ones but they also become accountable when they are openly involved in the panchayati raj institutions. The view that political parties are a species of impurity from which the rural local government in India needs to be shielded failing which the rural life would get polluted carries little meaning. Political parties are an essential ingredient of the democratic process. But the political parties must re-orient themselves and learn a new style of functioning at the local level. As visualised by the Committee, the panchayati raj elections are to be based on political parties with reserved constituencies for scheduled castes and tribes, a minimum of two reserved for women. The election will be conducted by the chief electoral officer of the state in consultation with the Chief Election Commissioner.

The Committee has also made some very interesting recommendations favouring the creation of certain monitoring forums to safeguard and promote the interest of the vulnerable social and economic groups in the villages. It suggests a regular social audit by a district level agency as well as by a committee of legislators to check whether funds allocated for these groups are actually spent on them. This is a wholesome recommendation. An absence of such bodies in the present structure has made it easy for smart operators to monopolise the benefits at the expense of who they profess to serve. The Committee had also proposed a 'social justice committee' in each zila parishad to ensure that panchayati raj bodies function so as to show keen interest in the welfare of these groups. These bodies proposed by the Committee have great potential, provided their members are carefully selected and they are truly representative of the diverse interests in the locality. Further, the state legislatures will have a committee on panchayati raj with adequate representation for scheduled castes and tribes and this body will attend to the needs of the weaker sections.

An important recommendation of the Committee is that the state government must not supersede the panchayati raj institutions on partisan grounds. If, however, the supersession of a body becomes necessary, there should be an election within six months. This is a salutary recommendation. It should be remembered that the local government is as much representative of its area as the latter is of the state as a whole. Having been elected by the freely expressed will of the people, a local government ought to run its full course set out in the governing statute itself. Punitive actions like suspension and dissolution of local governmental institutions may be invoked only when absolutely necessary, and even in such cases, it would be a good practice if the state government puts itself under an obligation to seek its legislature's endorsement of such a measure. Supersession and dissolution of the grassroots government must not occur except with the approval of the state legislature and what is more, there must be a fresh election within six months.

The Asoka Mehta Committee treats rural development as part of the urban-rural continuum and therefore argues for the provisions of urban amenities, such as roads, potable water, medical care, employment and education in the rural areas to weaken or even neutralise the pull for migration to urban centres. This is good insofar as it goes, but on closer analysis, it does not seem to go very far. The present pattern of local government in India is essentially based on rural-urban dichotomy; the two arms of local government, urban and rural, presently constitute two separate independent entities with little organic inter-relationships characterising their activities. The fact, however, is that today the points of contact between a town and its adjoining villages have multiplied enormously so much so that they have come to constitute more or less one broad entity. The mass media, the rapid means of communication, the inter locking nature of the economy, the growing political socialisation, and above all, the revolution of rising expectations have been bringing about the social and political mobilisation of the people. The correct solution may perhaps lie in a sharper definition of relationships between the urban and local government, or even in the creation of a single 'area government' in which all the urban and local governments of the area would get merged.

It is to Balvantrai Mehta Committee that the present pattern of panchayati raj owes its parentage. It was given to Asoka Mehta Committee to take a close look at the institution with a view to revitalising it. Between the two Mehtas lie two decades of the functioning of this grassroots government. Both are easily the two landmarks in the history of local government in India though each has its distinctive conceptual angle to inform parts of its formulation. In certain aspects, the second Mehta builds upon the first, but in many others seeks a deliberate departure from his predecessor. While the first Mehta made the block as the level of decentralisation and thus the cornerstone of panchayati raj structure, the second one treats the district level zila parishad as the lynchpin of the new proposed pattern. The block is a standardised unit being a product of thinking in the developmental context. The same may not perhaps be claimed in favour of the districts. Districts vary considerably both in size and population.

The state governments have not been very equitable in their relationship with the infant panchayati raj institutions. The financial resources developed on them have been meagre and measly. Elections to these bodies have been repeatedly postponed: there is a state having the dubious reputation postponing panchayat elections over a hundred times! Supersessions of local bodies are too common. The painful fact is that the state governments in general have not so far shown much sustained enthusiasm for panchayati raj institutions. They have even given an impression of being unwilling to curtail even a portion of their executive power. The higher level governments in India have been rather allergic to the concept of sharing of power with the lower level ones. It is hoped and expected that the state governments would now be more kindly disposed towards panchayati raj in view of the formidable challenges of both democracy and development. They must not forget that local government is the oldest one, much older than themselves. Man first evolved his neighbourhood government, the village government, before he could visualize or even succumb to a more remote authority like the state or central government. Chronology apart, functionality too imparts rationality to this demand. Democracy at higher levels is bound to have a weak foundation unless there is its habitual practice at the local level.

# 19

# The Generalists and The Specialists

The subject of the role of specialists in the Indian administrative system has of late come to the forefront of the problems in public administration. It has emerged as perhaps the knottiest internal problem facing the country's civil service today, which can be easily sensed from a dangerously mounting frequency and intensity of agitations on the part of the various groups of specialists, especially engineers and doctors. A satisfactory solution of this problem can brook no delay in the context of the admittedly vast responsibilities resting on all sections of the country's bureaucracy for making a success of the plans and programmes being taken up by the Government. Partly, this problem has been bequeathed to the present-day public administration by history but partly also it is of our governmental leaders' own making—in the sense that they have tended to let things drift and not to fully recognise the gravity of the problem, and even its belated recognition has not till now given sufficient evidence of a firm determination to adopt the necessary corrective measures.

## Problem in its Historical Perspective

Historically, the civil service in India has been designed as a generalist one with the leadership role at all levels and in all spheres of administration reserved for the Indian Civil Service, set up in 1854. This was the conception of the Northcote-Trevelyan Report on the 'Organisation of the Permanent Civil Service' in Britain, submitted in 1853. The Report laid stress on the superior positions in the civil service being manned by "the most promising young men of the day by a competing (literary) examination on a level with the highest description of education in this country" arguing that "men capable of distinguishing themselves in any of the subjects we have named and thereby affording a proof that their education has not been lost upon them, would probably make themselves useful wherever they might be placed." This was the contention—but elaborated with much greater pains—of the Report on the Indian Civil Service, submitted, in 1854, by Lord Macaulay, Ashburton, Melvill, Sowett and Lefevre (popularly known as the Macaulay Report). As the civil service in India continues to be constituted on the basis of what these 'gentlemen' (to use Charles Wood's expression) recommended, it is appropriate to recall the philosophy enunciated by them. "We believe", they observed "that men who have been engaged, up to one or two and twenty, in studies which have no immediate connection with the business of any profession, and of which the effect is merely to open, to invigorate, and to enrich the mind, will generally be found, in the business of every profession, superior to men who have, at 18 or 19, devoted themselves to the special studies of their calling. The most illustrious English jurists have been men who have never opened a law book till after the close of a distinguished academical career; nor is there any reason to believe that they would have been greater lawyers if they had passed in drawing pleas and conveyances the time which they gave to Thucydides, to Cicero, and to Newton. The duties of a civil servant of the East India Company are of so high a nature that in his case it is peculiarly desirable that an excellent general education, such as may enlarge and strengthen his understanding, should precede the special education which must qualify him to despatch the business of his cutchery." This has since become the classic of generalism.

Unquestionably, the Indian Civil Service was designed and groomed as the elite service. It was the master of all it surveyed, and there was no inch of the Indian administrative territory which it could not and did not survey. In the days of the raj, the experts and the specialists were fewer in number and, moreover, were kept on top as a matter of deliberate administrative policy. The members of the Indian Civil Service were deployed on positions of administrative leadership practically in the whole field of public administration, not excluding the specialist posts like the Director of Agriculture, Inspectors General of Police, Post-Masters General; they were also manning the higher judiciary.

The solitary exception was the Chief Engineer of the province who also functioned as *ex officio* Secretary to the Government in the department of public works/irrigation—an arrangement which, however, was discontinued soon after independence.

The predominance of the generalist could not remain completely unchallenged and unquestioned. Though independent India took over predominating the generalist administrative culture, the voices of discontentment and indignation at such an administrative ethos began to be heard from various quarters, slowly but unmistakably. In the fifties, when India launched her First Five-Year Plan, a large number of personnel possessing technical and professional qualifications were inducted into the Government at various levels. The inflow of such personnel inevitably became larger in the sixties as a result of bigger and bigger Five-Year Plans. In short, the number of experts and specialists employed in the Government shot up since the launching of socio-economic planning in the country and has been continually increasing ever since. In 1971, they constituted 6.4 per cent of the total manpower on the payroll of the Central Government, as would be evident from the following table on page 276.

The specialists have been directly engaged in carrying out the developmental and promotional functions of the Government. These are the persons who construct dams and bridges, cure patients and man medical hospitals, generate and distribute electricity, undertake researches in physical, biological and social sciences, to mention only a few of their many faceted activities. While engaged in the performance of these complex tasks, they have frequently felt curbed and constrained by the barely concealed authoritarian habits on the part of the Secretariat—Central or State. They have also not been very happy with the attitude and behaviour of some at least of the personnel at the controlling levels of the

**Break-up of Manpower in Central Government**

| | *Group* | *Per cent to Total* |
|---|---|---|
| 1. | Administrative | 0.5 |
| 2. | Specialists (like doctors, engineers, scientists, etc) | 6.4 |
| 3. | Clerical | 17.9 |
| 4. | Production process workers | 20.5 |
| 5. | Others like unskilled workers | 54.7 |
| | | 100.0 |

Government. As the Secretariat has normally been the citadel of the generalist ICS or IAS, the specialists' already simmering discontentment with the administrative system received eloquent confirmation, even reinforcement. The specialists began showing signs of uneasiness at the role traditionally set for them and a demand for a basic change both in the structure and style of the country's bureaucracy was gathering momentum. They derive strength from their ever expanding number in public administration and from their increasingly momentous role in the modernisation process of the country. Equally firmly implanted on the mind of the many groups of specialists is the proud thought of a bright university career—brighter indeed than the scholastic achievements of many of the generalist-administrators of the day who are 'bossing over' them. Nor do they find the outer environment completely unsympathetic towards their demands. The former Prime Minister's observation made in 1967 became a most powerful morale-booster of the specialists in public administration. She said: "It is odd that the greatest doctors and engineers in the country, who would be rated as the leaders of the profession and who save lives or add permanent assets to the nation can rarely hope to receive the pay or status of secretaries of Ministries. The brightest of our young men and women choose engineering and medicine. If they happen to go into Government they are very soon overtaken by the general administrator. This must change and I am trying to change it. The administrative system must reflect an individual's contribution to human welfare and economic gain."

**Who are Specialists?**

The specialists figuring on the pay-roll of the Central Government are presently grouped into a number of organised civil services. There are also a number of them who do not belong to any of the organised civil services and are clubbed together and deemed to be included in what is called as the General Secretariat Service. The more prominent of the specialist service are as follows:

1. Archaeological Service.
2. Botanical Survey of India.
3. Central Electrical Engineering Service.
4. Central Engineering Service.
5. Central Health Service.
6. Central Legal Service.
7. Central Revenues Chemical Service.
8. Geological Survey of India.
9. Indian Economic Service.
10. Indian Meteorological Service.
11. Indian Statistical Service.
12. Overseas Communication Service.
13. Survey of India.
14. Telegraph Traffic Service.
15. Telegraph Engineering Service.
16. Zoological Survey of India.

A definition of the term 'specialist' becomes necessary in the interest of a rational discussion of the present theme. Those who are recruited to the civil service on the basis of their specialist qualifications are the specialists. It needs to be mentioned that the public personnel in India fall into two broad categories. The first one includes those who already possess recognised professional qualifications before their entry into Government and are recruited to the public service on the basis of their professional qualifications. The examples are doctors, engineers, meteorologists, statisticians, geologists, etc. The services enumerated in the preceding paragraph belong to this area. There are also persons who possess the general educational qualifications and are, as a rule, inducted into the civil service on this basis. The members of the IAS, IPS and of non-technical civil services fall in the second group. This category may be further divided into two streams. Members of all these services except those of IAS are uni-functionaries: they remain in the particular field of activity for which they have been selected and, thus, acquire expert knowledge of that field. The IAS has been an all-, or general- purpose service and thus constitutes an altogether different species; its members man the higher positions in different fields of public administration.

## All-India Confederation of Central Government Officers' Associations

The specialists of the first category mentioned above and the public personnel belonging to the non-technical central civil services do not have similar or identical professional background. Indeed, each service has evolved its own distinct personality and culture in the course of its growth and development and has been content to hoe its own row. Surprisingly, they seem to have achieved, in a short period, a measure of unity amongst themselves. They today, seem to share one trait in common, which is their united stand against the predominance of the generalist IAS in the public administration of the country. It is this negative community of interests which impelled both specialists and members of other non-technical central civil services to come together and form a common forum to seek re-adjustment of relationship within the civil service. In March 1970, all their service associations formed the All-India Confederation of Central Government Officers' Association, pledged to break what it calls the 'monopoly of the IAS'. As a direct consequence of this, the question of proper relationship between the specialists and the generalists has threatened to get reduced to a dispute between the non-IAS and the IAS civil servants. The Indian Administrative Service, the Indian Foreign Service, the Indian Police Service and the Central Secretariat Service have kept themselves out of the Confederation. The Confederation has as its preamble the following:

1. that an efficient and dedicated administrative machinery competent to carry out the tasks of democratic development is essential for the rapid progress of our country;

2. that a set-up involving attitudes of administrative overlapping, authoritarianism and non-accountability, which results in outmoded procedures and unresponsiveness to the needs of the community leading to general inefficiency, is unsuited to serve the needs of a democracy;

3. that in the modern context in which governmental activity covers many specialised fields, administrative efficiency can be maximised only by a set up in which all officers have the fullest scope for disciplined self-expression;

4. that sound policy decisions can be made only if the popularly elected Government receives direct expert advice and support in the various fields of governmental activity; and

5. that the officers who bear the real burdens of developmental activity and who are equipped with the necessary skills, can contribute in the evolution of a sound administrative policy by common action over and above the areas of separate action.

The move towards 'polarisation' between the specialists and the members of non-technical civil services on the one hand and the generalist IAS on the other hand began in a slow but sure way with the appointment of the Administrative Reforms Commission in 1966. This occasion imparted a sense of obvious urgency to some form of joint action on the part of the first group to aggregate and articulate its demand for a suitable re-structuring of the country's public administration. The process of polarisation reached a fairly advanced stage by 1970 consequent upon the emergence of the All-India Confederation of Central Government Officers' Association. It has been virtually completed in 1973 when the Third Pay Commission published its report containing a note of dissent by some members.

The All-India Confederation of Central Government Officers' Association is, today, the premier institution to spearhead the cause of the specialists and non-technical civil services. It seeks:

1. to evolve an administrative set-up in which power and responsibility to produce results will be combined and vested only in those who by qualification and training are competent to deal with the worker entrusted to them;

2. to ensure that the administrative set-up is so refashioned as to secure the full benefits of science and technology and modern techniques of management for the rapid development of the country; and

3. to foster an *espirit de corps* among the members of the Confederation and, consistent with the objectives listed above, to promote and safeguard and common interests of all the members so that they may have full opportunities to give of their best in the service of the country and to secure for them a fair deal.

The Confederation, with its headquarters in Delhi, has quickly shot up into prominence as the articulator and aggregator of the specialists' demands for reform of public administration. Although the various positions in the Confederation are filled up through election by its affiliated members, its leadership since the inception of this body flows almost completely from the medical doctors, the engineers (especially power engineers) and the members of the Central Information Service. This is not merely accidental. The medical doctors and the engineers easily command various ways of displaying their strategic place in the society's life. The members of the Central Information Service are naturally quite articulate personnel and provide a bridge with the media of mass communication. It is not likely that their pressure towards remodelling of the administrative system would relent in the foreseeable future; rather there is a fear of their taking increasing recourse to tactics like work-to-rule, pen-down, mass casual leave, processions, marches, etc. Further, it is safe to speculate that its posture of militancy is likely to prove rewarding in this era of the permissive for, 'submissive'?) state.

**Views of Various Committees**

It is not that the case of the specialist has not been scrutinised or commented upon by the committees set up by the Government. The Second Pay Commission (1957-59) to which their memoranda calling for remedial measures, observes "Proposals were made to us on behalf of officers belonging to the specialist classes, *viz.*, scientists, engineers, etc., that they should be more freely appointed to administrative and secretariat posts. It was urged that the principal specialist officer should have direct dealings with the Minister, and that there should be no interposition of an administrative officer who could only become a transmitter of professional or specialist advice, not unoften failing to transmit or interpret the advice with the clarity and precision with which the specialist officer himself could do. It was further stated that the present arrangement does not afford to a specialist adequate opportunities to influence policy or otherwise to make the maximum contribution he is capable of. We do not wish to make any recommendations on this subject: though raised as one having a bearing on conditions of service, it involves issues which extend beyond the scope of our enquiry. We, therefore, content ourselves with making a few general observations. Where the work of a department is mainly technical it is desirable in our view, that the Secretary should be a person who, while possessing administrative ability and capable of taking a broad government-wide view of matters, has a technical background in the particular field. In a department which has a considerable amount of technical as well as administrative work, the Secretary may be either a technical officer with proved administrative capacity, or a generalist administrator; technical officers should not be excluded from the field of choice on priority considerations, but should be considered on merits. Further the top technical advisers or heads of departments should have full opportunity to have their views considered by the Minister, alongwith any views which the Secretary of the department may have; for which a suitable arrangement may be a joint discussion with the Minister, whenever there is an unresolved difference of opinion between the technical head and Secretary. The basic idea governing the relationship between the two must be the recognition that the former should have an effective share in the framing of policies and programmes at the highest official level. We are, however, clear of the view that the functions of head of department and Secretary should not normally be combined—whether the Secretary is a general administrator or a technical or a professional officer. This view corresponds with the government's stand on the relationship between generalists and the specialists in public administration. Nearly a decade later, the Estimates Committee of Parliament gave its attention to this question and lend its support to the appointment of increasing number of specialists in positions of administrative responsibility. "The (Estimates) Committee hope that Government would take practical steps to induct a larger number of officers with technical background, training and experience as administrative heads of institutions, departments/Ministries dealing with scientific, industrial and technical subjects. The Committee would also like the secretaries of Ministries/departments to deal with matters of technical nature that the technical advisers do not have the apprehension as expressed to the Second Pay Commission that their views do not get properly transmitted to the Minister. The Committee would like to observe *en passant* that there is a widespread feeling among the services that the officers belonging to the ICS and IAS regard themselves as an exclusive group, unnecessarily exacerbating feelings that generate inter-service rivalry. The Committee hope that members of the ICS and IAS would avoid such attitudes towards the other "services and would, instead, by their conduct set high example of dedicated service which may inspire the other services." It may be of interest to note the views of the Government on this recommendation. It, in its reply to the Committee, observed: "While, the recommendations that practical steps should be taken to induct a larger number of officers with technical background, training and experience as administrative heads of institutions, departments and Ministries dealing with scientific, industrial and technical subjects is unexceptionable, there are practical difficulties in providing that posts in Ministries/departments dealing with technical subjects such as agriculture, science, education, economic matters, etc., would be filled only with officers of respective technical services. Senior posts under the Government are of two kinds. In the first category are posts in institutions and departments outside the Secretariat organisation where the departmental or institutional hierarchies are utilised to man the top posts. It is seldom that the generalist administrator is placed at the head of any such organisation. In exceptional cases where this is done, it is usually for the reason that job content of a particular post is more administrative than technical. In the second category fall Secretariat posts. It may be mentioned that the secretariat type of work is quite different from that done in the specialised departments. While under the present rules, secretariat appointments can be manned by officers of any of the central services class I, most scientific and professional officers would continue to make their careers in their own fields and may indeed wish to do so. Up to the level of the heads of departments, certainly technocrats, scientists, educationists, etc., are essential so that government's examination of the technical and scientific side is well informed, but it is not necessary that certain departments of the Secretariat should be manned only by officers belonging to those specialised services. Therefore, while maintaining the flexibility of staffing and keeping the senior posts open to all groups in the services, the professional aspects of the generalist services cannot be ignored.

It was, however, left to the Administrative Reforms Commission (1966-70) to examine this problem in a much more comprehensive way and to make its own outline of reform. The Administrative Reforms Commission's principal recommendation was that a functional field be carved out for the IAS. This should consist of land revenue administration, exercise of magisterial functions and regulatory work in the states in fields other than those looked after by other financial services. All posts in a functional area whether in the field or in the Secretariat should be staffed by members of the corresponding functional services. There should be clearly defined schemes for staffing the middle and higher levels in each functional area. Post of Under-Secretary in the Secretariat and the Attached Offices should first be classified as falling: (i) with in functional or (ii) outside functional area. These posts should be filled by personnel of the corresponding functional service. The tenure for the post of an Under Secretary should be three years and for that of a Deputy Secretary four years. Finally, the posts at the level of Deputy Secretary at the central headquarters, which do not fall within a particular functional area, should be demarcated into the following eight areas of specialism, selection, to them being made from among all class I officers on the basis of a written examination: (i) economic administration, (ii) industrial administration, (iii) agricultural and rural development administration, (iv) social and educational administration, (v) personnel administration, (vi) financial administration, (vii) defence administration and internal security, and (viii) planning. The senior administrative posts in functional areas should be filled by members of the respective functional services but the posts falling outside the functional areas should be filled by personnel who have had experience in one of the eight specialisms. Although the ARC made this recommendation in 1969, no action on it has followed so far. Meanwhile, the internal harmony within the civil service is getting repeatedly broken.

**Pakistan Moves Forward**

It should be of more than ordinary interest to note that Pakistan, which inherited the same administrative system and culture as India, introduced, in August 1973, a fundamental change in the structure of its civil service by replacing the familiar framework of a four-fold class structure, service cadres and the elite service—the Civil Service of Pakistan, the successor to the old ICS—by a unified civil service. The newly created unified civil service has the following features:

1. All the services and cadres have been merged into a unified grading structure with equality of opportunity for all who enter the service at any stage based on the required professional and specialised competence necessary for each job.
2. All 'classes' among the public personnel have been abolished and similarly replaced by a unified grading structure, a peon at the bottom, a Secretary or departmental head at the top. The existing classification of the services into class I to class IV was, thus, put an end to. This has the effect of opening the road to the top to all on merit. In all, a unified twenty-two grade pay scale has been introduced, thus doing away with over 600 salary scales which were in operation.
3. The unified structure of the civil service enables promotions to the higher posts throughout the range of the public service, for horizontal movements from one cadre to another including the movement of technical personnel to the cadre of general management.
4. The correct grading of each post is determined by job evaluation.
5. There is provision for lateral entry into government service.

Consequent upon the creation of a unified services structure, each of the existing services has become converted into a functional branch of the Single Unified Service retaining its separate occupational identity but no longer constituting a separate service as such. A few new functional branches may be instituted to accommodate such occupational or professional personnel who did not have a regular service identity and who, at the same time, cannot be classified under one of the existing functional branches.

The following table gives the classification of functional branches relating to the existing services and some identifiable occupations:

**Central Services**

| *S. No.* | *Name of Service* | *Functional Head* |
|---|---|---|
| 1. | Civil Service of Pakistan | Administrative |
| 2. | Provincial Civil Service (Listed Posts) | Administrative |
| 3. | General Administrative Reserve (General Wing) | Administrative |
| 4. | General Administrative Reserve (Special Wing) | Administrative |
| 5. | Pakistan Military Land and Cantonment Service | Administrative |
| 6. | Officers of Investment Promotion and Supplies Department (Non-Technical Personnel) | Administrative |
| 7. | Police Service of Pakistan | Police |
| 8. | Pakistan Foreign Service | Foreign Affairs |
| 9. | Pakistan Audit & Accounts Service | Accounts |
| 10. | Pakistan Military Accounts Service | Accounts |
| 11. | Pakistan Railway Accounts Service | Accounts |
| 12. | Pakistan Taxation Service | Central Revenue Collecting Agency (Taxes) |
| 13. | Pakistan Customs & Excise Service | Central Revenue Collecting Agency, (Duties) |
| 14. | Central Engineering Service | Engineering |
| 15. | Officers of Investment Promotion and Supplies Department (Technical Personnel). | —do— |
| 16. | Telegraph Engineering Service | T & T (Engineering Branch) |
| 17. | T & T Traffic Service | T & T (Traffic Branch) |
| 18. | Pakistan Postal Service | Postal Branch |
| 19. | Central Information Service | Public Relations |
| 20. | Central Secretariat Service | Secretariat |

*(Contd...)*

| S. No. | Name of Service | Functional Head |
|---|---|---|
| 21. | Trade Service of Pakistan | Commerce & Trade |
| 22. | Geological Survey of Pakistan | Geological Survey |
| 23. | Transportation (Traffic) and Commercial Department of P.W. Railways | Railways (Commercial) |
| 24. | Railways Engineering Service | Railways (Engineering) |
| 25. | Economists in Planning Commission, Central Statistical Organisation and elsewhere | Statistics |
| 26. | Statisticians in Planning Commission, Central Statistical Organisation and elsewhere | Statistics |
| 27. | Technical Officers of Ministry of Agriculture | Agriculture |
| 28. | Professional Officers under Ministry of Education | Education |
| 29. | Professional Officers under Ministry of Health | Health |
| 30. | Scientists in Pakistan Council of Scientific and Industrial Research and elsewhere | Scientific |
| 31. | Scientists in Pakistan Atomic Energy Commission | Atomic Energy |
| 32. | Labour Officers | Labour Welfare |
| 33. | Officers of Civil Aviation Department | Civil Aviation |
| 34. | Officers of Civil Meteorology Department | Meteorology |

## Provincial Services

| S. No. | Name of Service | Functional Head |
|---|---|---|
| 1. | Civil Service (Executive Branch) | Administrative |
| 2. | Co-operative Service | Administrative |
| 3. | Prisons Service | Administrative |
| 4 | Officers under Food Department | Administrative |
| 5. | Civil Service (Judicial Branch) | Judicial |
| 6. | Secretariat (Section Officers) Service | Secretariat |

| *S. No.* | *Name of Service* | *Functional Head* |
|---|---|---|
| 7. | Agriculture Service | Agriculture |
| 8. | Forest Service | Forest |
| 9. | Fisheries Service | Fisheries |
| 10. | Excise and Taxation Service | Revenue Collecting Agency |
| 11. | Industries Service | Industry |
| 12. | Printing and Stationery Service | Printing and Stationery |
| 13. | Education Service (Collegiate Branch) (Men's Section) | Education |
| 14. | Education Service (Collegiate Branch) (Women's Section) | Education |
| 15. | Education Service (Administrative Branch) (Men's Section) | Education |
| 16. | Education Service (Administrative Branch) (Women's Section) | Education |
| 17. | Technical Education Officers | Education |
| 18. | Medical Service | Health |
| 19. | Engineering Service (Roads and Buildings) | Engineering |
| 20. | Engineering Service (Irrigation) | Engineering |
| 21. | Engineering Service (Electricity) | Engineering |
| 22. | Animal Husbandry Service | Animal Husbandry |
| 23. | Information Officers | Public Relations |
| 24. | Labour Officers | Labour Welfare |

Announcing these measures to reform in the country's civil service Zulfiqar Ali Bhutto, the then Prime Minister of Pakistan, observed: "The scientific and technological revolution that has taken place in the twentieth century must be harnessed by a socialist country dedicated to satisfying the needs and expectations of the people. To an ever-increasing extent, therefore, the Government will rely upon an effective corps of technical experts working in conditions which enable them to exercise their talents to the best advantage of the country... The new service structure will enable the Government to gain the full contribution of scientists, engineers, doctors, economists, accountants, statisticians and other professionals and specialists in policy-making, management and administration. We have indeed already taken steps to ensure that the Government can draw on the widest possible range of talent. We invited applications last year (i.e. 1972) for lateral entry into Foreign Service and the senior secretariat posts. Over 200 candidates have been given suitable appointments. We intend to continue this search for talent."

The reforms of August 1973 are of truly historic significance in the administrative annals of the Indian sub-continent. For the first time in her administrative history, a radically new public personnel system has been designed and put into operation in Pakistan which till 1947 was a part of India; for the first time it enables engineers, doctors, scientists and other technical specialist staff to be drawn into the stream of higher management from which they had been barred so far, thus making their advice and expertise directly available to Government at the highest policy-making level. As the direct result of these reforms, the road to top management gets opened up to all scientific and technical personnel. It remains to be seen if India would remain content with the Macaulay-bequeathed structure of her civil service when both Britain and Pakistan have decisively voted this model out, Bangladesh, too, has adopted in effect the Unified Civil Service.

**Re-adjusting the Relationship**

Whatever be the precise outfit to respond to the corollaries and compulsions of national commitment to development, a measure of ascendancy of the specialist appears to be certain in the very logic of modernisation to which the country is resolutely committed. Not only will their number increase but areas of specialisation will also become more diversified. Further, a new development is likely to characterise Indian public administration—the short-term appointment in Government of technical personnel. And in this context the fear voiced in some circles about the 'destruction of democracy by the technocrats', even if completely well-founded, may not succeed in reversing this process, at least in the forseeable future: However, the word 'specialist', like socialism, has become a rather loose one, so much so that it has begun to be employed to refer to all the existing civil services other than the IAS. This may perhaps be the surest way of letting the important question of proper relationship between the specialists and the generalists spend itself through its own extravagance. In the true sense of the term, only those who are recruited to civil service on the basis of their specialist qualifications are the specialists.

The demands of the specialists are principally two: parity with the IAS in the matter of pay-scales and service conditions and, secondly, access to administrative positions at the policy-making levels in government. The pay-scales and service conditions of doctors, engineers and scientists, etc.—have remained less attractive than those of the IAS which is illogical and indefensible. In 1972, 30.5 per cent members of the I.A.S. were in the pay-band of Rs. 2000 per month and above. The corresponding percentage in the medical, engineering and scientific services have been 1.7, 2.1, and 0.6 respectively. 26.6 per cent members of the I.A.S. were in the pay-range of Rs.400-1100 whereas bulk of the medical (70.4%), engineering (81.1%) and scientific (87%) personnel have remained concentrated in this pay-range. The percentages of members in the pay-range of Rs.1100-1800 per month are, for these four categories of personnel respectively, 36.7, 27.2, 12.5 and 12.2. The above figures for the specialist services relate to the period before the implementation of the Third Pay Commission recommendations. But the changes made as a result of this Commission's Report do not greatly change the relative position. It is evident from the foregoing that the generalist service is designed mainly to man high-salary positions in public administration in India while the specialists are to pass their lives in lower and middle salary-range.

Indeed, a specialist ought to receive by way of his emoluments as much as, if not more than, a generalist does. The cost of social reproduction of his skills is admittedly high, and, moreover, his capacity to build permanent assets for the society is much greater. At the same time, the specialists, particularly the engineers, must evolve suitable professional ethics against corruption by no means negligible among at least some of their lower ranks.

But one is not very sure if the specialists should be thoughtlessly encouraged to migrate on a very large scale to administrative positions in the Secretariat. It may perhaps be a prudent national policy to deploy the admittedly scarce specialist human resources on the urgent tasks for which the society has subsidised the specialists' education and this should be secured by making these posts attractive in terms of emoluments, advancement and status. The administrative positions in the specialist organisations (e.g., executive organisations) must, of course, be filled from amongst the specialist personnel themselves and the practice, though not very regular or widespread, of appointing members of the IAS as heads of executive organisations must be discontinued. Moreover, such of the specialists as have shown a flair for administrative work must not be formally barred from the secretariat posts. In this context the ARC recommendation on this subject appears to be sensible and should be implemented. Besides, there is a need for the setting up of staff colleges at least for the numerically viable groups of specialists and one of the tasks of such institutions should be to formulate suitable administrative and 'de-specialisation' training courses for such specialist administrators.

At the same time it is necessary that there is a calculated de-emphasis of the role and authority of the Secretariat in the decision-making and implementation processes of the Government. The Secretariat must be obliged to shed both its non-essential functions and the personnel engaged in their performance. It must remain as a slim and sleek organisation performing its tasks of higher policy-making with utmost business and despatch. There should be a parallel development of enhancing the status and authority of the various specialist positions. Also, the specialists must be invariably consulted by the Secretariat while formulating policies.

It follows that there must be massive delegation of power and authority from the Finance Ministry to the spending Ministries and from the latter to their executive organisations. Consequent on a measure of planned deglamourisation of the Secretariat, the specialists will find the administrative infrastructure helpful for the practice of their skills in the field and may not be tempted to secretariat jobs.

**Role of the Generalist**

The forces that give rise to various specialisms and, what is more, impart significance to the specialists' roles in society also call for the stay of the generalist administrator. No specialism today stands complete in itself in terms of the problems confronting the society: several specialisms require to be integrated and put into a defined relationship in order to fulfil any large-scale tasks. Besides the specialists are not completely unpolitical beings: indeed, there have been instances of the specialists producing organisational bulges reflective of their individual specialisms. The foregoing makes it necessary that the specialist judgements be evaluated in the larger framework of social, economic, political and administrative considerations. These call for consultation, synthesis, coordination, control—the processes which are the true functions of a generalist administrator. Viewed in this way, both the specialist and the generalist have contrasting, nevertheless complementary, roles to play in public administration. Their roles are contrasting for they operate on generally different priority scales: to the specialist an administrative requirement appears to be only incidental whereas to a generalist the technical job is-subservient to the administrative problem. The truth is that both components are essential for successful administration and the part ought to be seen in relation to the whole. It would be idle to expect that the generalist administrator shall wither away. When the present author discussed this question with a very distinguished person known for his progressive views on administration, the latter observed: "I do not see any escape from a measure of generalism. People specialising in narrow fields seldom rise to the top of the organisation. Where we want one single project to go ahead without any regard for cost, then put in the specialist as its head. Similarly, the *ex officio* secretariat status to a specialist may be workable only in an emergency—when, for instance, one particular project is concerned. There are three reasons for the stay of generalism in

Indian public administration. First, the Ministers are enabled to get two lines of advice on a given problem. Secondly, the specialist is an over-enthusiast and, to this extent, he disqualifies himself to take final decisions. Finally, the co-existence of the generalists and the specialists creates and maintains 'constructive tension' which should be helpful in matters of governmental decision-making." But measures would have to be adopted to make the members of the IAS more knowledgeable and more competent in terms of their tasks. Career planning should be introduced in the IAS without any further delay so that there develop linkages in the experience of the members of this service. Indeed, the members of the IAS must specialise by choosing an area of administration, getting an indepth specialised training in that area, and stay there sufficiently long to acquire relevant experience. At senior levels, where inter-disciplinary approach is indispensable, their transfer should be restricted to linked fields only. The future seems to stand in need of such of its members who combine in themselves a modest measure of technical competence in one of the fields and a high degree of administrative skill—by no means an unattainable combination. Simultaneously, efforts must be directed at making the generalist administrators out of such specialists as have demonstrated an aptitude for administration.

Both the generalist administrator and the specialist will have to travel a long way to arrive at such a stage. At present, the good generalists and the good specialists continue but a fraction of their respective numbers in the public service.

# Civil Servant of Tomorrow

It would sound a cliché to say that our future is built on our past and on our present. Also if we want to address ourselves to the task of defining the civil servant of tomorrow and the set of conditions in which he would be required to function, we would necessarily have to look at the past and the present before we envision the future.

Let me at the outset state the obvious. The term 'civil servant' does not refer to the individual who is a member of the Indian Administrative Service or a member of any of the state administrative services. The term generically refers to that large group of civil servants who comprise the major services of the central and the state governments and on whom lies the burden of discharging the government's commitment to the people. These include the members of the Indian Administrative Service, the Indian Police Service, the Indian Forest Service, the central services and the major services of the state governments—who collectively constitute the 'civil services' I have used the expression in that sense. These are the persons who are generally in the public eye and whose actions and behaviour have an impact not only on the affairs of the state but also on the lives of the people.

Secondly, when one talks of the role of the civil servant or the attributes of the civil servant of tomorrow, one will have to understand the context in which the civil services would be required to operate and function in the foreseeable future: the overall milieu which would be a combination of social, political and economic forces superimposed by the impact of the global society. In short one will have to first consider what will be the shape of the Indian society and the Indian nation in the years to come, what will be the expected role of civil servant and, flowing from these two, what would be the characteristics, qualities or attributes of the civil servants of tomorrow.

The third aspect which needs to be clarified is the use of the expression 'tomorrow'. Obviously, it does not mean tomorrow in the literal sense nor does it mean the distant perspective of 50 or 100 years from now. What I have in mind is a future timeframe of 10 to 20 years, say, what may be obtaining in the year 2010 to the year 2020—the years comprising the first quarter of the 21st Century.

In November 1949 the people of India adopted, enacted and gave to themselves the basic law which encapsulated the aspirations, the hopes, the assurances, the ethos and the genius of the Indian people. When it was promulgated, it came to be known as the Constitution of India which came into force on the 26th January, 1950. It would be worthwhile to recall the original Preamble to the Constitution to remind ourselves of the commitments our leaders made to the people of this country in terms of liberty, equality, fraternity, human dignity and national unity. It said,

"WE, the people of India, having solemnly resolved to constitute India into a Sovereign Democratic Republic and to secure to all its citizens.

JUSTICE, social, economic and political;

LIBERTY of thought, expression, belief, faith and worship;

EQUALITY of status and of opportunity; and to promote among them all;

FRATERNITY assuring the dignity of the individual and the unity of the Nation;

In our Constituent Assembly this twenty-sixth day of November, 1949, do hereby adopt, enact and give to ourselves this Constitution."

A close perusal and a moment of reflection on the Preamble would immediately suggest that what we wanted to ensure was liberty, equality, justice, human dignity and national unity—absolutely unexceptionable objectives but each one of them calling for certain preconditions and certainly casting heavy obligations on each one of us, particularly those in authority. What follows in the shape of the Articles of the Constitution and their Schedules is a delineation of the basic concepts and philosophy set out in the Preamble.

When we look back at our achievements in the last 50 years we find that, as a nation, we have many reasons to feel satisfied. The biggest of them is preserving the unity of the nation which, in spite of some aberrations and periodic shocks and jolts, has endured. Along with that or as part of the mechanism to ensure national unity we have a fairly elaborate edifice of public administration: an instrument for the governance of this country including the political executive, the permanent civil service and the judicial system. Each one of them finds a respectable mention in the Constitution and has a major and specific role to perform. Any suggestion that any one of them is superior to the others is both inappropriate and unfair. Each one has a designated role to perform and this delicate balancing is one of the features of the basic structures of the Constitution. Eliminate any one of them and the consequences will be disastrous. Therein lies the status, dignity and the obligations of the civil service.

The other noteworthy achievements of the last 50 years include the development of the political system, achieving the higher rate of literacy of 55 per cent or so, reaching a much higher longevity of about 65 years and strengthening and deepening of Indian economy. Above all we have been able to build solid blocks in agriculture and industrial production which not only made us self-reliant but also generated surpluses for export.

While we have enough cause for satisfaction arising out of our achievements, there is an equal measure of dissatisfaction and unhappiness, on a number of counts. The first and foremost is in regard to the maintenance of law and order, which is the basic responsibility of the state. The violence which keeps on erupting in certain parts of the country at regular frequency, makes the average citizen rather apprehensive and worried. Security of life is the first precondition for socio-economic growth and if life is not secure, the citizen cannot look forward to an assured future. The second major area of concern is our inability to generate adequate employment and to eradicate poverty. It is more than 25 years since we coined the populist slogan of 'Garibi Hatao', but unfortunately the number of people below poverty line has increased during these years. Even if 25 per cent of our population, if not 33 per cent, lives below poverty line it would mean that 250 million of people or 50 million families, approximately, are living below poverty line. What sort of a certificate can we give ourselves if this is so. The misery caused by our poverty levels is further aggravated by a vast multitude of illiterates numbering 450 Million or so. Certainly the majority of the Indian women continue to be illiterate, their literacy rate as per 1991 Census being below 40 per cent. Even if we assume a slight increase in female literacy in the last seven years, it is doubtful if even 50 per cent of the Indian women would have become literate by now. Reaching higher level of literacy or education is not only a milestone by itself, it is also a necessary precondition to attain better levels of socio-economic growth including realising the dream of an electronic society.

In this chiaroscuro of achievements and failures lies the gist of our achievements in the last 50 years. Again it is in this background that we have to envision our tomorrow. When I some time reflect on what will be the shape of India in the year 2020 when some of us may, fortunately, still be alive, I immediately think of about half a dozen factors which will be impacting the Indian society. These include, the pace of economic growth – the 5 to 7 per cent GDP growth; the percentage of literacy; the health services and the average longevity; the forces unleashed through the implementation of the Mandal Committee Report; the whole gamut of reservations in services and in legislators etc.; pressures of global competitiveness i.e., global economy, global trade, global management, global services; and finally the onslaught of the information technology including office automation and artificial intelligence. Also the current phase of political unrest, coalition politics etc. Could we put all these factors together and try to envision the Indian society and the Indian nation in the future years and the civil servant as a critical part of it?

It may perhaps be possible to use all these inputs and prepare some Computer Model and study, analyse and assess what will be the shape of the Indian society in the year 2020 or 2025. I am not sure whether one could really run a computer model on these factors. Nonetheless, what one could do is to pose some questions. Whether India in 2020 will be a modern society or a feudal society; whether India of 2020 will be fully integrated to the global economy or will be isolated; whether the Indian society will be cohesive or will it be a fragmented society; whether we will be part of a civil society or we will be clamouring over privileges; whether we shall be a fully educated country or would we have large pockets of ignorance and so on. It is from the assumed answers to these questions that the role of public administration and the attributes of the civil servants of tomorrow will emerge.

Addressing myself to the question of the role of civil services and the attributes of the civil servants of tomorrow, the first thing that strikes me is that the state shall still be required to provide the three basic services, namely, securing the life and property of the citizen commonly known as maintenance of 'law and order', dispensation of justice and maintenance of the public record of urban and rural immoveable property. To these can be added a long list of other desirable functions of the state, namely, defence, education, health, transport, communications, currency, coinage, banking international exchange etc. Many of these can be passed on to the non-state sector and for valid reasons. Of course, as years roll by, more and more of the activities in these areas should shift from the state or the government to the non-state organisations, the NGOs, the groups of citizens and to the people themselves. Not only for the reasons that we have now started realising that the citizen can look after himself better but for other equally strong reasons like the financial and managerial limitations of the state which are under severe strains both at the Union Government level and in the States. With the Central Government running into a hefty deficit on current account and all the states except may be half a dozen or so, not only having a negative revenue account but even having a negative balance on current revenue (the BCR), it would be impossible for the state to continue with the type of activities it has taken upon itself in the last 50 years of administering an independent India. With the adoption of the recommendations of the Fifth Pay Commission, the situation is bound to get worse whatever be the demands placed before the Eleventh Finance Commission and whatever be their recommendations, it would be well nigh impossible for any financial wizard to satisfy all demands placed on the government. Hence the wisdom in the state shedding some of its functions by empowering the people themselves.

In the context of government becoming leaner and more efficient the civil servant of tomorrow will have to show a number of qualities and traits. Firstly, as an advisor to the government and an aide to policy makers, he will have to play a positive role in persuading the government to streamline itself and to reorder its priorities. In this context it would be useful to refer to the new situation created by the 73rd and 74th amendments to the Constitution which were effected with lot of fanfare and have generated great hopes, aspirations and even ambitions. As we know, the 73rd amendment seeks to empower the Panchayati raj institutions. The 74th amendment seeks to empower municipalities, that is, the urban local bodies. The reports emanating from the states indicate that while follow up legislations have been enacted by the States and even State Finance Commissions have made their recommendations, the actual transfer of authority, responsibility and power from the state headquarters to this third tier of administration has not yet taken place. Whether in doing so, the basic structure of the Constitution has been violated or not is another matter and we need not go into it. Nonetheless, the civil servant has a critical role in inducing and effecting a genuine devolution of power and responsibility from the state government to the Panchayati Raj institutions and the urban local bodies. What is perhaps, not being appreciated in the midst of a tussle for power among the variously elected peoples' representative is that concentration of authority and responsibilities at the state level would only delay the social transformation and empowerment of the people which is badly needed. The other role that the civil servant of tomorrow would have to play effectively is to assess the effectiveness of the PRIs and the urban local bodies to discharge their responsibilities in a manner that the public interest is subserved and not private agendas. The general impression is that management of the affairs of the local bodies, whether urban or rural leave much to be desired. This may be so in many cases. But what they deserve is not envy but empathy and this has to come both from the civil servant as also from his political master.

As a spin-off of our democratic process, there is a greater awakening among people and the citizen is becoming more demanding. Education, transport and communications, media, and the socio-politico-economic process itself have created an atmosphere where the citizen is seeking more and more. That being so, those who deal with public affair, and are entrusted with any aspect of the citizen's care and well-being will have to show greater sensitivity, greater caution and greater maturity in managing public affairs. The civil servant will have to play the role of an enlightened provider of services in a dispassionate, objective and selfless manner. He may not be the leader of the society as a public man is. But nonetheless he will be a leader in his own right, even sometimes a role model.

At the time of Independence and in the pre-Independence era the society could boast of a large number of voluntary organisations and many achievements could be counted to the credit of the citizens' voluntary efforts. It is an irony of the post-Independence social development that we lost out heavily on the voluntary efforts. However, lately the NGOs are seeking a greater role in managing public affairs. In this scenario the civil servant will have to define his role *qua* the NGOs and social groups. He would be required to show a positive attitude to the non-government efforts in nation building and will have to strike the right chord on behalf of government. He will have to forge the public-private synergy for socio-economic development. At the same time, it would also be expected of him to maintain an objective distance from the citizen pressure groups. For decades the citizen has been trying to get close to the administration. The civil servant has been keeping himself away. But as state withdraws from many areas of activities, as the NGOs come into their own and as the citizen starts taking better care of his affairs, the civil servant would have to act as one of them without abandoning his responsibilities as part of governance. It would require a delicate balancing act. For that reason he will have to ensure equi-distance from the warring political factions.

There has been a long debate on the generalist versus the specialist. It is difficult to take a view because human affairs are intricate and the situation is ever changing. However, as far as the civil servant is concerned, there is no denying the fact that he will have to be a much better professional tomorrow than what he was yesterday or even what he is today. Not so much in the sense of technical qualifications, but in the sense that his attitude and approach to the job will have to be more professional and scientific. He cannot muddle through his affairs. He will have to be fully cognizant of his goals, fully cognizant of his role in administration and would need to have a clear understanding of how to go about his job in a professional manner. He will have to be result-oriented but in a manner that human values are not sacrificed. I had earlier referred to the financial problems which the state has run into. The civil servant as a part of its professionalism, will have to inculcate the habit of being cost conscious, would have little time to waste on non-issues and will be required to optimise on investments in costs, time and energy.

Every employee costs government a tidy sum. Every matter which is kept hanging for a decision results in a heavy economic costs, and therefore sensitivity to costs: financial, social and economic, will have to be one of the primary considerations of the civil servant of tomorrow, much more than what it is today.

One criticism against the civil servant, a widespread and frequent criticism, is his insensitivity to the problems of the citizen to the extent of being callous. Unfortunately, there is some basis for this criticism. In the first place it is often noticed that he does not take a stand if a wrong decision or an unfair decision is being taken against the larger public interest. Secondly, it often happens that even where there is no pressure on him, political or otherwise, he fails to act either out of *malafide* or pure inaction. Every year there are dozens of cases of stand-off between the citizens and the police because the FIR has not been registered at the police station in a case of rape, or murder. Let us ask ourselves: Is the citizen asking for too much if he insists that an FIR be registered in a rape case, that the matter be investigated and the accused apprehended? No, I think it is a legitimate demand. When the head constable who is supposed to record the FIR or the SHO fails in his duty, there are demonstrations against the police. In socalled self-defence, the police takes stern action. There is *pathrao*, there is arson. The police opens fire. What is the result? A few dead bodies, a burnt down police station and a badly shattered image of the government. It occurred because the concerned civil servants lacked sensitivity and showed scant regard to his duty. The civil servant of tomorrow has to show greater sensitivity and greater feeling for the misery and suffering of the citizen. Protecting one's colleagues and subordinates is alright up to a point but beyond that it is unwarranted, improper and even counterproductive.

Do we need a committed civil service? This question has come up again and again. Perhaps, the term was coined after the Emergency was imposed in 1975. Strictly speaking, the civil servant is committed. He is committed to the Constitution of India, to the people of the country and to the goals and objectives of the organisation, where he works. But the new concept of commitment, namely, personal commitment to the man in authority has proved disastrous. It has led to distortions both in the system of governance and in the work culture of the civil servant himself. When Bhishma and Dronacharya kept quiet at the time of utter humiliation of Draupadi in the Court of Dhritarashtra one wonders to whom was their commitment ascribed: to Dhritarashtra; the ruler, to his sons who were the extra-constitutional authorities, or to the kingdom of Hastinapur? Had they been committed to the state, the story would have been different. Therein lies the message to the civil servant. If he could stay committed to the people of the country, to the Constitution of India and to the objectives of the organisation he is serving, perhaps, no other commitment would be needed. A personal commitment, working to the detriment and in contradistinction to the public interest should have little meaning for the civil servant. I am not for a moment suggesting that a civil servant should be unreliable, untrustworthy or disloyal to his superiors, including the political masters. But loyalty includes the courage of conviction and the ability to advise the superiors and political masters on what is in public interest and what is otherwise. Loyalty and trustworthiness do not mean a blind implementation of the instructions of a superior. I think it is an attribute which the civil servant has to inculcate in a greater measure in times to come. Also for the reason of pure self interest.

The judiciary is unfolding new dimensions in its functioning which some people call 'judicial activism', while others call it 'judicial aggressiveness'. One can give it any name but what is evident is that the judiciary is showing a marked sensitivity in public matters and is not hesitating to call in question the decisions of the executive and the motives of decision makers. The civil servant cannot hide behind the civil service anonymity or seek privilege when ordered to produce documents before the court. It would become increasingly more difficult to do so. Coupled with the demand for a transparent system of governance which is a direct antithesis to the code of secrecy the civil servant of tomorrow will be left with hardly a few fig-leaves to cover himself if he cannot defend his own actions. The society and the individual citizens are fully entitled to know from us as to how we conduct ourselves and what goes behind our decision-making. That being so, the civil servant will have to be more accountable.

The role of the future civil servant in poverty alleviation is much too obvious to be emphasised. While the country has registered impressive economic growth, the question remains whether growth will be sustainable and whether the growth is coupled with social justice. The role of the civil servant in formation of new policies and in the modification of the existing policies and in the implementation of policies and programmes is critical, to say the least. One would not say that poverty is confined to the villages of India. It shows its ugly face even in cities and towns. Whether it is Rojgar Yojana or it is the rural development schemes, the citizen is in the centre stage and his continuing poverty and misery will remain a cause of concern and a task to be attended to by the civil servant till the need to have a poverty line disappears.

Similarly his role in the other major task as a provider of services, namely, the maintenance of law and order, dispensation of justice and other basic goods to be provided by the state: in short creating and sustaining a civil society. In the performance of this task, not only the members of the executive services but also those in the judiciary are included. Justice not only needs to be done but it should seem to be done. At the same time social justice calls for sensitive handling of the poor,. the weak and the downtrodden. The instruments of the state and the agencies of the state carry a big responsibility on their shoulders, namely, dispensation of social justice, maintenance of law and order and ensuring equal treatment to the citizens of this country irrespective of caste, creed, colour or sex. Sometimes it may appear that under social or political pressure or as a consequence of vested interest, fairness, objectivity and judiciousness are being sacrificed for the sake of expediency. Such situations are most unfortunate. No society can be sustained and no society can remain strong unless the citizen has the assurance that he will receive a fair treatment at the hands of those in whose hands his destiny has been placed.

The political system has seen a major change in the last few years, namely, the challenges of coalition governance. The full impact and the administrative implications of governance through coalition are yet to be comprehended *Prima facie* it would seem to put a severe strain on the administrative system. One thing is apparent: coalition governance requires an extra ounce of wisdom, competence, forbearance and integrity on the part of the civil services. Some may be tempted to become the active members of the political camps who constitute the coalition government; but one should ask whether that is the right course of action. Some others may suffer by totally staying away and becoming unmindful of the legitimate demands of coalition governance. The civil servant of tomorrow would require a much better understanding of his own capabilities and of the programmes and policies of governments. Nothing, perhaps, can be taken for granted. For the same reason he will have to be more skillful and more adroit. Only then he will be able to discharge his responsibilities more effectively.

The world over there is a sudden realisation for need of ethics in government and there is a renewed insistence on good governance. As a child we often read that even kings were expected to be benevolent and caring. It therefore looks strange that after 50 years of post-colonial era, we are still looking for '*good governance*'. What exactly is good governance? To my mind it means caring for all citizens, keeping the interest of the state and of the nation as first priority, being accountable for one's action, being as transparent as possible, and being professional and ethical in one's conduct. These are age old values: the insistence on them is recent. Suddenly, everybody has woken upto it: United Nations, the World Bank, the multilateral agencies and even some national governments. One could suspect some of them of hypocrisy, but one cannot quarrel with the stated objectives particularly when these include greater sensitivity in dealing with the citizen, transparency and efficiency in government, containing costs and the like. The civil servant of tomorrow will have to be fully responsive, and a positive promoter of all these values because these would be insisted upon even more keenly. There is a comprehensive programme for civil service reforms and as the programme is being put through these qualities and attributes will be in sharper focus.

I have given a long list of the desired characteristics and attributes of the civil servant of tomorrow. Situation is changing in a manner and demands of the society are growing at a pace that the civil servant will have to do many things to many people at the same time. Shri B. Mehta whose memory has brought us together today, stood for integrity, for sagacity, for maturity, for impartiality and for equanimity of mind. I commend to the civil servant of today and of tomorrow to imbibe these attributes and qualities.

It may be debatable whether the civil service is the oldest profession in the world or is the second oldest. One thing is sure, though. After mankind organised itself into a society and once the society organised itself into a system of government, the civil servant became an integral part of it. In any system of governance, he has a critical role to play by whatever name you call him. Changing times and changing values require reorientation of the philosophy of government: the civil servant also has to reorient himself. The higher civil service in India had a different task to perform under the colonial rule; the civil services were called upon to shoulder added and more complicated responsibilities in the last fifty years; and the next 25 years will seek more qualities in the civil servants. The system is becoming more demanding, the citizen is more wide awake, the political culture is getting more aggressive. To cope with them the civil servant will have to show greater wisdom, greater competence, greater professionalism and above all, greater humanism.

*—M.C. Gupta*